Murderous
LEEDS

Murderous LEEDS

The executed of the Twentieth Century

John J. Eddleston

In association with

YORKSHIRE Evening Post

The Breedon Books
Publishing Company
Derby

First published in Great Britain by
The Breedon Books Publishing Company Limited
Breedon House, 44 Friar Gate, Derby, DE1 1DA.
1997

ISBN 1 85983 084 6

Printed and bound by Butler & Tanner Ltd., Selwood Printing
Works, Caxton Road, Frome, Somerset.

Colour separations by RPS Ltd, Leicester.

Jackets printed by Lawrence-Allen, Weston-super-Mare, Avon.

CONTENTS

Acknowledgements

My thanks must go to a number of people whose help has been greatly appreciated in the preparation of this work.

The staff of the Public Record Office at Kew have proved to be most helpful and I would especially like to express my gratitude to Edward Tilley and Josephine Matthews of the image library there for their extremely valuable assistance in providing some of the illustrations in this volume. I would also like to thank Brian Carter, the image library photographer at Kew, who has copied pictures from various trial depositions.

In addition to the above, I would like to acknowledge the help of the staff of the British Newspaper Library at Colindale.

Once again, I want to make a special mention of Yvonne Berger, my research assistant who did a great deal of work on many of the cases in this book. As always, her valuable assistance made my task of writing that much easier.

INTRODUCTION

THE city of Leeds and its nearby partner, Bradford, have seen some of the most intriguing cases of murder this century. This book opens with the story of the man who killed both his daughters because he couldn't afford to take care of them. He was subsequently told by the jury which found him guilty of murder that he had been kind to his children. The book ends with the murder of a man who had bragged about a win on the football pools. Other chapters, though, are equally fascinating.

The reader will find the story of William Horsely Wardell, who wormed his way into his victim's affections and then brutally battered her to death. Imagine his horror when his description was published in a newspaper and all his friends rushed to give him up to the police.

Alternatively, what of the story of William Batty who shot his rival in love, or of Eric Briggs who killed his wife after she discovered that he was having an affair with his own step-daughter. Or Walter Sharpe, who with an accomplice shot a shopkeeper during a robbery.

Finally, read of the mysterious death of Emily Yeomans and decide for yourself whether David Maskill Blake was guilty of murder.

Remember that in this country, a man is not required to prove his innocence. All that is necessary is that you, as a member of the jury, have a reasonable doubt as to his guilt.

Leeds and Bradford have indeed seem some fascinating murders and not only does this book catalogue all those this century which ended in the execution of the convicted, it also includes many illustrations never before published.

Finally, after nearly 60 years, it names the other suspect in the Blake case, and for the benefit of the true crime historian it contains a complete list of all the executions at Armley jail since 1900.

John J. Eddleston
Sussex
Summer 1997

CHAPTER ONE

KILLING BY KINDNESS

URING the early hours of Saturday, May 12th, 1900, William Wilson was enjoying a quiet walk along the banks of the Leeds and Liverpool Canal at Glebe Road, Holbeck, when he noticed something floating in the dark and murky waters. Looking more closely, Wilson saw that what had attracted his attention was the body of a small girl. And as if this were not horror enough, floating nearby was a second body, also of a little girl, and she appeared to be even younger than the first. Wilson ran for a policeman as fast as his legs could carry him.

Within minutes, he had found Constable Byrom and together they returned to the canal and steeled themselves for the task of fishing out the bodies. From the girls' facial similarity and the fact that both had red hair, Byrom assumed that they were related and might be sisters. The two girls were taken first to Hunslet Road police station and then to the Millgarth Street mortuary to await identification.

No children had been reported missing so this did not look like a case of accidental death. Indeed, the police already felt that they were dealing with a double murder.

Inquiries soon revealed that a man had been seen in the company of two little girls the previous evening and eventually a description was pieced together. It was not long before officers found a man with short red hair, who fitted the description they had been given, standing at the corner of Water Lane and Bridge Road. He was taken to the police station so he could be questioned further.

The man was 29-year-old Thomas Mellor, who was known to have two red-haired daughters aged six and four — ages which fitted with the apparent ages of the girls found in the canal. While Mellor was being questioned by senior officers, neighbours were brought from Fourth Court, off Bridge Road, and they identified the girls as Ada and Annie Beecroft, the daughters of Thomas Mellor.

Ada and Annie were Mellor's illegitimate daughters, their mother, Ada Beecroft having been committed to the Menston Asylum where she died in November 1899. Mellor had cared for his children alone until his common-law wife had passed away. After her death, though, Mellor had moved in with another woman, Priscilla Redshaw, in what was little more than a hovel at 6 Fourth Court. This particular thoroughfare was a small passageway in the shadow of the London & North Western Railway bridge. The 'home' the four now lived in was nothing more than a derelict property where the broken windows were stuffed with rags.

In fact, there should really have been six people living in those dreadful conditions at Fourth Court, but Priscilla had sent her own two children to live with her mother so she would be able to devote more time to looking after Mellor and his two daughters, the eldest of which, Ada, was a cripple. Both Mellor and Priscilla were working, he at the gas works and she as a cleaner, but even so, they never had enough money to feed and clothe the family, due mainly to the fact that Mellor was not particularly forthcoming with his cash. The financial upkeep of the family was left mostly on Priscilla's shoulders. As a result, even though the rent on Fourth Court was only 2s per week, the family soon began to fall into arrears.

It was inevitable that Mellor and his family would be told to quit and so it was no surprise when, on May 4th, they were evicted. The few possessions the family had were stored in a disused stable and for the remainder of that day Priscilla and the children toured their neighbours' houses while Mellor was at work. For the rest of the week, the family would wander the streets during the day and then, each night, drag their bedding back into the house, to which Mellor had retained a key. Early the next morning, the bedding was stored away and the routine began all over again.

After a week of this, Priscilla had had enough. Early on the evening of May 11th, she took the two girls to their father who was in a nearby public house. She handed the children over, told Mellor she was leaving him, then turned on her heel and walked away, intending to look after herself from that moment on.

The last sighting of Mellor that night was when he was walking along by the canal, holding Ada's hand and carrying Annie. No one ever saw the girls again until they were seen floating in the water by William Wilson. On the strength of this evidence, Mellor was now charged with two murders.

His first appearance at the Leeds police court was before Mr Atkinson on May 14th. Details of the arrest were given and Mellor made a statement to the court in which he claimed he had tried his utmost to find a home for the children between 7.00pm and 11.00pm, but to no avail. He had even been before the Holbeck Guardians to see if they would take the girls in the workhouse but after all avenues had failed, he had taken them down to the canal and put them in the water in the hope that someone would find them and take care of them. After this and other evidence, Mellor was remanded in custody. Further hearings followed before Mellor was sent to the assizes on the two charges.

Thomas Mellor's trial took place at Leeds before Mr Justice Ridley on July 28th, 1900. The prosecution case was led by Mr Harold Thomas, assisted by Mr Edmondson, while the defence lay in the hands of Mr Horace Marshall. The only charge which was proceeded with was the murder of six-year-old Ada Beecroft.

Esther Ann Mellor, who lived at 13 Forest Street, Leeds, was the accused man's sister-in-law, being married to his brother, Arthur.

After explaining the circumstances of Mellor's relationship with the mother of the two girls, her subsequent death in an asylum and of his new relationship with Priscilla Redshaw, Esther went on to tell of the recent financial problems the family had suffered. After the eviction, Mellor had asked his brother, for lodgings but they had not had the room and so Arthur had reluctantly refused the request. Concerned for his well-being, Esther had asked Mellor what he would do with the girls if he couldn't find anywhere for them. Mellor had replied that, "The water is big enough to hold them and me and all. I have said it and it will be tonight." He did not, however, carry out his threats on that occasion.

Priscilla Redshaw, Mellor's long-suffering partner, explained how although he had a good job at the gas works and earned 17s per week, he only ever gave her 3s to look after the family and pay all the bills. When she had handed the children over to their father, on May 11th, he had said that he "would go to the bottom of the water with them".

Pamela Bramham who lived in Crossland Street, told the court that just before 11.00pm on the night of Friday, May 11th, she had seen Mellor with the children in Fourth Court after she had visited a friend who lived there. As Pamela passed the little group she heard Mellor say to his youngest daughter, "Don't cry little Annie." He turned to Pamela and asked her if she had seen Priscilla. She hadn't and after she had told him that, Mellor had commented that he had no idea what he was going to do with the children. She had suggested he might take them to his father's house, but Mellor had apparently not thought this a good idea. By bringing forward these witnesses, the prosecution were, of course, seeking to show that this was no spur of the moment act, but something that Thomas Mellor had been considering for some time.

Evidence was given that a man had been seen by the side of the canal at around 11.00pm on May 11th. At the time he was near Half Moon Bridge and had two young girls with him. It was too dark to identify either the man, or the girls but the witnesses noted that the elder girl wore a shawl over her head. The bodies were found floating near the same bridge at 5.00am the following morning and a shawl, identified as Ada Beecroft's, was found amongst the grass underneath the bridge. Further, at 11.30pm on May 11th, Mellor had been seen in a local restaurant and by that time, he was certainly alone.

Telling testimony was given by Constable Ernest Rodgers, who had been on duty in the cells at the Town Hall on Saturday, May 12th. At 5.30pm, he had checked on the prisoners, who included Thomas Mellor. As Rodgers looked in on Mellor, the prisoner began crying and then, without being prompted, made a lengthy statement which Constable Rodgers noted in his book.

In this statement, Mellor said that he had taken the girls to the workhouse and offered to pay for their upkeep but the authorities there had refused to take them, saying that they were not destitute. On the Friday, May 11th, he had taken them around all the neighbours' houses but no one would offer them a bed. Finally, out of desperation, he took them down by the canal.

Ignoring the fact that he had no right to question the prisoner, Constable Rodgers now prompted, "And threw them in?" Mellor was silent for a few seconds before replying, "No, shoved them in." Rodgers continued, "It is a wonder they didn't scream." To this Mellor had said, "The first one was very quiet but the other was the strongest and youngest and cried out 'Oh dada!'" In court, Mellor denied that he had said any of this.

For the defence, Mr Marshall asked for a verdict of manslaughter. Mellor had done all he could for his children and had placed them in the water with the expectation that their cries would attract the attention of some passer-by. The deaths were accidental and Mellor was therefore not guilty of murder. In his summing up, though, the trial judge pointed out that if this had been Mellor's intention, it surely made more sense to abandon the girls on the streets of Holbeck, where they would not have been in danger of losing their lives.

The jury retired at 3.05pm and took only 17 minutes to decide that Mellor was guilty of murdering Ada Beecroft, although they added a strong recommendation to mercy on the astonishing grounds of his previous kindness to his children. Since no evidence had been offered on the specific charge of murdering Annie Beecroft, and there was no point in pursuing that when Mellor would already face the death sentence, the judge directed the jury to return a formal not guilty verdict on this charge. Technically this meant that the murder of Annie Beecroft remains unsolved although, of course, the circumstances of the case are such that the man responsible for Ada's death was undoubtedly also the man who had taken Annie's life.

Asked if he wished to say anything, Mellor replied, "I do not see how the jury can convict me on the evidence of one lying constable. I have no recollection of making the statement than the paper on the wall. If I had made it, I should have some recollection of it. I don't think there is one spectator in court who will agree with the verdict."

In 1900, there was no appeal court, so a reprieve was now Mellor's only hope. Soon, the Home Secretary announced that he had found no reason to interfere with the sentence of death and Mellor's fate was sealed.

Thomas Mellor passed a fairly quiet last night on earth, rising at 6.00am the next morning and having a good breakfast at 7.30am. At 9.00am on Tuesday, August 16th, 1900, he was taken into the execution chamber at Leeds prison where he was hanged alongside Charles Benjamin Backhouse, who had shot a policeman, John William Kew, at Swinton, near Rotherham. The executioner was James Billington, assisted by his son, William. It was the fourth double execution at Armley.

CHAPTER TWO

THE DEATH OF MARY ANN

THERE appeared to be something very curious going on at 7 Star Fold, Beeston, in June 1900, for the 8th of that month, a Friday, was the last time anyone could recall seeing 33-year-old Mary Ann Blewitt or her husband Charles.

Robert Coffey, who lived at number 8, had seen Mary Ann at 8.30am on that day, when she was busy washing her doorstep. Some 12 hours later, at around 8.45pm, Robert had seen Mary Ann's husband, Charles Oliver Blewitt, pass by number 8 and apparently go to the back door of his own house. Just 15 minutes after this, at around 9.00pm, Sarah Harrison, who lived at 4 Star Fold, had seen Mary Ann at her doorstep. That, though, was the last time anyone had seen either Mary Ann or Charles and now the door was locked and the blinds had been pulled down.

Three days later, on June 11th, the landlord of the houses, Thomas Armitage, called to collect his rent. There was only one house where he failed to gain admittance and that was the Blewitt house at number 7. Thomas made several other attempts to gain admittance, all unsuccessful, until finally, on June 17th, he called again, this time accompanied by James Bunney and his wife, Jemima, who was also Charles Blewitt's mother.

Mr and Mrs Bunney had themselves been trying to get an answer at 7 Star Fold because Jemima had some belongings there which she wished to collect. They eventually went to Thomas Armitage who, ever a businessman, agreed to open the property for them, providing they first of all paid the rent arrears of 5s 6d. Once more Mr Armitage tried to gain access to his property and when there was again no answer to his knocking, with James and Jemima looking on, he broke open the front door with a pickaxe.

James Bunney was the first person to go into the house and there, in a chair, he found the body of Mary Ann Blewitt. A large shawl had been thrown over her and when this was removed, the horrified onlookers saw that her throat had been cut. The police were called and a search of the premises revealed a number of possible weapons. Two hatchets and three carving knives were found and all had been recently sharpened. More important, a couple of the knives appeared to be stained with blood. There was, however, no sign of Charles Blewitt, a man who the police now desperately wanted to interview.

The inquest on the dead woman opened at the Railway Hotel, Beeston, on June 18th before the city coroner, Mr J.C. Malcolm, and only evidence of identification was given by George Jackson, the dead woman's brother. The proceedings were reopened on June 25th when matters were once more adjourned for a further week. The third hearing took place on July 2nd when it was stated that by all accounts, Charles and Mary Ann Blewitt had lived happily together. No one could be found who had seen them engaged in arguments or rows. However, medical opinion was given that Mary Ann's wounds could not possibly be self-inflicted.

Further evidence was given that on July 1st, a second search of the house had revealed a six-chambered revolver and in a chest of drawers, Superintendent Gillespie had found a marriage certificate showing that Charles Oliver Blewitt, a native of Copper House in Cornwall, had married Mary Ann Jackson on August 20th, 1896. A note found with the marriage certificate read, "Please save these marriage lines for me while I want them. Your sister, Mary Ann Blewitt, No. 7, Star Fold, Beeston." The handwriting was identified as being Mary Ann's by her brother, George Jackson, who confirmed that his sister had given them to him for safekeeping. She had asked for their return some two months ago. Mary Ann had given no explanation for any of this behaviour but the inference was that she might have been concerned over the security of her marriage.

After hearing all the evidence, the inquest jury decided that they were looking at a case of murder and that the man responsible was the missing husband, Charles Oliver Blewitt. It now became all the more urgent to find him and bring him to justice.

There were two witnesses who were able to shed some light on what had happened to Charles Blewitt. James Boshell was an engineer but also helped his uncle in his hairdressing business situated at 59 Town Street, Beeston. On June 8th, at some time between 7.00pm and 8.00pm, Blewitt came into the shop and had a full moustache and a week's growth of beard removed. With hindsight, it was apparent that he was trying to change his appearance.

The second witness was Constable Blackburn, who was stationed at Staincliffe, Batley. He had been on duty in Halifax Road at 3.30am on June 9th when he noticed a man coming from the direction of Dewsbury. It was an unusual hour for someone to be walking the streets and the man was a stranger to him, so Blackburn asked him what he was doing. The man said he had come from Morley and was going to Heckmondwike to see if he could get work at the collieries there. He added that if he was unsuccessful, he would go on to Barnsley. The policeman walked with the stranger for perhaps half a mile before bidding him goodnight. Constable Blackburn believed that the man, who he had observed to be clean shaven, was none other than Charles Blewitt.

The breakthrough, when it came, was from information given by a number of men in Halifax that their new workmate fitted the description of the wanted man. This man had also admitted that he had recently arrived from Leeds. So it was that on July 3rd, at 10.00am when a man calling himself Oliver Jackson arrived for work at the foundry of Redman Brothers, machine tool makers of

Parkinson Lane, Halifax, he was told that he was wanted in the manager's office. Thinking that he might be in trouble for coming in late, Jackson duly went to the office where a gentleman introduced himself as Detective Inspector Bradley of the Halifax Borough Police. Inspector Bradley asked the man his name and received the reply, 'Oliver Jackson'. Bradley asked what his name was before he came to Halifax. Jackson hesitated for a moment and said, "Well, my name's Charles Blewitt." He was arrested and subsequently charged with the murder of his wife.

Blewitt's first appearance before the magistrates at Leeds came on July 4th where he was represented by Mr Arthur Willey. Only the most basic details of the case were given by the prosecutor, Mr T. Thornton, before Blewitt was remanded to July 12th. On that second date, the story of Blewitt's flight to Halifax was given and the fact that he had taken lodgings with a Mrs Elizabeth Ann Lamb at Dunkirk Street, on June 12th. Blewitt had arrived there at about 5.30pm and said he had come from Leeds. That night, as Mrs Lamb hung his coat up for him, a razor fell from his pocket. This was, of course, not an unusual item for a man to carry, but Mrs Lamb did find some of her new lodger's behaviour strange. The following morning, after 'Jackson' had gone to work, Elizabeth had gone to his bedroom and found that his bed did not appear to have been slept in. Further, she found a pair of underpants and a singlet which had been left on the floor. These were soiled and apparently bloodstained and, far from being satisfied with her guest, when he returned home for his dinner the landlady told him to find other lodgings.

That same evening, Blewitt, still using the name Jackson, had taken fresh lodgings with Hannah Chapman at Kings Cross Road, where he remained until his arrest. At one stage during his stay there, Hannah had read some details of the murder at Beeston and remarked that she had some relatives living quite close by. She asked her lodger if he knew that area to which he had replied, "Not much, I live at the other end."

The evidence was not completed on July 12th, so a further

remand followed, this time to July 17th. It was on that occasion that Blewitt was sent for trial at the next assizes. That trial took place on July 30th, 1900, before Mr Justice Ridley. Blewitt's defence rested in the hands of Mr W.J. Waugh and Mr C. Felix Palmer, while the prosecution was led by Mr Banks, assisted by Mr F. Brent Grotrian.

James Bunney explained how, having heard that the house at Star Fold was locked, he had visited a number of times to try to gain entrance before he finally returned on June 17th, with the landlord. Bunney described finding the body of Mary Ann Blewitt with a shawl thrown over her face and upper body and confirmed that there was no razor or other weapon which might have caused her wounds, anywhere near the body. He also told the court that he had never heard Charles and Mary Ann argue and intimated that there was nothing inherently suspicious in Charles shaving off his moustache. It was something he had done many times before and he often walked about clean shaven.

Charles' mother, Jemima, agreed that her son and his wife had always seemed to be happy together and added that it was not unusual for Charles to use the name Oliver Jackson. Indeed, some eight months ago, he had taken out an insurance policy in that name.

Many of the neighbours in Star Fold told the court of their last sightings of Charles and Mary Ann. Robert Coffey, who reported that he had seen Charles at around 8.45pm on June 8th, said that at the time, he was clean shaven. He was asked how he could be absolutely sure that this sighting was on June 8th and replied that he knew only because the police had told him. In effect, he was not claiming that the police had 'manufactured' his evidence, but that they had pointed out when Blewitt had vanished and he was assuming that this was the same day. Pressed by the judge to clarify the matter, Coffey became more and more confused until finally Mr Justice Ridley said to Mr Banks, "Have you a plan of this place. This witness is so stupid I can make nothing of him. I think he knows more than he has told us."

James Edward Smith was a planer at the tool makers where

Blewitt had obtained employment in Halifax. He told the court that Blewitt had started work on June 12th. Six days later, on June 18th, Smith saw a report of the murder in a Leeds newspaper and the following morning, mentioned it to Blewitt, saying, "Do you come from Leeds?" Blewitt had replied in the affirmative and Smith had added, "You will know about this murder at Beeston then." Blewitt had replied, "I do not come from that quarter," and added that he had not seen the report, claiming that he was not a good scholar and so did not read much. Four or five days later, Smith read another report, stating that Blewitt had shaved his moustache off. "Look out" said Smith, "The bobbies is after all them that's without a moustache." Blewitt had made no reply.

John Boyle was another fellow worker and he, too, had spoken to Blewitt about the murder. Blewitt had said he was not in Leeds at the time it took place and denied that he had ever been married. When other reports said that Blewitt had been in America, Boyle's workmate also denied that he had ever set foot out of England.

When the trial was resumed after lunch, there occurred a strange affair in the public gallery. In their eagerness to get seats, a group of women fell over each other and in the crush that followed, began to scream and shriek. The judge ordered the court officers to turn some of the women out and ensure that there was no further overcrowding in the gallery.

Medical evidence proved to be crucial to the case, for the defence were claiming that Blewitt had merely gone to Halifax to find work and knew nothing of the death of his wife, who must have killed herself. Dr George Henry Heald, the police surgeon, stated that there were wounds on Mary Ann's throat and hands and this was more consistent with homicide than suicide.

The neck wounds were irregular and this in itself implied that this was a case of murder. If Mary Ann had decided to kill herself, she would have had no interference and so the wound would have been more smooth and regular. This, of course, took no account of the fact that she would have been nervous and her hand would almost certainly have shaken. More telling, however, was the fact that the wounds on Mary Ann's hands were such that if she had cut her throat first, she would have been unable to inflict the cuts on her hands and if she had cut her hands first, she would not have been able to hold the razor to inflict the wound on her throat. Added to this, of course, there was no weapon found near the body so Mary Ann would have had to cut herself and then conceal the weapon. Finally, on the shawl there were no bloodstains which could have come from Mary Ann's hands, so how could she have thrown the shawl over her own head without staining it?

The jury retired to consider their verdict and after 70 minutes returned to announce that they were hopelessly deadlocked and there was no hope that they would come to a verdict. Mr Justice Ridley had no option but to order a retrial.

Mr Justice Bruce had been hearing civil cases at the assizes but on August 6th, he found himself presiding over the second trial of Charles Blewitt. The same prosecution and defence teams were assembled and this time, the evidence took two days to be heard. Perhaps the biggest difference was the summing up at the end of the trial when Mr Justice Bruce made much of the fact that Blewitt had made no fuss over the news of his wife's death. Surely if this were a suicide, he would have been distraught upon hearing this terrible news and would have flown back to Beeston to see what he could do. There was also the fact that a half-finished meal lay on the kitchen table in Star Fold. Was it reasonable to assume that a woman would rise, halfway through a meal and kill herself? This time the jury were out for only 45 minutes before deciding that Blewitt was guilty as charged.

On August 18th, Blewitt wrote a last letter to his mother and father. It read, "My Dear Mother and Father, I received your letter this morning, and was pleased to hear from you, but was sorry to hear that grandfather was so ill. When you come you might all come at one time. You can come when you can make it convenient for you to do so, and I hope that Ernest and Lizzie will do so. Give my regards to all the family — From your loving son, Charles O. Blewitt."

Blewitt could not write, so the letter would have been dictated, and it was noted that no mention had been made of the crime for which he had been sentenced. This indifferent attitude was confirmed when someone once mentioned that he had only a few days left to live. Blewitt had remarked, "What does it matter? A fellow's got to die some time."

On August 21st, no fewer than seven of Blewitt's relatives visited him and again he never spoke about the crime. On the night before his execution, Blewitt sat on his prison bed, enjoying a large cigar when one of the warders started to leave his cell. "I say, where are you going?" shouted Blewitt. The warder replied that he was going off for a half a pint to which Blewitt had said, "Well old man, remember me when you are drinking it."

Charles Oliver Blewitt slept well until the small hours of Tuesday, August 28th, 1900, but from 3.00am onwards he was very restless. He ate little of the breakfast provided but offered no resistance when the executioners entered his cell and pinioned him. At 9.00am Blewitt was hanged at Leeds by James Billington who was assisted by his son William. A large crowd had gathered outside the prison gates for what was the third Leeds hanging of 1900.

The inquest afterwards was held before Mr J.C. Malcolm. Here some of the history of Blewitt was revealed. He had lived in America for 11 years and been joined there by an uncle, three years before his return to England. That journey home had taken place in 1895 and on the boat he had fallen down a hatchway and badly bruised his head. It was also stated that before this crime, Charles Blewitt had never been in trouble with the police.

CHAPTER THREE

A CALLOUS MAN

GEORGE SMITH could not have been described as the best husband in the world. A bricklayer by trade, he much preferred not to work and live instead on the money his long-suffering wife, Martha, brought in. She worked as a domestic servant and by all accounts was a hard working and dedicated employee, supporting not just her idle husband, but also their two children, Ivy and George. It was Martha's second marriage and she also had two grown-up children from her first marriage but they no longer lived at home.

In June 1905, Martha Smith left her second husband. She took her children to live with their grandfather and then went to work for Mr Harold Skelton, a pawnbroker who lived in Burley Road, Leeds. This position did not last long but that was no reflection on Martha's work. One day, soon after Martha had started work for Skelton, he came home to find her hiding in the kitchen. Mr Skelton noticed that her face was bruised and heavily plastered. After much cajoling, Martha told him that George Smith had been around to visit, they had argued and he had beaten her.

While Martha might have been one to accept this sort of behaviour from George, Harold Skelton certainly wasn't. The next morning, Smith visited his wife again only to find himself on the receiving end of a severe tongue lashing from Mr Skelton who berated him for the way he had treated Martha. Smith was contrite and promised not to do it again, but the day after he returned once more and demanded that Martha leave Mr Skelton's employ there and then. After some argument, Martha reluctantly complied.

Martha, though, was not about to move back in with her husband. At first she went to live with her mother at Wakefield but on Saturday, September 9th, 1905, she found new employment with the Glendinning family who lived in The Kells, Riddings Road, Ilkley. Meanwhile, George Smith had taken new lodgings with Mrs Storey at 199 Park Lane, Leeds, making a point of telling his new landlady that his wife would be providing the money to pay for his rooms.

The Glendinning family had three members living at The Kells. In addition to Mr and Mrs Glendinning, their daughter Catherine also lived at home, but on Tuesday, September 12th, only Miss Glendinning was there, her parents being away on holiday. At 9.00am even she went out, telling Martha that she was going into Leeds. When Catherine left, Martha was washing some clothes downstairs in the basement of the house.

Catherine Glendinning returned home at 7.00pm and entered the house by the front door. Going through the house, she found to her surprise that the back door was locked and there was apparently no sign of Martha Smith. Catherine called out a couple of times, but did not receive a reply. After looking all over the house, she went down into the cellar which was the last place she had seen Martha. The room was in darkness but there, lying on the floor, Catherine could make out a shape which she assumed was Martha. Thinking that the poor woman might have fainted, she took some water and threw it over the still form, but this did nothing to revive Martha.

Only when she moved closer did Catherine Glendinning see that Martha Smith was covered in blood. Help was summoned but it was too late for Martha. She was dead and Dr T. Browne Hearder who attended the scene counted 49 separate wounds including a cut throat which was the direct cause of death.

It was not only the circumstances of Martha's relationship with her estranged husband that led police to start looking for George Smith. Witnesses had seen a man fitting his description in the area on the day that Martha met her death. At 2.00pm, a man in Wheatley Lane had asked Ada Finch for directions to Miss Glendinning's house at Ilkley, saying he wanted to speak to a Mrs Smith who was in service there. Later still, in The Grove, Beatrice Cryer was stopped by a man she subsequently identified as Smith. Again he asked for directions and was last seen heading towards Riddings Road.

It was also possible to pinpoint exactly when Smith had finally arrived at the house where his wife was working. Margaret Watson was a maid at the house next door to The Kells and she had passed the time of day with Martha as she was hanging out some washing in the garden. This was at about 4.00pm and before this, at soon after 2.30pm, Margaret had seen a man enter the Glendinning house without knocking. The man went in through the back door and, once again, he fitted the description of George Smith.

When the police went to interview Smith, though, they found that he was no longer at his lodgings. Mrs Storey reported that he had left the house at 9.00am on September 12th, taking his tools with him and saying that he was going on a bricklaying job in Halifax. However, just a few minutes after saying this to Mrs Storey, Smith called at a neighbour's house and left the tools there with the occupant, Mrs Wright. Further, upon checking her kitchen, Mrs Storey had noticed that a sharp pork butcher's knife was missing from the house.

The inquest on Martha Smith opened on September 13th before the deputy coroner, Mr C. Percy Charlesworth. After hearing evidence of identification, given by the dead woman's sister, Jane Crook of 2 Clement Street, Orsett Road, Wakefield, he adjourned matters until September 28th.

In the meantime, a detailed description of Smith was sent to all police stations in the area and it was this which led to his arrest. At 5.00am on September 14th, Constable John William Eason was on duty near the Wakefield town boundary when he noticed a man who fitted the description of Smith. Since this man also had what appeared to be bloodstains on his clothing, he was stopped and escorted to the police station. Here he admitted his identity but denied vehemently that he had anything to do with the murder of his wife. Smith appeared in the Otley police court the same day where, in addition to evidence of arrest, the court heard Dr Bennett, the police surgeon, testify that upon examining Smith he had found recent cuts on both his hands. There were bloodstains on his clothing and heavy bloodstaining around his right knee. Told he would be remanded for one week, Smith was asked if he had anything to say. He replied, "No, you can remand me." Later that day, Martha Smith was laid to rest in Wakefield.

The final hearing took place on September 21st before the stipendary magistrate, Mr R.P. Arnold-Foster, the case for the Director of Public Prosecutions being put by Mr Edgar C. Newstead. All the evidence was heard before Smith was sent for trial at the next assizes. One week later, the inquest returned a verdict of wilful murder against Smith.

George Smith faced his trial at Leeds on December 7th before Mr Justice Jelf. Smith was defended by Mr E.H. Chapman while the prosecution case was led by Mr Harold Thomas, assisted by Mr R.A. Shepherd.

All the witnesses previously mentioned repeated the evidence they had given at both the police court and the inquest. Two letters, sent by Martha to her husband, were also read out. In the first of these, Martha had written, "My dear husband, I wish you had not taken that money. It has caused me a lot of trouble this week, and I cannot help thinking about it.

"I do hope you will try and pay it back, for I don't see what I can earn towards it. I have had to work for a bit of something. I don't know what you are doing for your living, but you don't seem to get work. Aren't you ashamed of yourself that me and the children had to go on other people's fireside? …I expect you are carrying on a fine game, but don't you forget it, I get to know of your games. You might wish me out of your way.

"Our Ivy has not been very well this week, but she is all right again. I wish you could send me something. George and Ivy send their love, and keep asking me if you are working, where you are living… I think I will conclude with kind love, as I am in a hurry, going out to do a bit more work. Good night and may God Almighty bless you. From your wife, in name only…"

The second letter was filled with talk of the work she was now doing but ended, "…I wish you had some work. I am tired of thinking. I hope you won't be disappointed that I cannot meet you tomorrow [Sunday] but I will meet you on Monday… With kind love to you, and may God help you to be a better man. I hope you will get work before Bank Holiday."

It was not until Smith stepped into the witness box that the trial took a sensational turn. To begin with he gave some basic details about himself and then admitted, in the most matter of fact way, that he had taken Martha Smith's life. He began, "She was an affectionate wife. I was very fond of her. I did not take a knife from my lodgings. On the afternoon of September 12th, I went to Mr Glendinning's house at 2.30 and went into the kitchen. I found my missus there and had some talk with her. She tried to keep me from her, saying she had somebody else. She shoved me away and, as I had a penknife in my hand, I went for her. She went for me, and hit me on the shoulder with square board. We had a struggle and I dabbed the knife at her. I don't think she had any sharp instrument. She cut my hand as she was taking the knife from me."

Smith was asked if he had done this to his wife because of what she had said to him about having another man in her life. He admitted that this was so and added that he thought a great deal about her and had often walked 20 miles in a day just to see her. His barrister, Mr Chapman asked Smith if he had acted in the passion of the moment. He said he had and that he suffered from a short temper.

Questioned about the knife, which had never been found, Smith said that he had thrown it away somewhere in Ilkley as he was walking back to the railway station, but it was when he was asked about the bloodstains on his clothes, and his right knee, that the people listening to the case began to gasp in disbelief.

Smith admitted, "I stayed with her until the finish. I kissed her as she lay on the floor and she kissed me. I got on my knees and lifted her out of the blood and put her where she was found. She was not quite dead then." Smith had never admitted cutting his wife's throat and he was now pressed on this point but replied, "I didn't do that, I'm sure about it." The judge intervened at this point and again asked Smith to clarify what he was saying.

Smith turned to face Mr Justice Jelf and admitted, "I certainly did it sir. I don't say I made such a gash. It was only about one and a half inches I did." He went on to confirm that he must have given her all the wounds but he could not say exactly how many as he just kept on jabbing at her. Finally, when asked if Martha had any means of defending herself from this onslaught, Smith had replied, "Certainly. Her hands."

The jury retired at 3.40pm and took only 13 minutes to decide that Smith was guilty. At 9.00am on Thursday, December 28th, 1905, George Smith was hanged at Leeds by Henry Pierrepoint, who was assisted by John Ellis. The drop was reported to be 6ft 9ins.

CHAPTER FOUR

A BIT OF BOTHER

FIFTY-eight-year-old Thomas Wilkinson had been a cashier for Messrs Fieldhouse & Jowett, dyers and sizers of Fieldhead, for more than 14 years. The company had their factory at Legram Street, Listerhills, Bradford, but they also maintained a small office in the town at 18 Swaine Street.

The office in Swaine Street was really only ever used on a Friday. It was on that day that Wilkinson would go into the city centre, carrying out banking operations for the company and cash a cheque to cover the weekly wages. The single room office contained nothing more than a desk, a chair and a high stool and was approached by a long corridor. Off that corridor there were a number of other offices belonging to many other businesses and it was in one of those that Samuel Jowett, who had no connection with Fieldhouse & Jowett, was working on the afternoon of Friday, July 31st, 1908.

It was at 2.30pm when Jowett, a warehouseman for George Armitage Ltd, returned from a late lunch and heard a thud coming from the office of Fieldhouse & Jowett, which happened to be next door to his own. At first, Jowett thought nothing of this but when a number of low moans also emanated from next door, he rushed to investigate.

Looking through the small glass window, Jowett saw nothing

except for a hat resting on the desk and a walking stick hanging upon the wall. Of Mr Wilkinson there was apparently no sign, but when Jowett opened the door and walked into the office he found Thomas Wilkinson lying face down on the floor, his feet close to the door. Wilkinson was seriously injured. He had a severe head wound and lay in a pool of blood. Jowett wasted no time in running for the police.

The first officer on the scene was Constable Laycock. He had been on duty in Forster Square when Jowett ran up to him and told him what had happened. Laycock had not been at the scene long when other officers arrived, including a constable who by coincidence, was also named Wilkinson. Between them they did their best to dress the victim's wounds and it was Laycock who went with him in the ambulance to the Royal Infirmary. In the meantime, an initial search of the office had revealed a poker lying on the floor. This was covered with blood, hair and brain matter and had obviously been used to batter Wilkinson into unconsciousness. Blood was splashed on the office walls to a height of six feet.

At the infirmary, Constable Laycock searched Wilkinson's pockets. Here he found a gold watch and chain, nine cheques and less than £1 in coins. There was no sign of the small purse that Wilkinson was known to always carry.

The initial police investigation threw up a number of valuable witnesses. Harry Jowett was the manager at Wilkinson's place of work and he told the police that Wilkinson had left the factory at 11.30am on July 31st. Jowett had given Wilkinson two cheques to a total of £63 to cover the wages, but having checked with their bankers, Jowett was able to confirm that these had not yet been cashed. Other cheques had also been handed over for Wilkinson to pay into the company account. These had totalled £116 10s 4d, and they had not been paid in either. This information could, of course, have indicated a possible motive. Someone who knew Thomas Wilkinson's routine might have gone to the office, believing that the banking had been done and hoping to steal the wages of £63 now in cash. The assailant had merely arrived too early, for Wilkinson had not yet had time to go to the bank, and as some sort of compensation the robber had stolen Wilkinson's purse instead.

Albert Ashton was an office boy for Fieldhouse & Jowett and at 11.00am he had answered the telephone at the factory. The caller asked for Mr Wilkinson but did not identify himself. Ashton could, of course, hear only half the conversation that followed. Mr Wilkinson had been explaining to someone exactly what time he would be in the town office. Could it be that his attacker had actually made an appointment to see him? If so, this indicated that the assailant might be someone who Thomas Wilkinson knew.

The office boy also supplied another piece of interesting information. At 9.00am Mr Wilkinson had handed young Albert a note and asked him to deliver it to 44-year-old John William Ellwood at his home. When Albert arrived at the house, Ellwood was not at home, so the letter was left with his wife. It did not escape the attention of the police officers that Ellwood knew Wilkinson and had, until fairly recently, worked for Fieldhouse & Jowett and would therefore know about Wilkinson's Friday routine.

Meanwhile, at the Royal Infirmary, Thomas Wilkinson was not responding to treatment. At 5.00pm his wife was summoned to his bedside and at 7.30pm, he died. This was now a case of murder and it was news of that crime which brought forward another witness, one whose evidence would give the police the breakthrough they needed.

Isaac Pollard was a cart driver who lived at 6 Back William Street. At some time between 2.00pm and 2.30pm, Pollard had been on his way to his employer's premises in Swaine Street and had passed number 18. As he reached that address, Pollard heard a cry of, "Oh!" and stopped to look down the corridor which led to all the offices. A red-faced man came out of one of the rooms, carrying a long thin object which was wrapped in newspaper. Pollard asked if there was a problem.

"We are having a bit of bother," replied the man. Thinking that whatever was happening had nothing to do with him, Pollard went to his employer's office at 12 Swaine Street, but stayed there for only a few minutes. As he left, he saw the red-faced man coming out of number 18 and asked him how he had got on. The man said, "Oh all right." But as he walked off, Pollard could see that the man was rubbing his hands together and they appeared to be covered in blood.

Curious, Pollard now followed the man along Swaine Street to Charles Street, across Leeds Road and into Hall Lane. At this point he lost his quarry, so returned to Swaine Street where he spoke to a man he had seen previously, sitting on the steps of number 20. This man, Henry Mason, was not known to Pollard but in the brief conversation that followed, Mason said that he, too, had seen the red-faced man going in to number 18, and re-emerge out not long afterwards. There was, however, no sign at this stage that anything untoward had taken place and so both Mason and Pollard went about their own business.

At 10.30pm on July 31st, by which time, of course, Thomas Wilkinson was dead, Isaac Pollard first heard that there had been a brutal murder at 18 Swaine Street. Pollard immediately went to the police and told them what he had observed that afternoon. He also gave them descriptions of the two men he had seen, Henry Mason and the red-faced man. He told the police, "The man was about 40, 5ft 10ins tall. He was broad set with a very red face and a black, heavy, drooping moustache and a prominent nose. He was wearing a brown mixture cloth suit with a green stripe running through it. He also wore a gold albert with a dog-link pattern, which had some sort of shield attached to it. This shield had either a coat of arms or an enamelled figure emblazoned upon it. Finally, the man wore a billycock hat."

It was late that night when the first of the men Pollard had described was traced. Henry Mason admitted that he was sitting on the steps of 20 Swaine Street. It was just after 2.00pm when he had seen a man enter number 18. The man had been carrying a long, thin parcel wrapped in newspaper. This was at least 18ins long and may have been 2ft. The man had been inside for two or three minutes, after which he came out and had a brief conversation with another man, who, of course, was Pollard. This latter man walked away while the first man returned to number 18. Just minutes later he was back outside and had another brief talk with Pollard, who by this time had returned.

The description the two men had given fitted the man whose name had already been mentioned by Albert Ashton, the office boy. This was why, at 4.00am on August 1st, Detective Sergeant Knowles and Detective Constable Pounds called at the house at 62 Edinburgh Street where John William Ellwood lived. Told that he was being interviewed about the murder of Thomas Wilkinson, Ellwood replied, "I know nothing about it, but I will go with you." Ellwood was taken to the Town Hall where later that day he was placed into an identification parade and picked out by both Isaac Pollard and Henry Mason. John Ellwood was then charged with murder.

Later that day, August 1st, Ellwood made his first appearance at the police court. He was not legally represented and the proceedings lasted for only a few minutes.

It was also on August 1st when the inquest opened before the city coroner, Mr J.G. Hutchinson. Only evidence of identification was given by the murdered man's wife, who also said that Wilkinson had arrived home for dinner at 1.00pm and returned to the office at about 2.00pm.

Ellwood was back at the police court on August 8th, by then having obtained representation in the form of Mr C.L. Atkinson. The prosecution were not ready to proceed and Ellwood was again remanded, this time until August 15th. Before that, on August 12th, the inquest re-opened and a verdict of murder against Ellwood was returned.

There were three more appearances at the police court. On August 15th, Ellwood was remanded to August 18th and his final appearance took place on August 26th when, after hearing all the evidence, the magistrates sent him for trial at Leeds. That trial opened on November 10th before Mr Justice Pickford. The prosecution case was led by Mr C.F. Lowenthal, assisted by Mr Frank Newboult, while Ellwood's defence lay in the hands of Mr Charles Mellor, who was assisted by Mr J.J. Wright and Mr Godfrey Ellis.

Albert Ashton repeated his evidence about the telephone call he had taken for Mr Wilkinson. He heard Wilkinson say, "I can't be there. I am going to my dinner at one. I shall be there between two and two fifteen."

In addition to the details of the cheques he had given to Thomas Wilkinson, Harry Jowett confirmed that he had seen Ellwood on the day Wilkinson was attacked. At 4.30pm, Jowett noticed the accused in Back Edinburgh Street and told him that something had happened at the town office. At the time, reports were unclear and Jowett was not sure whether Wilkinson had suffered an accident or not. He said to Ellwood, "There has been an accident or something at our town office and Mr Wilkinson has either cut his throat, tumbled off a stool, or there has been foul play."

Ellwood made no comment and when seconds later, Jowett's brother had come up to him and said that medical opinion was that there was no hope for Wilkinson, Ellwood maintained his silence. Harry Jowett was also able to confirm that Ellwood had worked for his company but had been discharged in April 1908 because he had had a disagreement with Walter Jowett, another of the company directors.

Mary Craven was employed by Constantine & Son, umbrella and stick manufacturers of Swaine Street. At around 2.10pm on July 31st, she had seen a tall, well-built man standing in the doorway of number 18 and had later seen him talking to Mr Pollard. She, too, had picked out Ellwood at an identity parade, two days after he had been arrested, so now there were three witnesses who swore that Ellwood had been at the town office at the time of the attack.

Joseph Mason, who was no relation to Henry, worked at the Fountain Brewery and at some time between 1.30pm and 1.45pm

33

on July 31st, he had seen Ellwood in Manchester Road. He had known Ellwood for 16 years and they had served together as soldiers in South Africa. The two fell into conversation and went for a drink together. At first this evidence might not appear important but it put Ellwood in Manchester Road where someone bought a poker which might have been the murder weapon.

Samuel Ellis worked at a shop at 89 Manchester Road and sometime between noon and 3.00pm a man came into his shop and purchased a poker for 3d. Ellis had a habit of wrapping purchases in newspaper and this is exactly what he did with the poker. Mr Ellis' evidence, though, was strange to say the least. At the inquest, Ellis had said that he could not identify Ellwood, but later, at the police court, he changed his evidence and said that he now certainly could. He also confirmed that he had known Ellwood for many years and had not given a positive identification before only because he wanted to be 100 per cent sure. This ambivalence perhaps damaged the effect of his testimony.

The police, of course, held that the motive for this crime was robbery. Attempts were made to show that Ellwood had financial problems. William Richardson was the landlord of the Gardener's Arms in Melville Street. Ellwood was the secretary of a money club at this establishment and on July 30th, contributions of more than £184 had been given to Ellwood for distribution amongst the club members. Unfortunately for the prosecution, Mr Richardson was able to confirm that every single penny had been properly paid out. Richardson also mentioned that Ellwood had been in his pub at 5.00pm on the day of the murder and had said, "Have you heard the news about Tom Wilkinson? It is a terrible affair. It has been more than a one-man job."

Evidence was given that the brown suit with a green stripe had been found in Ellwood's house and had shown evidence of blood-staining. Then the time came for the medical evidence. Dr Frederick William Eurich had performed the post-mortem with Dr William Wrangham. He described at least ten violent blows with the poker found at the scene of the crime. The bones forming the back and sides of Wilkinson's skull had been broken into many pieces and the posterior third of the left half of the brain had been excessively lacerated and reduced to a pulp.

The defence called a number of witnesses. Norah Gledhill lived in Cobden Street and she saw Ellwood on the day of the murder. At the time he was wearing a light green cap, not a billycock hat. She remembered it well because it was a windy day and the cap blew off near her gate.

Thomas Gawith was the superintendent of the British Homes Assurance Company and he confirmed that Ellwood had been employed by his company from April 18th at a salary of 15s a week. He also earned a small amount of commission which added perhaps another shilling per week to his income. He was therefore in regular employment with a regular salary.

Ellwood went into the box to give evidence on his own behalf. He explained that before his marriage he had been in the West Riding Regiment and was discharged in 1894 after serving his country for 12 years. He claimed that he had not been near the office in Swaine Street on the day that Wilkinson had been attacked but agreed that he had received a letter from the dead man on the morning of July 31st. This letter was about a new situation that Wilkinson was helping him to find and read, "Dear Ellwood, I have not seen the gentleman I was telling you about, but will let you know in the course of a few days." Unfortunately the letter had been destroyed after Ellwood had read it, although he had shown it to his wife first. As for the bloodstains on his clothing, that was easily explained. His wife looked after a child during the day and on July 25th the child had fallen in the yard and bled badly. He had picked the boy up and would have blood on his clothing from that accident. As for his movements on the day of the attack, he had left home at 8.45am but did not feel well so did not go on his rounds and returned home in the early afternoon. As for the shop where the poker was purchased, he had never been inside it and did not even know where it was.

This was in part confirmed by two witnesses. James Francis Gregory was Ellwood's brother-in-law and lived with him. On July 25th he had heard a cry from the yard and was there as Ellwood rushed out and picked up a small boy who had fallen over, cutting his face badly.

Ada Ellwood had been married to the accused man for 22 years and they had four children. Not only did she corroborate the evidence of the child falling and cutting himself but added that her husband had been at home between 2.00pm and 2.20pm on July 31st. She also confirmed the contents of the letter her husband had received from Thomas Wilkinson.

Ellwood's defence team claimed that there was no motive that could be put at their client's door. He had been fond of the dead man and had no reason to kill him. The purse was missing but there was no evidence that it had contained any cash at the time. Ellwood was not in financial difficulties and had £1 6s 10d on him when he was arrested. The witnesses who said they had seen him were simply mistaken.

The jury retired at 1.45pm on November 11th and returned at 2.53pm to announce that Ellwood was guilty as charged. In response Ellwood said, "I have nothing to say, not guilty of the charge." He was sentenced to death.

In the condemned cell, he apparently slept well and showed no loss of appetite. At 9.00am on Thursday, December 3rd, 1908, John William Ellwood was hanged at Armley jail by Henry Pierrepoint who was assisted by his brother, Thomas. He made no confession to the murder of Thomas Wilkinson.

CHAPTER FIVE

DEAD AS A MACKEREL

I**T IS** perhaps a truism that most couples who live together argue from time to time. It may also be a fact that sometimes these arguments develop into serious altercations where even physical violence may be used. Of course, some people seem to do little else but argue. One such couple were Thomas Mead and Clara Howell.

In 1908, Thomas and Clara, who had been together for seven years, lived in Crook's Yard, Well Street, which was off West Street, Leeds. Thomas was a gasworker, Clara was a tailoress and they had lived at various addresses in Leeds and Bradford before, around late July 1908, they finally settled down in Crook's Yard. There were only three houses there, which meant that only two neighbours had to put up with the constant bickering, fighting and shouting that emanated from Thomas Mead's house.

One of those neighbours was Sarah Whittaker and she had first-hand experience of the volatile nature of Thomas and Clara's relationship. In mid-November, Sarah had been woken at 3.00am by a policeman who told her that Clara was asking for her. When Sarah went next door she found the poor woman nursing a nasty injury to her head. Her partner denied that he was responsible, insisting that Clara had hit her head on the edge of the sink — and since Clara made no official complaint, no further action was taken.

On the night of Friday, November 27th, 1908, Clara spent some time in Sarah Whittaker's house but later she and Thomas went out together for the evening. When they returned, though, Sarah could hear yet another argument. Mead shouted, "Where's that two shillings you took out of my pocket?" Sarah heard Clara deny over and over again that she had stolen any money. Then followed the sounds of what was probably a violent attack. The police were called and two officers paid a visit on Thomas Mead. The argument ended and for once, all was quiet in Crook's Yard. The silence did not last for long, however. At 1.00am, the noise started again and now that there were no police on the scene, it went on and on. It was not until 3.00am on the Saturday that the racket finally subsided.

Just a few hours later, Sarah Whittaker heard someone bang on the shutters of Mead's house and shout, "Get up Tommy, it's Saturday morning." Shortly afterwards, when Mead had still not appeared, Sarah herself knocked on the door and cried out, "Get up Tommy, it's a quarter to six." From inside, Mead's voice replied, "I am up." Satisfied that all was well, Sarah returned home and attended to her own family.

It was not until 9.00am that Thomas Mead finally left his house, locking the front door behind him. At the time, Sarah Whittaker was cleaning the steps of a shop in West Street and as Mead passed, they exchanged pleasantries before the subject of the last argument was broached. "What do you think of her, Sarah?" asked Mead, referring, of course, to Clara. Sarah replied, "What do I think of you both? If there's not an alteration soon, there'll be murder." Mead stood in silence for a few seconds before muttering, "There will an' all." Finally, since Sarah had seen nothing of Clara that morning, she asked where she was. Mead said that she had gone to her mother's and that he would be going up there later after he had collected his back pay. Mead strolled off down West Street and was not seen again that day.

Clara Howell had often visited her mother's house but had never before stayed away all day. As Saturday wore on, Sarah Whittaker grew suspicious and eventually, on Sunday morning, satisfied that something was wrong, she again contacted the police. In due course, Constable F. W. Garbutt appeared and having failed to gain entry to Mead's house, and noting that the shutters were still closed, he decided that further investigation was necessary.

Finding a ladder, Constable Garbutt climbed up to a bedroom window, smashed the glass with his truncheon and gained entry. The room was empty of any furniture but there was a pile of rags and sacking in one corner. Underneath that sacking lay the body of Clara Howell. She was wearing only a pair of stockings and her face was a mass of bruises, as was the upper part of her body. Medical attention was summoned but Clara was already dead and the initial opinion was that she had been kicked to death. Not surprsingly, a full-scale search was launched for Thomas Mead.

In fact Mead had not gone far and had been telling as many people as possible what he had done. In the early evening, Mead had gone into the Railway Hotel on Spence Lane. Here he fell into conversation with John William Prenderville and mentioned that Clara had taken two shillings out of his pocket. Mead went on to tell Prenderville that he had struck Clara and she had fallen over. He had gone to bed but when he woke later, Clara was moaning and groaning. Mead had carried her upstairs where she died after a few minutes. He stayed with her body until 9.00am when he went to collect his pay.

Not long after this first 'confession' Mead involved himself in a conversation with some other drinkers. They were talking about football and after some opinions had been expressed, Mead swore at one of the men who punched Mead in the face, knocking him to the ground. The landlord, Mr R.A. Burns, realising that Mead was already drunk and would almost certainly cause more trouble, threw him out into the street whereupon Mead shouted at him, "I have done one in. Let me go back and chivy him. If you don't believe me, take the key and go look."

By now it was 6.00pm and as Mead picked himself up from the

roadway, a friend of his, Robert Prust, came up and asked what had happened. Mead shouted, "I have been in yon boozer." At this he gestured towards the Railway Hotel and complained that a man had hit him in the eye. He went on, "If I could have got hold of him I would have pulled his throttle out and swung for two instead of one." He paused, looked directly at Prust and said, "I have done the missus in Bob." This last sentence was repeated several times before Mead elaborated by saying that they had argued and he had left her 'as dead as a mackerel'.

By 7.00pm Mead had arrived at 5 Lisbon Court where the door was opened by Margaret Shuttleworth, a married woman who had separated from her husband and returned to her parents' house at Lisbon Court, a house owned by Mick Robinson and his wife, who were friends of Thomas Mead.

Mead asked Margaret if she thought her father would let him have a sleep there. She told him to make himself comfortable on the sofa and then asked him why his eye was bloodshot. Mead told her about the fight at the Railway Hotel.

After Mead had been at Lisbon Court for some time, Margaret Shuttleworth asked after Clara but Mead would only say, enigmatically, that if Mick Robinson knew what he had done, he wouldn't let him stay there. He said that he had given Clara two black eyes and killed her, but since he also said that Clara was at her mother's, Margaret did not take this confession, his fourth of the night, seriously and at about 11.00pm went to her own bed, leaving Mead on the sofa. During the night, however, she heard him shouting about 'the murder' again.

The following morning, Mead again repeated that he had killed Clara and suggested that when it got dark, he was going to make for Bradford. Soon afterwards, a neighbour's little girl ran into the house and told, breathlessly, of how the police had found Clara Howell dead. Mead immediately leapt to his feet, asked for his cap and ran out of the house.

After speaking to Margaret Shuttleworth, the police established that Mead was still in the immediate area and appeared to be visiting his usual haunts as though nothing had happened. They decided to visit Mead's known friends and it was this that lead to the fugitive's arrest. It was 10.20pm when Detective Inspector Wilson and Detective Constable Wright called at 14 Chadwick Place, Whitehall Road, where they found Mead warming himself by the fire in the kitchen. He was taken to New Wortley police station and on the way was heard to say, "She is dead. As dead as a mackerel. If you had been an hour later, I should have done myself in." After being interviewed, Mead was taken to the Town Hall where he was charged with the murder of his common-law wife.

The inquest on Clara Howell opened at Leeds before the coroner, Mr J.C. Malcolm, on December 2nd. Mead was present at the hearing and when asked if he had any questions to ask, replied sullenly, "I have nothing to say." There were, in fact, too many witnesses for the matter to be concluded on this first day, so the hearing was adjourned until December 4th when after a short deliberation, the jury returned the expected verdict of wilful murder against Thomas Mead.

Meanwhile, Mead had made his first appearance before the magistrates at the Leeds police court on November 30th. He was not legally represented at the time and was remanded to December 2nd. Further remands followed until December 4th, December 11th and December 18th. At these later hearings, Mead was represented by Mr E.F. Maud and on the last occasion, all the evidence being heard, Mead was committed for trial.

The hearing against 33-year-old Thomas Mead took place at Leeds before Mr Justice Coleridge on February 10th, 1909. Mead was defended by Mr J. Willoughby Jardine while the case for the prosecution was led by Mr H.T. Waddy, who was assisted by Mr Bruce Williamson.

Evidence was given that the neighbourhood of the tragedy was a squalid one. The house in which Clara Howell had died had two storeys and when the police had entered the house, they had found the living room downstairs in a state of disorder. Neighbours had reported that the only item of furniture normally kept in that room was a wooden chair and this had been found smashed to pieces.

Clara's clothing had been found in a heap at the foot of the stairs and bloodstains found at the scene indicated that the dead woman had been attacked in a downstairs room, stripped of her clothing, with the exception of her stockings, and carried upstairs. Perhaps the most poignant detail was the finding of a card on the mantelpiece. It bore the motto, 'Watch and Pray'.

Emily Barker was Clara Howell's sister and she had seen Clara in Park Lane, Leeds, on the Tuesday before she met her death. At the time, Clara was sporting fresh bruises and Emily reported that this was nothing unusual. Clara was always battered and her eyes were constantly black from the beatings she received at the hands of Thomas Mead.

John Prenderville told the court of his discussion with Mead in the Railway Hotel on the evening of November 28th. Mead had told him that he had killed Clara and after the fight, and Mead's ejection from the pub, Prenderville had seen him outside and Mead had told him he was going to go to Bradford to do himself in.

Robert Prust told of finding Mead in the street after he had been ejected from the pub. The reason that Prust had first approached his friend was because he had heard that Mead had 'chucked his job'. It was after this that Mead mentioned the trouble he had had with Clara and at one stage had said, "About one o'clock this morning we had a bit of bother and I gave her two." At this point, Mead put his fist underneath Prust's jaw in order to emphasise his words.

Margaret Shuttleworth, to whose house Mead had gone on the Saturday night, gave details of him and Clara calling at Lisbon Court on the night of Friday, November 27th. There were other people there and everyone was drinking beer and whisky. Mead and Clara finally left at 11.15pm and Margaret said that Mead had had 'plenty to drink'.

Medical evidence was given by Dr G.P. Humphrey who visited

the scene of the crime and put the time of death at around 1.00am on November 28th. Clara was bruised from head to foot, had abrasions on her head, a black eye and a broken nose. There were no fewer than ten bruises on her arms and the backs of both hands were black. Dr Humphrey had also examined a broken broom handle found at the scene and confirmed that there were bloodstains and human hairs on this. Death was due to shock following the rupture of Clara's small intestine and he believed that the injuries had been inflicted upon her after the removal of her clothing.

Detective Constable Wright, one of the arresting officers, had placed Mead in a cell. It was then that Mead began to talk about the crime so Wright cautioned him again and said he would note down anything that Mead said. After asking Constable Wright if he had seen the body, Mead went on, "Well, I have done it. I shall have to swing for her. She made me do it. I woke on Saturday morning. She had taken all my money. We then got on about it. I gave her a good hiding. I hope to God they will hang me. I didn't want to live. How long shall I have to wait?"

For the defence, Mr Jardine argued that Mead had been so unhinged by drink that he had not known what he was doing. As a result, he was therefore guilty of manslaughter only. In his summing up, Mr Justice Coleridge told the jury that they must return a verdict of murder unless they were convinced that Mead was incapable of forming the intention to kill, when they could return one of manslaughter. In the event, the jury felt that they were looking at a case of murder and Mead heard the resultant death sentence apparently unmoved.

An appeal was entered and this was heard on February 22nd before Justices Darling, Walton and Pickford. There were two main grounds, first that Mead's reason had been disordered by drink so this should have been a case of manslaughter, and second that since Mead admitted he had used his fists on Clara, and as the fist was not classed as a deadly weapon, the offence could not be one of wilful murder.

Both of these arguments were dismissed but the appeal was adjourned to the following day on the defence claim that there had also been misdirection of the jury. Eventually, this, too, was dismissed and the appeal was lost, the judges pointing out that drunkenness was not held to be an excuse in law for the taking of a human life.

In the condemned cell at Leeds, Mead spoke little and never expressed the slightest regret over what he had done. He was ill for a few days after the original trial but soon recovered and maintained a healthy appetite throughout. On the day of his execution, he rose early and ate a hearty breakfast.

On the morning of Friday, March 12th, 1909, Thomas Mead was hanged by Henry Pierrepoint who was assisted by John Ellis. It was reported that he walked bravely to the scaffold and did not utter a single word. A small group of mostly women and children waited outside the gates but dispersed as soon as the prison bell began to toll.

CHAPTER SIX

JUST THE DRINK TALKING

THERE were three people living in the dingy house at 4 Springfield Place, Rook Lane, Dudley Hill in Bradford. The house was rented by 32-year-old John Raper Coulson, an iron moulder at the Prospect Foundry premises of Cole, Marchant & Morley, and he lived with his wife, 29-year-old Jane Ellen Coulson, known to all as Jenny, and their five-year-old son, Thomas. The family was not a happy one, though, and there were frequent rows between Coulson and his wife, many of which ended in physical assaults upon her.

Jane Coulson was employed as a weaver at Cawthra's Mill, not far from where she lived, and she usually started work early in the morning. Each morning it was the custom of her neighbour, Clara Spark, who also worked at the mill, to knock on Jane's window to ensure that she would not be late. So it was on the morning of Tuesday, May 24th, 1910. Clara, who lived at 2 Springfield Place, left her home at 6.00am and as she passed number 4, tapped on the window and called for Jane. Within seconds, Jane's voice called from somewhere inside her house, "All right." Satisfied that she had done her duty, Clara walked on to the mill.

Jane Coulson, however, did not arrive for work on that Tuesday morning so when Clara returned home for breakfast later that morning, and again at lunch-time, she considered knocking for her friend but on both occasions the front door was locked, the blinds were up and there was apparently no one at home. She thought perhaps there had been some trouble in the family and Jane had been forced to minister to a sick relative or friend.

Sarah Fieldhouse had known Jane Coulson for 16 years and had worked with her at the mill for the last eight. She, too, noticed that Jane had not come into work on the morning of May 24th and so at 9.00am when she took her breakfast break, Sarah went around to Springfield Place in a bid to find out what was wrong. She knocked on the front door, but received no reply so returned to work. It was just ten minutes later that Sarah noticed John Coulson standing near the factory gates. Going back outside, Sarah asked him if he was looking for Jenny as she had not come in to work. Coulson seemed to be surprised at this news and said that as far as he knew, Jenny was supposed to be coming in but then explained her absence by saying, "Well, she has gone away then and hooked it and taken the lad with her."

Emily Size lived in a house directly at the back of 4 Springfield Place and knew the Coulson family well. It was around 9.00am on May 24th when she looked out of her window and saw John Coulson standing at the top of her yard. Going out to see what he wanted, Emily heard Coulson ask, "Mrs Size, have you seen Jenny this morning?" Emily replied that she had not seen Coulson's wife since the previous evening to which Coulson remarked, "I suppose you know she has a summons out for me?"

Emily knew nothing of this and told Coulson that it was none of her business but he seemed not to hear what she had said and continued, "She will have gone where she went before and will have a warrant on me now." With that, Coulson went back into his own house, but Emily saw him again at 10.15am when he walked down Rook Lane, carrying a sack on his back.

Coulson had also been seen at around this time by another neighbour, Sarah Pearson, who lived at 6 Springfield Place. It was about 10.00am when she saw Coulson leave his house, walk past her, turn around three times and walk down a passage which led to the rear of his house. About 15 minutes later he emerged again, carrying a sack on his back and having closed and locked his front door, walked off down Rook Lane, continually turning his head back as if looking for someone following him.

By noon, Coulson was knocking on the front door of Emily Size's house and when she answered, he again said that he was looking for his wife. He also said he had been to the mill where she worked but the overlooker there had said Jenny had not been in all day. Emily said she had seen no sign of Jenny or the boy and could do nothing to help. She next saw Coulson at around 3.00pm when he was going back into his own house.

At 6.00pm, Harry Stead, who lived at 132 George Street, walked into his local, the Hand and Shuttle public house, and there he saw, amongst a group of perhaps a dozen men, John Raper Coulson. Stead had known Coulson only for a couple of months and usually only saw him inside this pub, but they had taken a few pints together in that short time so it was perhaps no surprise when Coulson walked over to Harry and said hello.

Coulson handed Stead a shilling which he owed him and the two fell into general conversation. Suddenly Coulson asked a man named Crossman if he would nip out and post a letter for him. Crossman, indignant, told Coulson to post his own letter but eventually another man, who Stead knew only as Josh, volunteered to take the letter to the nearest post box and Coulson handed it over. It was then that Coulson's mood appeared to change and he turned to Stead, showed him a summons and said, "I've killed both my wife and child. I asked her to withdraw the summons this morning and she refused and I did it with a carving knife." Stead assumed that since Coulson was the worse for drink, it was the alcohol talking and did not believe what his friend had just told him. Once again the conversation returned to more general matters.

By 7.00pm, Coulson was asking Stead if he would like to go home with him where he would cook him some bacon and eggs.

At first Stead refused but when Coulson insisted, Stead walked back to Springfield Place with him. As they went into the house, Stead noticed that it was cold and remarked that there was no fire lit so Coulson would be unable to cook anything. Coulson ignored this remark and in a matter-of-fact tone asked, "Are you going upstairs with me to look at the bodies of my wife and child?"

Although Stead still believed that this was the beer talking, the stillness of the house and the iciness of Coulson's tone bothered him and he walked out. As he left number 4, Clara Spark stopped Stead and asked him if Jenny was in. Stead replied that she wasn't and returned to the warmth of the Hand and Shuttle.

Harry Stead had not been back in the pub for long when he saw, to his dismay, that Coulson had also returned. Now, though, other people had noticed that he was drunk and his behaviour was so obnoxious that the landlord refused to serve him. Coulson, loathe to leave the premises, simply sat down. The other customers soon tired of his drunken ramblings and one of the regulars gave him twopence and told him to clear off home. Coulson left, but minutes later he was back again, although again he was not served with any drink.

It was about 7.45pm when Constable George Ernest Gill walked into the Hand and Shuttle and asked which man was named Coulson. Having had his man pointed out to him, Gill walked over and asked if he was John Raper Coulson. He replied, "No, they call me Fletcher." Thinking that he had been directed to the wrong man, Constable Gill paused, whereupon Coulson leapt to his feet and dashed out of the pub. Gill ran after him, caught him within a few yards and demanded to know if there was any truth in the tales he had heard of Coulson harming his wife and child. Coulson denied the stories and reluctantly agreed to accompany the officer back to 4 Springfield Place, so that he could check for himself.

It was 8.00pm when Coulson and Constable Gill arrived at the house in Springfield Place and almost at the same time, two other police officers, Sergeant Walker and Constable Wiley also appeared. They, too, had heard the stories about Coulson having killed his wife and child and Sergeant Walker asked Coulson what was the truth of the matter. He told Walker that there had indeed been a bit of bother, but that his wife had gone out early that morning, taking their son with her and he had not seen them since. The rooms downstairs were in order, nothing was out of place and the three officers saw that Coulson was the worse for alcohol and assumed that his stories had been nothing more than the ramblings of a drunk. They were about to leave when Coulson, who had been sitting in an armchair, pulled himself to his feet and announced that he was going out for a pint. Sergeant Walker stopped him in his tracks and warned, "You must have no more drink tonight, you appear to have had enough." The police left the house, having spent no more than ten minutes there.

Clara Spark had seen the police take Coulson into his house and she had also seen the officers leave. Now, perhaps 20 minutes later, Coulson was knocking on her front door and when she opened it, he asked if Jack, her husband, was in. Clara told him that he wasn't and saw that Coulson was soaking wet from head to foot. She watched him walk off down the street, away from his house.

The stories of what Coulson claimed to have done to his family continued to circulate and at 11.00pm Sergeant Walker, having been approached by one of Coulson's workmates in Tong Street, decided to pay another visit to Springfield Place and this time make a more thorough search of the premises. Upon his arrival he and Constable Carter, who had accompanied him, found the house locked. There was no answer to his repeated knocking but luckily a neighbour's key fitted the lock and finally Walker was able to gain admission.

The rooms downstairs were still neat and tidy but now, for the first time, Sergeant Walker went upstairs. It was there that he found the body of Jane Coulson, lying on the bedroom floor in a pool of blood, her head almost severed from her shoulders. There were two beds in the room and on the larger of these, Walker also found the body of little Thomas, his throat also gashed. It was obvious that both had been dead for some time and near the child's head lay a 12-inch long bread-knife, heavily encrusted with blood. Walker dashed downstairs to summon help but as he opened the front door to leave, he bumped into John Coulson, his clothes still dripping with water.

Coulson was arrested on the spot and told he would be charged with the murder of his wife and son. In reply he said, "That's right. I've done it. I've been in the Lower Lane dam to drown myself but I thought I would come and give myself up." Coulson went on to say that he had chosen that particular spot to do away with himself because it was notorious for claiming lives but to his chagrin he had found that he was too good a swimmer and decided instead to 'face it out like a man'. Going back inside the house, Coulson pointed to a piece of paper on the kitchen table and said, "That will tell the tale, I've written it."

Sergeant Walker picked up the paper and read, 'I have killed my wife and child on 25 (*sic*) May, so that we shall have peace for the future, more so the child. She has brought a summons from the Town Hall for me for assault, so tell my sister and her brother, and share the home and give brother Joe some. You will find me in the Lower Dam.'

Coulson took from his pocket another piece of paper which turned out to be a court summons. On the back of this he had written, 'I have murdered my wife and child for this paper being brought to me at my work. She has been nothing but a ★★★★ for some time. This done 24th May. You will find me in some dam round about cold dam, Lower Lane.'

The inquest on the two victims opened on May 26th before the coroner, Mr J.G. Hutchinson. The jury first visited the scene at Springfield Place, then travelled to the mortuary to view the bodies before returning to the Town Hall where the formal proceedings opened. The only evidence heard was that of identification, after which matters were adjourned until June 1st. On the same day, Coulson made his first appearance before the stipendiary magistrate, Mr H.W.W. Wilberforce. After details of the arrest were given, he was remanded until June 2nd.

It was on June 1st that matters began with a remarkable outburst from the coroner. He was extremely angry that Coulson had been remanded until June 2nd and not June 1st. This meant that he was unable to be present to hear matters that affected him and such a state of affairs was not acceptable. Nevertheless, a good deal of evidence was heard and matters again adjourned but only until the next day. It was then that the evidence of the previous day was repeated for Coulson's benefit. The inquest was concluded on June 2nd, but matters at the police court were still unresolved and further appearances followed on June 8th and June 13th when Coulson was committed for trial. Meanwhile, on May 28th, the two victims had been buried at the Bowling cemetery. All of Jane's workmates took the day off so that they could pay their last respects.

The trial opened at Leeds on July 21st, 1910, before Mr Justice Coleridge. The case for the Crown was led by Mr Waddy who was assisted by Mr Coutts Trotter, while Coulson was defended by Mr Mockett.

Harry Edmondson worked at the same foundry as Coulson and he told how, on the afternoon of May 23rd, Coulson had been called to the foreman's office. Returning a few minutes later he had seemed to be totally dejected and said, "I am going to leave you. I have had some bother at home with the wife and I shall be dead before morning." Coulson shook Edmondson's hand and continued, "Goodbye, I hope you have good luck. I hope you don't come to what I have come to."

The next day, though, Coulson was in work again and said to Edmondson, "I have done for her. When I awoke this morning I asked her if she was going through with this summons and she said she was. I said to her, 'Then you are going on with your old games,' and she said she was. The little boy woke and I told him to go downstairs and put his trousers on and I would get him ready for school" At that point the foreman came up and Coulson had walked away.

Later that day, Coulson had collected his wages and walked out of the foundry saying that he did not intend doing any more work. At lunch-time, Edmondson saw Coulson again, this time in Wakefield Road and he offered to buy a pipe as a remembrance. Edmondson insisted that he did not need a pipe but Coulson pushed sixpence into his hand saying, "I shall be dead before morning." At the time, Coulson had obviously been drinking and Edmondson had not taken his words seriously.

Jane Coulson had been heard replying to her neighbour at 6.00am on May 24th and at 8.45am, her husband had pawned her wedding ring. The inference was that the crime had been committed between those times. Later still, of course, Coulson had been seen leaving the house carrying a sack. This it turned out contained various items of clothing which belonged to his wife and which were also offered to the pawnbroker.

That night, Coulson had tried to get a fellow drinker in the Hand and Shuttle to post a letter for him. Joshua Mortimer testified that he was the man who had finally agreed to post it and had been given twopence for doing so. He noticed that it was addressed to Coulson's sister, Isabella Wilkinson.

Isabella lived at 25 Archibald Street and she had received the letter on May 25th. She confirmed to the court that it was in her brother's handwriting and the letter was read out in court, much to the distress of both Isabella and John Coulson himself. It read, 'Dear Sister, I am sorry to let you know that my wife has had me up at the Town Hall again, for she has been at her old game again, and told me that she would not give it up, so I thought I would put an end to it by cutting her throat and bonnie child.

'So goodbye and God bless you sister and brother. You will find me dead. This was done on the Tuesday morning, May 24th, 1910. Let them know that Mrs Gried, Coventry Street, has the insurance policy both for me, wife and little boy, in the middle drawer with all the policy and grave papers.'

The catalyst for this dreadful tragedy appeared to be the summons. Warrant Officer Brear gave evidence that on May 23rd, Jane

Ellen Coulson had been granted a summons against her husband, John Raper Coulson, for assault, and at 3.45pm that same day he had served it on Coulson at his place of work. At the time, Coulson had replied, "It is her that wants the summons for her drunken habits and going with men." Coulson was due to appear in court in answer to that summons on Friday, May 27th.

Dr William Wrangham was the police surgeon who had examined both bodies at the scene. He reported that Jane had a wound in her neck which was four inches long and two and a half inches wide. There were signs that there had been at least three or four cuts inflicted and her head had been hacked almost from her body. The boy, Thomas, had one clean wound, three inches long and two inches broad. In both cases the cause of death was shock and haemorrhage. There were also signs that there had been some sort of struggle between the murdered woman and her assailant. The body had moved after the injuries had been inflicted and bloodstained fingerprints were found on the window sill.

There were drops of blood on the window ledge below which showed that she had managed to open the window either to escape or to call for help. There were also deep cuts on the ball of her right thumb where she had grabbed the knife to fend off the attack upon her. Surprisingly perhaps, none of the neighbours, who in the past had heard many arguments from the Coulson household, had heard anything on the morning that Jane and Thomas had met their deaths.

Some of the history of the accused man was given. He had married Jane at Bradford Parish Church some six years before and, in the early days at least, their relationship was a happy one. Three years earlier, Coulson's father had died and left money and property to be shared amongst his children. Coulson had received £580 in cash and a house in Wakefield Road. Unfortunately, over the next few years he squandered this away on drink and eventually, at Easter, 1910, he had to sell the house and move to Springfield Place. The money from that sale was also soon spent, again on drink, and this led to the many arguments between Coulson and his wife, especially when he had drunk too much.

During his time in Armley prison, Coulson had displayed some strange behaviour and muttered constantly and incoherently about the crime. Despite this, the prison medical officer, Dr J. Exley, stated that there were no signs of insanity or delusional behaviour although he could not swear that at the time Coulson committed the crime, he knew right from wrong.

In the event, the jury did not even bother to leave the court before returning their guilty verdict and the prisoner was sentenced to death. On August 9th, 1910, that sentence was carried out when John Raper Coulson was hanged at Leeds by Thomas Pierrepoint and William Warbrick. On the same day, John Alexander Dickman was executed at Newcastle for the murder of John Innes Nisbet and the publicity his case received greatly overshadowed the crime committed by Coulson.

CHAPTER SEVEN

THE MAN WHO CHANGED HIS STORY

B Y 1910, 35-year-old Mary Jenkin, whose real name was Mary Letitia Whittaker, had been living with 45-year-old Henry Ison at 47 Boynton Street, Leeds, for some 13 years. The address was in a squalid area of the city but, unlike most of their neighbours, Ison and his partner had few financial problems. Indeed, they seemed to be comfortably off and with a reasonable disposal income they both enjoyed a drink, often to excess. Such was the case on Saturday, July 23rd, 1910.

That afternoon, Ison and Mary were drinking heavily in the Yorkshire Hussar in the company of Kate Crowther, a man named McHugh and another woman friend of theirs. By 5.00pm, Ison had invited the company to return to their house at Boynton Street to continue drinking, but after a while he and McHugh argued and Ison eventually threw McHugh out of the house. A fist fight developed in the street and Ison fell, banged his head and had to be helped back into his home where he, Mary and the other women continued the drinking session. By 6.30pm, both Ison and his lover were very drunk and Ison, deciding that he had had enough company, ordered Kate Crowther and the other woman from his home. He was not in the best of moods and they did not argue, leaving Ison and Mary Jenkin alone in the house.

It was around 8.20pm when a neighbour, Kate McQuire, heard what sounded like a scuffle coming from Henry Ison's house. A minute or so later she saw Mary Jenkin, on her hands and knees, crawl out of her front door. She got no more than seven or eight yards when Ison appeared, grabbed her by her hair and dragged her back into the house. Although upset, Kate McQuire thought this was nothing more than a domestic dispute between a man and the woman he called his wife. It was certainly nothing to do with her.

Later that evening, Henry Ison called at the house in Shears Court occupied by Mary's sister, Elizabeth Bradshaw. Although he was still extremely drunk, Ison managed to ask Mrs Bradshaw if she would go to his house and attend to Mary as they had had 'a few words'. Elizabeth Bradshaw hurried to 47 Boynton Street where, to her horror, she found her sister lying unconscious on the kitchen floor and a policeman already on the scene. Elizabeth tried to rouse Mary but when she failed, she turned to Ison and cried, "You've killed her." Ison did not reply.

The house was in a state of disorder and there were signs of a struggle having taken place. Lying on the floor near Mary was a bent poker and it was natural to assume that this had been used to batter her, especially as police inquiries established that the poker had not been bent on the Saturday morning. Since the only other person in the house had been Henry Ison, he was the obvious suspect, suspicions which appeared to be confirmed when he said, "There the drunken ★★★★ is. I gave her a sovereign and when she returned home, she said it had been taken from her. This will teach her a ★★★★★★★ lesson."

Mary was rushed to the infirmary, Ison was taken into custody and when, on Sunday, July 24th, Mary Jenkin died without regaining consciousness, Henry Ison found himself facing a charge of murder.

There were a number of remands at the police court, the first taking place on July 25th before the stipendiary magistrate, Mr Horace Marshall. Here it was reported that a neighbour had contacted the police to say that she believed a woman was lying dead in the house at number 47. Two officers had been sent to the address and found Mary Jenkin lying on the floor.

Ison's second appearance took place on July 28th, by which time Mr Arthur Willey had taken on the case for the Director of Public Prosecutions. A large number of witnesses were called and at one stage, Ison, with tears in his eyes, shouted, "They are trying to swear my life away. I can feel the flesh and blood creeping. I would sooner be shot straight away than have them swearing this pack of lies. I will go down. You can do what you like with me." Ison turned and tried to leave the dock but was prevented by the police officer set to guard him. Further appearances took place on August 4th and August 11th, when Ison was finally sent for trial. This took place at Leeds on November 24th, before Mr Justice Hamilton. Ison was defended by Mr Charles Mellor, while the case for the prosecution was led by Mr Edward Shortt, who was assisted by Mr J. Willoughby Jardine.

Amy Northrop was a next-door neighbour of Ison's, living at 49 Boynton Street, and she seen Mary at 6.00pm on the evening of July 23rd when Mary paid a brief visit to her house. Amy claimed that at that particular time, Mary was certainly not drunk. The next time she saw Mary was shortly after 8.00pm when Mary had left Ison's house and he had dragged her back inside. Amy Northrop testified that Ison hit Mary and kicked her on the thigh while she was still on the doorstep. When they had gone back into their house, the door was slammed and locked behind them. Amy heard the noise of a continuing scuffle and Mary shout, "Don't Harry! Haven't you done enough?" The sounds of that quarrel continued upstairs for some time and ended with a dull thud. Soon afterwards, Amy heard Ison call Mary's name three times. Another neighbour, Frederick Wadsworth, also heard the sounds of a scuffle which he said ended with a loud thud. Silence reigned for a few moments and then a male voice was heard saying, "Won't you speak to me? You will have me lagged for this." Those words were heard by Amy Northrop and she stated that there were frequent rows between Ison and Mary, especially on a Saturday night when they had been out drinking.

After being taken to the infirmary, Mary had been examined by Dr Richardson and he told the court that she had bruises on several parts of her body, including two or three severe blows to the head. These were several inches long and extended from her forehead over her skull. An operation had been carried out but this had not proved successful and Mary had never regained consciousness. The cause of death was given as concussion of the brain. More important for Ison's defence, Dr Richardson said that in his opinion, the injuries to Mary's head could have been caused by her falling downstairs.

Kate Crowther told the court of the evening she had spent with Ison, Mary and the others. Not long after the fight with McHugh, Ison had told her and the other woman to leave the house as he and Mary wished to lie down. Mary had seemed nervous at the thought of being left alone with him and had said to Kate, "Don't leave me or when you've gone, he'll kill me."

Henry Ison had first been arrested on a charge of causing grievous bodily harm. He had been charged with this offence by Inspector Oxterby and in reply had claimed that Mary had inflicted her injuries upon herself, saying, "I have done nothing to her, if anybody has, she has done it herself. She was drunk".

Ison was searched and as this was being carried out, he said to Inspector Oxterby, "I gave Jenkin a sovereign of my wage of 28s. I afterwards went to bed leaving her drinking with two other women downstairs. On getting up again I found her drunk and tumbling about. I asked her where the sovereign was and she said it had been 'done in'." Even later, when charged with murder, Ison had appeared not to know anything about it. Superintendent Bulmer had read the charge to Ison who had said, "It's no use talking now. It's the booze I suppose." He asked if Mary had 'come to'.

The basic defence Ison was putting forward was that both he and Mary were drunk. They had argued over a sovereign she claimed to have lost but he dragged her back into the house only so that he could put her to bed. Ison said that he had carried Mary up to bed that night but found it a difficult task as she was struggling all the time. He went to bed himself but later, when he went downstairs, he found her lying on the hearth rug. She must have fallen down the stairs, hurt herself, crawled to the rug and fallen unconscious. He had not hit her and had certainly not used the poker on her.

The poker had been examined by Dr Frederick William Eurich, professor of medicine at Leeds University, and he had found no trace of blood upon it whatsoever. It was true that he had found four human hairs, each one-quarter of an inch in length, but much more would have been expected had the poker been used to batter Mary Jenkin about the head. Dr Eurich had also examined two pieces of woodchip, a piece of linen sheeting and two pieces of mattress and all of these items had shown a positive reaction for mammalian blood.

In his summing up for the defence, Mr Mellor made much of the fact that there was no blood on the poker nor indeed splashed about the room where Ison was supposed to have battered his common-law wife to death. Also, there was no sign of bloodstaining on his clothing. The only appreciable amount of blood found at the scene had been a small pool underneath where Mary lay. Finally, although Dr Eurich had stated that he did not believe the injuries could be caused by a fall downstairs, Dr Richardson had given the opposite opinion and there was therefore a reasonable doubt as to Ison's culpability.

Despite all this, Ison was found guilty, although the jury added a strong recommendation to mercy. Asked if he had anything to say before the sentence was passed, Ison replied, "I think it is a very unjust sentence. I am innocent. I am not guilty of murder."

Ison's appeal was heard on December 12th before the Lord Chief Justice, Lord Alverstone and Justices Pickford and Avory. For the defence, Mr Mellor complained that in his summing up, the trial judge had omitted to put the question of drunkenness before the jury in such a way as to suggest that it might reduce the charge to manslaughter. Lord Alverstone considered the matter but said he could find no evidence of misdirection and consequently, the appeal was dismissed.

His last hope gone, Henry Ison was hanged at Leeds on Thursday, December 29th, 1910. The executioner was Thomas Pierrepoint and he was assisted by William Willis. Right up to the end, Ison denied that he had been responsible for Mary Jenkin's death.

CHAPTER EIGHT

A TWIST OF TOBACCO

IT WAS 9.20am on Wednesday, February 28th, 1917, when 65-year-old Robert Gadsby walked into the house where he lodged in Park Place, Bell Lane, Bramley, Leeds. The house was rented by Gadsby's married daughter, Mathilda, known to all as Tilda, and her husband Benjamin Hart.

As Benjamin watched, Gadsby took his watch and chain from his waistcoat, placed them gently on the kitchen table and said in a low voice, "That is for little Fred." Gadsby then took his purse from his pocket, placed it next to the watch and continued, "And that is for Jack." Before Benjamin could ask his father-in-law why he had decided to give away his most treasured possessions, Gadsby had strolled over to the foot of the stairs and called upstairs to his daughter, "Goodbye Tilda." He washed his hands and made to leave the house. Mathilda, puzzled by this strange behaviour, asked her father what was wrong, but all he would say was, "Goodbye forever. I am going to the police station to give myself up."

Constable Triffet was on duty in Bramley police station when Robert Gadsby walked in and announced, "I have murdered my sweetheart." He was cautioned but continued, "I have cut my sweetheart's throat," and he handed over a bloodstained three-bladed penknife. He went on to make a voluntary statement which read, "I have been courting a woman named Julia Johnson. She started swearing and ordered me out of the house. Knowing that she had been with other men, I took my knife out of my pocket and at the same time got hold of Johnson and cut her throat. I did not speak to her. I have been a widower for 12 months." It was a clear enough confession, but when his words were written down, Gadsby refused to sign the statement.

Immediately, officers went to 3 Thrift Crescent, Waterloo Lane, Bramley, and there they found the body of 54-year-old Julia Ann Johnson, lying on the hearth rug in the lounge. Her throat had been gashed and the police surgeon certified that she was dead.

That same afternoon, Robert Gadsby appeared before Mr Horace Marshall, the stipendiary magistrate. Throughout the short hearing, Gadsby, a short, stout man, leaned against the top of the dock and appeared totally disinterested in what was going on about him. Asked if he had any objection to being remanded until March 7th, Gadsby replied, "You can shoot me as soon as you like."

The inquest on the dead woman opened on March 1st, at the Kirkstall Congregational schoolroom. Formal identification was given by Julia's estranged husband, Thomas Johnson, who said that Julia had been his wife for 20 years but left him in 1914 after getting mixed up in 'bad company'. During their marriage, she had borne him six sons and one daughter. Having heard all this, the coroner adjourned the proceedings until March 7th.

It was on March 7th that the inquest returned a verdict of murder against Robert Gadsby and sent him for trial on the coroner's warrant. Later, at the police court, all the evidence having been heard, Gadsby was once again committed for trial.

Matters moved quickly and since the assizes opened soon afterwards, Gadsby found himself facing his trial on March 19th, 1917, before Mr Justice McCardie. The case for the Crown was put by Mr W. Valentine Ball and Gadsby, who despite his statements to the police had pleaded not guilty, was defended by Mr Gingall.

Benjamin Hart testified that on February 28th, Gadsby had first left their house at around 5.15am. He had returned at 5.45am without saying where he had been. He had gone back out at 7.45am and Hart went on to relate what had happened after Gadsby came back to the house. It was then about 9.20am and this was when Gadsby gave away his possessions and said he was off to the police station.

Clifford Johnson was the dead woman's 19-year-old son and lived with her at Thrift Crescent. He told the court that he had breakfasted with Julia on the morning she was killed. Although he did not know Gadsby personally, he did recall his mother talking about someone she was seeing, a man named Bob, and confirmed that this Bob had apparently been visiting the house for some time.

Alice Dowgill was Julia's married daughter and at 9.00am on February 28th, had gone to visit her mother. The front door was locked so Alice looked through the window and saw Gadsby, a man she knew as Bob, kneeling on the floor in his shirt sleeves. At the time Alice had simply believed that her mother was out and that either she had first let Bob in before she left, or that he had let himself in with a key that was usually kept on the windowsill. Alice walked away but had not gone far when she turned to look back and saw Gadsby leave her mother's house, lock the door behind him and put the key in his pocket.

Medical evidence was given by Dr Hopton, the police surgeon, who testified that there were two separate cuts on Julia's throat and in addition to these, there were slight cuts on her face and on one hand, indicating that a struggle had taken place. Also, the wounds seemed to indicate that Julia had been attacked from behind. As for Gadsby, Dr Hopton had examined him at the police station after he had given himself up. There were five scratches on Gadsby's neck, which might have been caused by fingernails, and a good deal of blood on his clothing.

Gadsby did not deny that he was responsible for Julia Johnson's death but was now claiming that it was an accident. At the inquest he had already made a passionate statement, denying that he was a murderer. Gadsby had said, "I say the woman never stood with her back towards me. We stood face to face. I was not in the house five minutes altogether. I say I was not in my shirt sleeves, nor yet on my knees. I went to speak to Mrs Johnson… She scratched my neck with a knife and said 'I will make you get out'. I never thought about hurting the woman."

Gadsby now elaborated on this saying that as he walked into Julia's house on February 28th, she had greeted him with the words, "Well kid, I know what you have come for. You have come to play the devil with me about Sunday night." This was a reference to the fact that after Gadsby had said goodnight to her on Sunday, February 25th, he had later seen another man waiting for her. For his part, Gadsby told Julia that he had not come to see her about Sunday. He just wanted her to return a ring he had given her and also to pay him back £4 of the £8 15s she owed him.

Julia became upset at this and reminded Gadsby of a promise they had once made, swearing on her mother's grave that they would never part. To underline that she did not want the relationship to end, she had thrown her arms around Gadsby's neck whereupon he had tried to push her away. Seeing that her words had not mellowed him, Julia grabbed a knife from the kitchen table and threw herself upon him. They struggled together and at the time, Gadsby, who had been cutting himself a plug of tobacco, had his penknife in his hand. Julia was accidentally cut during that struggle but Gadsby emphasised that there was no way he would have deliberately attacked her, saying, "I loved every hair on her head."

His story did not convince the jury and having been found guilty, Gadsby was asked if he had anything to say. He replied, "I am innocent and God is my judge." After being sentenced to death, Gadsby asked the judge if he could appeal and was told that he could.

The execution was originally set for April 13th, but this was postponed pending Gadsby's appeal. In due course, leave to appeal was refused and on April 12th, a new date was set, Gadsby soon becoming resigned to his fate. At 9.00am on Wednesday, April 18th, 1917, Robert Gadsby walked firmly to the scaffold at Leeds prison where he was hanged by Thomas Pierrepoint who was assisted by Robert Baxter.

CHAPTER NINE

ONE SHILLING SHORT

MARGARET Bell had enjoyed a blissfully happy marriage to her husband, Joseph, a marriage that had been blessed with three children, the eldest of which was Emily. But when war broke out in 1914, Joseph Bell was one of the tens of thousands of men who answered the call to the colours and one of those sent to the trenches of France. The following year, his 32-year-old wife and her young family received the news they had been dreading. Joseph had been killed.

It was not until 1917 that Margaret Bell found herself able to start socialising again and it was in that year that she first met Alfred Hird, a young man aged 27 whose real name was Lewis Massey. A relationship developed and finally, at Christmas, Margaret and Lewis married and began living together under the name Hird. In July 1919, a child, Albert, was born but by now there had already been a great deal of trouble between Alfred Hird and his wife. He accused her of drinking too much, going out too often and leaving the children to take care of themselves. She claimed that he treated her cruelly and beat her. That was certainly true, for Margaret Hird often sported bruises and other signs of violence.

Alfred Hird was also in the Army but every time he returned home there would be fresh arguments and more bruises for Margaret to show to her friends and neighbours. Eventually she decided that enough was enough and made an application for a separation order. This was granted, along with an order for Hird to pay his wife 17s a week maintenance.

Hird was demobbed in September 1919, and there followed a brief attempt at a reconciliation between him and his wife. He returned to their home at 8 Alfred Terrace, off Camp Road, Leeds, but when it became clear that nothing had changed and the relationship could not succeed, Margaret told him to leave and on September 14th he moved to Hunslet Road although he made further requests for Margaret to take him back. Alas, many of those attempts also ended in violence and only confirmed to Margaret that she had made the right decision.

On October 30th, Margaret Hird was back in court, applying to the magistrates for an increase in her weekly maintenance. She told the court of her husband's continuing cruelty towards her but omitted to mention that after he had come out of the Army, they had, albeit it just for a few days, lived together again as man and wife. As a result of her evidence, the court increased the weekly payment to 25s which caused something of a problem for Alfred Hird.

Hird had now obtained employment as a labourer at Atkinson Wheelwrights in Black Bull Street, Hunslet, for which he received a weekly wage of £2 18s. From that figure he paid 30s for his lodgings and a further 4s for his clothes and other living expenses. That left Hird just 24s and, of course, he was now supposed to pay his wife 25s. Every week, Alfred Hird was earning one shilling less than he needed in order to survive.

On Tuesday, November 4th, Hird called on his wife while a neighbour, Ada Clarkson was there. Once again he asked Margaret if they could try again to which she replied, "Ada knows I have been to the Town Hall and taken out a summons for threat. Do you think I am going to take you back to be done in? You know you said that if you do me in they will never hang you because of having lunacy in the family." Reluctantly, Hird left the house.

It was that same night, at around 9.25pm when Margaret's sister, Elizabeth Hackney, called on her. Not long afterwards, they asked Emily, by now aged ten, to go to the fish and chip shop to get them something to eat. Emily had not been gone for more than a few minutes when another caller arrived at 8 Alfred Terrace.

That caller was Alfred Hird and he began by asking his wife, "Maggie, will you forgive me and take me back again? I will be good to you if you will let me come back. What I have done to you has been done in my mad temper." Maggie was not to be moved and shouted at her husband, "If you do not shift out of here I will go to Sheepscar and fetch the police." As Margaret spoke these words she moved forward towards the door, at which point Alfred Hird placed himself in the way and turned the key in the front door lock.

Precisely what happened next differed in the accounts given by Alfred Hird and Elizabeth Hackney but the outcome was that Hird using first a poker and then a small hatchet which lay nearby, battered his wife repeatedly. Elizabeth, too, was injured and eventually both women were rushed to hospital. The wounds inflicted on Elizabeth Hackney were not life threatening but poor Margaret Hird died at 2.15am the following morning.

It was not until November 5th that Hird returned to his rooms in Hunslet Road and told some of the fellow lodgers that he had killed his wife. From there he walked to the house of his married sister who lived in Otley Road, Bradford, and it was there that he was picked up by the police during the early hours of November 6th, the arrest being made by Detective Inspector Dalton. Later that same morning Hird made his first appearance at the Leeds police court where he was defended by Mr J. Burrows. Evidence was given that on the way to the police station, Hird had first asked, "Shall I be tried today?" Told that he would be put before the magistrates, he paused for a few seconds and went on to say, "I did it because of the way she has been carrying on. She has been drinking every night with her sister and going out and leaving the children alone in the house."

Back at the police station, Hird had continued talking about the crime. At one stage he remarked, "She has been carrying on something awful. I have been sending her 16 or 17 shillings a week ever since I was in the Army. She has been drinking every night. She had me up in court a week ago and got 25 shillings a week put on me. I paid 30 shillings for my lodgings and four shillings for my clothes and I only get two pounds 18 shillings a week. I have been to see her every night this week and begged her on my knees to take me back."

Hird was remanded for a week and consequently made his second appearance on November 13th. On this occasion, the court heard that he was also known as Lewis Massey and was 29 years old. Witnesses were called to outline the case against Hird and after hearing all the evidence, the magistrates sent him for trial on a charge of murder.

The case against Alfred Hird opened before Mr Justice Coleridge at Leeds, on December 3rd, 1919. The case for the prosecution was led by Mr W.J. Waugh, who was assisted by Mr A.S. Matthews, while Hird's defence lay in the hands of Mr J.R. MacDonald.

Elizabeth Hackney was, of course, a vital witness for the Crown. She told of the words that had passed between Hird and his wife who, at the time she was attacked, carried four-month-old Albert in her arms. According to Elizabeth, as Margaret moved to unlock the door, Hird had struck her, knocking her to the ground. At this, Elizabeth had picked up a poker and rushed forward to help her sister. She lashed out at Hird but he managed to wrestle the poker from her, whereupon she also received a severe blow to the upper body. Rolling away a little, Elizabeth watched in horror as Hird continued to rain blows down upon his wife, later picking up a hatchet in order to finish the job. At one stage, Elizabeth had heard Margaret pleading for her life and screaming, "Don't kill me for the sake of little Albert."

Seeing that there was little she could do to help, Elizabeth dashed upstairs, smashed two panes of glass in a window and shouted into the street, "Murder, murder! He is murdering our Maggie." A few minutes later, all had gone quiet downstairs and Elizabeth ventured back down to see that Hird had left. Finally, Elizabeth denied that she and Margaret had been out drinking that night.

Mrs Ward was one of Margaret Hird's neighbours and she told the court that she had heard screams coming from number 7 and Elizabeth shouting for help from an upstairs window. As Mrs Ward reached her front door, Alfred Hird was just leaving number 7. He walked quietly away with his hands in his trouser pockets, as if he hadn't a care in the world.

Ten-year-old Emily Bell had returned to 7 Alfred Terrace with her parcel of fish and chips even as the attack upon her mother was ending. Finding the front door locked and hearing terrible sounds coming from inside, Emily had looked through the key-hole to see Alfred Hird striking Margaret with what looked to be a small hatchet.

Inspector Dalton told the court that when told he was about to be arrested for his wife's murder, Hird had said, "Is she dead? I am very pleased. I meant to do her in." However, the inspector also confirmed that Hird had been examined at the police station and he did have a mark on his head consistent with a blow from the poker found at the scene of the crime.

Alfred Hird went into the witness box to give evidence on his own behalf. He claimed that earlier that night he had seen his wife and her sister drinking in a local public house. Having followed them home, he went into the house but only because he wanted to see his baby son. Without any provocation from him, Elizabeth Hackney had struck out at him with the poker. This had made him see red and he had no recollection of what he had done after that. Basically, Hird was claiming that he was not responsible for his actions at the time of the attack and, as if to strengthen that argument, also pointed out that his sister had died in Menston Asylum and a brother of his was resident in that same establishment. There was, therefore, a history of insanity in the family. This evidence was in part backed up by Hird's father, Charles Massey, who agreed that his son had been 'queer in the head' when he was a child and had always been subject to fits.

Dr J. Exley was the medical officer of Armley jail where Hird had been held and he had examined the prisoner on a number of occasions. In Dr Exley's opinion, Hird was of sound mind and understood the consequences of his actions, although he was of low intelligence and could not answer simple questions that a child of 13 would be able to.

The trial ended after just a few hours and the jury had little difficulty in adjudging Hird guilty as charged. He was originally due to be hanged on December 23rd but the execution was postponed when Hird announced that it was his intention to appeal. That appeal was dismissed on December 19th and a new execution date now set.

At 9.00am on Tuesday, January 6th, 1920, Lewis Massey, who preferred to be known as Alfred Hird, was hanged at Leeds by Thomas Pierrepoint and William Willis. He was one of three men hanged that day, the other two being Hyman Perdovitch and David Caplan who were despatched at Manchester. All in all, 1920 proved to be a busy year for the executioners of England, with no fewer than 20 men meeting their deaths at the end of a rope.

CHAPTER TEN

FOR A PIECE OF PAPER

O N MAY 17th, 1917, widower Thomas Hargreaves Wilson married a woman whose surname was, coincidentally, Hargreaves. Annie Maria, who was two years older than Thomas, had also been married before and consequently, she brought a number of children with her to this new relationship. All told Annie had seven children but two were grown and had moved out so Annie, Thomas and five of the children set up home together at 41 Evanston Row, Kirkstall, Leeds. In fact, there was an eighth person living in the Wilson household, for Annie also took with her an invalid relative, Harriet Watson, her sister-in-law from her first marriage who was known to all as Aunt Harriet.

Soon after the wedding it became clear that Wilson had something of a temper and the relationship between him and Annie deteriorated rapidly. The problems were solved, however, at least in the short term, when Wilson was called up and joined the Army in July, 1917. He remained in uniform until February 1919 when he returned to Evanston Row and the problems began all over again. Eventually, Annie announced that she had had enough and on November 21st she was successful in obtaining a separation order on the grounds of Wilson's cruelty and neglect. As a result, Wilson moved out of the family home and into new lodgings at 24 Smith's Row, Bramley.

Over the next few months, Wilson returned to Evanston Row a number of times and almost always these visits resulted in arguments. Indeed, on one occasion the police had to be called to remove Wilson from the premises. Annie, concerned for the safety of herself and her children, took to making sure that the the house was secure. Unfortunately on Friday, January 16th, 1920 she forgot to do this and that day Thomas Wilson made his next visit to her home. At the time, Annie Wilson was in the house with two of her children, 20-year-old Annie Hargreaves and 11-year-old Mary. Harriet Watson was also there, sitting in a chair facing the fire, and in addition a friend of Annie Hargreaves, Margaret Joyce Hill, was present. Annie Wilson, her daughter Annie, Mary and Margaret were all gathered around a table in the kitchen, cleaning some knives when Wilson opened the door and walked in, carrying a piece of blue paper in his hand.

It was obvious to Annie Hargreaves that her stepfather was not in the best of moods. So much so that she beckoned for her sister Mary to get out of the room, but before she was able to move, Thomas Wilson locked the door and removed the key.

Mrs Schofield lived next door to Annie Wilson and at 8.00pm had just been outside to shake the dust from some door mats. As she returned inside and closed the door behind her she heard a terrible scream which came from next door. Mrs Schofield was fully aware of the problems Annie had been having with her estranged husband and, suspecting that he might have somehow got into the house, she opened her door again in order to see if she could offer any assistance.

No sooner had Mrs Schofield reached her doorstep than she saw the bedroom window next door smashed from within. Annie Hargreaves stuck her head out of the broken pane and shouted, "Murder! He's killing my mother. Go and fetch the police." Mrs Schofield now added her own screams to the cacophony by shouting for help and some of the other neighbours came running, while others dashed to fetch the police.

Mrs Schofield's daughter was ill in bed upstairs at the time and, concerned that she should be reassured, Mrs Schofield went upstairs to be with her. Almost as soon as she reached her daughter's room, she heard someone banging on her bedroom window. Annie Hargreaves and her sister Mary had climbed out of their broken window, along a small verandah that connected the two houses and now stood outside Mrs Schofield's window. Annie cried, "Do let me come in," and Mrs Schofield threw open the window and helped them both over the sill. Then, almost as soon as the window was closed again, there came another knock. Margaret Hill had followed the sisters along the same route. She, too, was admitted into the bedroom, by which time Annie Hargreaves had rushed downstairs, out into the street and tried to get back into her house so that she might help her mother. At one stage Annie looked through the window and saw to her horror that Wilson's arms were covered in blood up to his elbows.

The first police officer on the scene was Constable Russell who gained entrance to the house by smashing a window with his truncheon. As he entered the kitchen, Russell saw Wilson who was kneeling on the floor, having by now also inflicted a severe wound to his own throat. Despite this, as soon as Wilson saw the constable, he raised himself with his left hand and lashed out with the knife he was still holding. Russell gave Wilson a sharp crack on the head with his truncheon and the assailant collapsed and was eventually taken to hospital. Meanwhile, Russell discovered Annie Wilson lying underneath a bed which was also in the kitchen. Her throat had been badly gashed and even as Russell tried to administer basic first-aid, she passed away.

The inquest on 46-year-old Annie Maria Wilson opened before the city coroner, Mr J.C. Malcolm, on January 19th. Here it was stated that the man who would subsequently face a charge of murder was still in the infirmary but was improving and would be discharged in due course. Mr Malcolm adjourned the hearing until February 2nd, in case Wilson wished to be present.

In fact, Wilson was discharged from the infirmary on January 26th. He was arrested, charged with murder and made his first appearance before the Leeds police court that same afternoon. Details of the crime were given, as were the statements made by the accused man when he was charged. Wilson had apparently replied, "I don't know anything about it. Do you mean to say that my wife is dead?" Having heard all this, the magistrates remanded Wilson for one week.

Another person involved in this case also made an appearance at the police court on January 26th. Margaret Hill, the friend of Annie Hargreaves, faced a charge of having stolen a silk scarf from a fellow lodger at the Stead Hostel. The magistrates decided to give Margaret one more chance and dismissed the charge on condition that she spent the next three months living at the St Faith's Home. Margaret agreed to the condition and was released.

On February 2nd, the inquest was reconvened and returned a verdict of murder against Wilson. He made his second appearance before the magistrates on the same day but this hearing was again adjourned, this time until February 10th. On that date, all the evidence having been heard, Wilson was sent for trial. That trial took place at Leeds on March 18th, before Mr Justice Roche, the case for the Crown being put by Mr R. Watson.

Annie Hargreaves was an important witness who stated that after Wilson had entered the house, he had brandished a piece of blue paper and exclaimed, "You have got the receipt for this and I want it." Annie Wilson had refused even to look at the paper and had said, "I do not know what you are talking about. Go out of the house." Seeing that he was getting nowhere with his wife, Wilson handed the paper to his stepdaughter and asked her to read it. Annie saw that it was the separation order her mother had obtained and as she glanced at the words printed on it, Annie gestured for her sister, Mary to get out. The first time Mary did not see the gesture so Annie repeated it. Unfortunately, Wilson also saw it and now demanded, "Who lives in this house besides Aunt Harriet?"

Puzzled as to what Wilson was implying, his wife replied, "Only our own family." Wilson had called her a liar and claimed that a man named Franklin was also living under the roof, suggesting that he might be involved in a relationship with her. Annie Wilson told her husband that no one named Franklin lived there although a man with that name had visited once or twice. This infuriated Wilson even more and he turned to Mary and kissed her before locking the door and putting the key into his pocket. At this, Annie Wilson jumped to her feet and ordered her husband out but he merely pushed her back onto the sofa and seized something from the table. Annie Hargreaves tried to pull Wilson off her mother and when this failed, took a picture down from the wall and struck him hard on the back of his head. Seeing that Wilson had not been knocked out, Annie, her sister and Margaret Hill now ran upstairs to escape his wrath. From there, Annie took Mary out through the window and along the verandah to the house next door.

Annie's sister Mary had also been a witness to what happened in Evanston Row on the evening of January 16th. She said that Wilson had claimed that the receipt he wanted was on a shelf but her mother had replied that it could not be there as she had dusted the shelf several times and not seen anything. Before escaping through the bedroom window, Mary had gone back downstairs for a few moments. She had seen Wilson, his hands covered in blood, loosening his collar presumably so he could cut his own throat. Seeing her and Annie, who had followed her back downstairs, Wilson chased them and it was then that, fearful for their own safety, they got out of the window.

Margaret Hill testified that as Wilson entered the house, he had turned to Harriet Watson and greeted her with, "Good evening mother, how are you?" No sooner had she replied than Wilson turned to his wife and said, "Do you intend to ruin my life?" Later, during the attack on his wife, Margaret had also tried to pull him off but he was far too strong for her. After being chased upstairs, Margaret did not have time to get out of the window at the same time as Annie Hargreaves and her sister. Terrified, Margaret had hidden under the bed until she heard Wilson's footsteps going back downstairs. Only then did she feel that it was safe enough to follow them out on to the verandah.

Mrs Proctor was a neighbour and one of the first to answer the call for help from Annie Hargreaves. At the time, one of Annie Wilson's sons, Joshua, was in Mrs Proctor's house and they ran together to the front door of number 41 where they were soon joined by Annie Hargreaves. Together they beat upon the door but failed to get in. Annie shouted, "Are there no men about?" and kicked in a small window with her foot. Mrs Proctor poked a clothes prop through the hole in the glass and lifted the blinds. She saw Wilson standing in the middle of the room, holding a large knife in his hand. Throughout all these terrible events poor Harriet Watson, being paralysed, had remained sitting facing the fire and Mrs Proctor heard her pleading, "Annie, speak to me. Don't kill her Tom."

Dr Hopton was the divisional police surgeon and he had examined Annie Wilson at the scene. He reported that there were two deep slashes on her throat and ten separate wounds on her head. When Wilson had been admitted to the hospital his condition had been critical and he had been suffering from wounds on his head in addition to the gash in his throat.

Once Wilson had been charged, he had been held in Leeds prison and the medical officer, Dr Eric Craig, had examined him there ten days after the attack had taken place. Dr Craig testified that at the time the wound from the blow on the head inflicted by means of the picture frame had still not completely healed. However, there was no question that Wilson was perfectly sane. Having said that, Dr Craig did admit that a severe blow to the head could have temporarily have affected Wilson's state of mind.

Thomas Wilson went into the witness box to tell his own version of events. He claimed that he had only gone to the house to get a receipt for payments he had made to the court under the separation order. He had taken no weapon with him and had no intention of

harming his wife in any way. Noticing that his stepdaughter was mot-
ioning to her sister, Wilson believed that she was suggesting that Mary
should go for the police. This, of course, had happened once before
and Wilson was determined that he would sort this matter out before
his family should have the opportunity of throwing him out again.
This was why he had locked the door and pocketed the key.

At one stage during the conversation, Wilson picked up Mary and
kissed her but his wife shouted, "Put her down!" and ran to knock
on the wall to attract the attention of the neighbours so they might
call the police. This, too, was something Annie had done before so
Wilson pushed her back on to the settee. As far as he was concerned,
the incident would have ended there but without warning, Annie
Hargreaves smashed him over the head with the corner of a picture
frame. This angered him and he turned to face his stepdaughter and
said, "If you don't stop that and clear out, I will kill you, all of you."
Then to emphasise the point, he had chased the girls upstairs to get
them out of the way.

Returning downstairs, Wilson found his wife standing near the
kitchen door. He recalled receiving more blows over the head at that
point, but he had no idea who had inflicted them. From that
moment he had no recollection of anything until he woke up in the
infirmary. Finally, to illustrate that there was a history of insanity in
his family, Wilson pointed out that a brother and a sister of his had
both died in the Menston Asylum.

It took the jury only 15 minutes to decide that Wilson was guilty
of murder. His appeal against the death sentence was heard on April
19th before the Lord Chief Justice, Lord Isaacs. Once again Wilson's
defence claimed that as a result of the blow to the head from the
picture frame he had been temporarily thrown off balance mentally
and was, to all intents and purposes, insane. That claim was dismissed
and the appeal was lost.

On Thursday, May 6th, 1920, Thomas Hargreaves Wilson was
hanged at Leeds by Thomas Pierrepoint who was assisted by Robert
Baxter. Few people gathered to read the official notices.

CHAPTER ELEVEN

THE MYSTERIOUS MR GOODSON

SOME people really had no consideration for others. George Hall and his men had turned up at the appointed time at 23 Sunderland Road, Bradford, to move the furniture and contents of that house to an address in Buxton. Now, though, there was no answer to his repeated knocking and it appeared that the owner of the house had simply not bothered to be there to let them in.

George Hall worked for Swithenbank & Co, a company that had been in the furniture removal business for many years. As he stood in the street, talking to his workmate, George Renton, Hall shifted his weight from foot to foot and muttered something about some folk having no regard for others.

The two men had been in the street for perhaps ten minutes when Renton spotted a torn scrap of paper sticking out of the letterbox of number 23. He took the paper out, unfolded it and read a pencilled message: "Mr Wilson, have had to go to Buxton today. Come Monday, 8am, please." The note was not signed and turning the piece of paper over, Renton saw that it had been torn from an envelope which had been addressed, 'Messrs Driver and Pickersgill, House and Estate Agents, 33 Iregate, Bradford.'

The Mr Wilson referred to in the note was Arthur John Wilson, one of the managers of Swithenbank & Co, and now Renton and Hall thought it might be an idea to telephone their office and see if Wilson knew any more about this matter, or if possibly he had another job for them to do. Finding a telephone kiosk, George Hall rang his office and spoke to another manager, Thomas Adamson. George explained that he and his men had been unable to gain access to no. 23 and was told to return to base. Once there, Hall handed the scrap of paper to Thomas Adamson who said he was at a loss to understand what was going on.

Arthur Wilson had first called at 23 Sunderland Road on January 22nd, 1924. There he had seen the sole occupant of the house, 60-year-old Elizabeth Reaney, who told him that she planned to move to a new home, 'Hymen House' which was on Castleton Road, Buxton, in Derbyshire. In fact, Mr Wilson had called a total of three times to see Mrs Reaney and, having agreed a price for the move, arranged to send his men, with their van, at 8.30am on Saturday, 23rd February. From the wording on the note it now seemed that Mrs Reaney had changed her mind at the last minute and now wanted the move to take place on Monday the 25th instead. Arthur Wilson put the piece of paper to one side. He would sort it all out later.

Not long after George Hall and his men had driven away from Sunderland Road, another caller knocked on the door of number 23. Eliza Marshall lived at 27 Sunderland Road and had known Mrs Reaney for about five years. At 9.00am on February 23rd, Eliza went to visit her neighbour but again there was no reply. She tried the front door and found it locked, something that Mrs Reaney rarely did when she was at home. Eliza simply assumed that her friend had gone out and resolved to call again later.

The next callers at number 23 arrived at 1.15pm. John Driver and Herbert Pickersgill were partners in the estate agents that bore their names, Driver and Pickersgill. They had first met Mrs Reaney on December 7th, 1923, when she explained to them that she would be moving to Derbyshire some time in 1924 and wished to sell her house in Sunderland Road. Having visited the premises, the partners agreed to pay £390 for the house and as a sign of good faith, handed over £15 in cash as a deposit.

The sale had been completed on February 18th, 1924, and the conveyance duly executed. Arrangements had been made for the agents to be given vacant possession on February 23rd. Mrs Reaney had said that she had made arrangements to move on that date and would drop the keys in at the estate agents' office at around noon. Those keys had not been received and now the two partners were knocking on the door of a house that now belonged to them.

John Driver found both the front and back doors of the property securely locked. Admission had to be gained and it was Mr Driver who eventually forced open a cellar window, climbed into the house and opened the front door for his partner. The house was still furnished, although some items had been packed away in boxes. The two men began to look through the rooms to see if any clue could be found as to the whereabouts of Elizabeth Reaney.

It was Pickersgill who climbed the stairs and entered the upstairs back bedroom. Moving around a strange, empty house is always an odd feeling, but Pickersgill could never have been prepared for the sight which met his eyes. There on the floor, at the foot of the bed, lay the battered and bloody body of Elizabeth Reaney. She was quite obviously beyond all help and Pickersgill ran to fetch his partner. Neither man touched the body and the police were on the scene within minutes.

The officer in charge of the case was Detective Superintendent Frederick Petty, who made a detailed inspection of 23 Sunderland Road. A blanket and a folded piece of material had been placed underneath Mrs Reaney's head, apparently to serve as some kind of pillow. Near the body lay a bloodstained hammer. Someone had apparently searched the premises already for a trunk situated inside the doorway had been ransacked, yet whoever had carried out that search had obviously been in a hurry, for if they had been looking for cash they had missed £445 in £1 notes in a handbag which lay in a corner of the room. Superintendent Petty found other bundles of cash in a couple of envelopes. In all, £529 4s 11d was discovered on the premises.

On the stairway, newspapers had been scattered about and one of these bore the bloody imprint of a stockinged foot. The direction of the print was downwards. In the kitchen there were two glasses which had apparently contained stout, and the remains of a meal for two. More important, a number of letters were found and these went a great way towards clarifying the picture for Superintendent Petty.

The letters were signed either 'G. Goodson' or 'George Goodson' and were all couched in affectionate terms. One, dated January 20th, 1922, read, 'Dear Lizzie, Have had influenza and have not been able to get over. I am at Stanningley this morning and am waiting for someone so just have time to scribble you a note. I will come over as soon as I have a little time.

'As you know I am extra busy just now but shall have more time soon. Hope you are quite well and will escape the influenza. Best love till I see you. G. Goodson.' At the foot of the letter there were nine kisses and the dates on this and the other letters showed that Mr Goodson, whoever he was, had been acquainted with Elizabeth Reaney for some considerable time.

Superintendent Petty began by interviewing Elizabeth Reaney's neighbours. Eliza Marshall was able to provide them with some useful information. Mrs Reaney had once earned her living by taking in lodgers but the last of these, Mr David Neville, had left at the beginning of 1924. Since that time, Elizabeth had lived alone, but she did have a regular male visitor who was paying her a great deal of attention.

On February 21st, Mrs Marshall had visited number 23 at around 7.15pm. Although they only spoke at Elizabeth Reaney's back door, Mrs Marshall could hear voices from inside the house before the door was opened. The second voice was definitely male and when she came to the door, Mrs Reaney looked bright and happy.

The following day, February 22nd, Elizabeth Reaney had been wearing a new wedding ring and a dress ring. Mrs Marshall had called at 7.00pm and noticed a white tablecloth on the kitchen table and two places set. Mrs Reaney told Eliza that she was expecting a visitor. In fact she had announced, "I am expecting the man I am going to marry. I had expected him between six and seven o'clock." The man had obviously turned up later, though, for when Eliza Marshall passed the back of her neighbour's house at around 10.30pm, that same night, the lights were on, the blinds were drawn and voices could be heard from within.

The fact that Elizabeth Reaney had been expecting someone was confirmed by two other witnesses. Bertie Feather kept a grocer's shop at 46 Oak Lane. Elizabeth was a regular customer and often called in for a single bottle of stout. On February 22nd, though, at 9.15pm, she bought two bottles. In addition to this, Laura Weidman, who ran a tobacconist's at 1 Athol Road, said that on the same night, Elizabeth had come in and asked for a packet of Robin cigarettes, a brand she did not stock. Since Elizabeth Reaney did not smoke, it was natural to assume that these were for her mysterious gentleman friend.

Derbyshire police were contacted and they confirmed that the Buxton address given to the removal men by Mrs Reaney was fictitious. Finally, Alice Simons, who kept a stationer's at 7 Grand Arcade, Leeds, which was used by several people as an accommod-ation address, told the police that from 1921 onwards, letters had been received there for a man who gave his name as George Goodson. This gentleman had also collected mail in a second name, Musgrave.

The police were certainly thorough in their attempts to trace Mr Goodson. They knew that one way a gentleman might contact a lady was by placing an advertisement in a newspaper. Archives were checked and soon they had traced an advertisement dated July 2nd, 1921. This read, "Gentleman, private income £1,000, desires correspondence with refined lady, means, private, genuine." The box number was Q95 and that advertisement had been placed by a man who gave the name G.A. Goodson and the address of Alice Simons' office in Grand Arcade, Leeds. Unfortunately, the newspaper concerned had that very week sent the original advertisement request, along with tons of other material, to the council dump to be incinerated.

Sarah Howarth was Elizabeth Reaney's sister and lived in Blackpool. She told the police that her sister had married David Lewis Reaney, who had left her 24 years ago to emigrate to Australia. Many years afterwards, Elizabeth had 'married' another man named Herbert Gosling and they had lived together at Shef-field. Gosling had died four years previously and soon afterwards came news from Australia that David Reaney had only just died and left his wife some money. Only recently, however Elizabeth had intimated that she was thinking of getting married again to 'a very nice and cheerful sort of fellow, about 55 years of age'.

It all appeared so straightforward: Mrs Reaney had replied to Mr Goodson advertisement. He had represented himself as a wealthy man and had wormed his way into her affections. In time, he had proposed marriage and suggested that they move together to an address in Buxton. Mrs Reaney had sold her house and it seemed to have been Mr Goodson's intention to steal the proceeds of that sale from her. He had battered her to death, searched the house for the money which he knew she held, but had failed to find it before fleeing.

The inquest on Elizabeth Reaney opened on February 26th before the Bradford coroner, Mr J.G. Hutchinson. Only the most basic details were given before the proceedings were adjourned until March 12th. The crime had, however, been given a great deal of publicity in the local newspapers and this led to a number of valuable witnesses coming forward. One was a neighbour of Mrs Reaney's who told the police of a man he had seen calling at number 23 on several occasions. The mysterious Mr Goodson had been seen by several other people and some had even spoken to him.

With all this information, Superintendent Petty was able to compile a detailed description of the man the police were looking for, a description which he released to the newspapers on February 27th.

The following announcement was published: 'We are offering £100 for information which will lead to the arrest and conviction of the murderer. The person suspected has used the names of G. Musgrave and George Arthur Goodson. It is probable that both of these are fictitious.

'His age is somewhere between 40 and 50, but he may be a bit older. His height is about 5ft 9ins. He is believed to be clean shaven, and to be losing some hair. He may be partially bald on the top of his head.

'He is respectably dressed, and that is all we can say about his clothing. There is reason to believe that Musgrave or Goodson has recently received some injury to his face, possibly cuts and bruising or even black eyes. He accounted for these injuries by stating that he had fallen down the steps when getting out of a tram.' On the same day that this message was published, Elizabeth Reaney was buried at the Nab Wood Cemetery, Shipley.

Thousands of people in Bradford and Leeds read the description in their newspapers and began to puzzle over who it might be — but to one group of men it appeared to match precisely someone that they knew well. Ben Pickles was the landlord of the Peel Hotel, a public house on Longside Lane, Bradford, and as he read the report in the newspaper, he remarked to one of his regular customers, Leonard Heseltine, that the description matched a friend of theirs, a customer known as 'The Doctor' because of his fondness for giving people advice on what they should do if they had colds or other minor ailments. At this point, Heseltine remarked, "This is the doctor to a T. When he comes in, keep him until I come back. I'm just going for my tea and when I return, I'm off for that £100 reward." The real name of 'The Doctor' was William Horsely Wardell.

Even as the two men spoke, 47-year-old William Wardell came

into the bar. As Pickles put the newspaper down in front of Wardell, Heseltine said, "Here, the Jacks [the police] are looking for you, Doctor." Wardell replied, "Nothing of the sort." But Pickles interrupted. "My word, Doctor, they are after you." One of the waiters, Fred Mawson, added, "You are wanted old pal."

If these comments were meant as jokes, Wardell did not appear to see the funny side and disappeared into a private room at the back of the pub. In due course, Leonard Heseltine followed and in an attempt to cheer his friend up suggested, "Come on down to the Town Hall, Doctor. If you've nothing to do with it, you've nothing to be frightened of. They will fetch you about midnight if you don't go down now."

Wardell thought for a few moments and then asked Heseltine if he would go down with him. Heseltine said he would be happy to. Wardell seemed to recover a little and said, "We'll have a drink apiece and then I'll go down with you." On the way to the Town Hall, though, Wardell's depressed mood returned and he muttered somewhat prophetically, "They will keep me all night."

As the two men stepped inside the Town Hall, Wardell was shocked to hear someone in an adjoining office giving not only a description of him, but also his name and address. This man was a hairdresser, Mr Topham of 69a Little Horton Lane, Bradford, who recalled shaving Wardell, a man he knew well, on the previous Tuesday. He, too, had recognised the description in the newspapers. Wardell tried to look through a frosted window to see who was speaking, but was unable to make out anything. In due course, at 9.00pm, Wardell was seen by Superintendent Petty.

Petty began by saying, "I understand you match the description of the man wanted for the murder of Elizabeth Reaney." Wardell replied, "Yes, it's ridiculous." He went on to detail some of his past history and said that although he was not in work at the moment, he had no financial concerns as he had owned two houses in Scarborough, 55 and 57 Prospect Road, and had recently sold them to a Mr Ellinson for £500.

Superintendent Petty had not failed to notice that Wardell's face was discoloured and bruised on the left side, and inquired about this. Wardell explained that he and an old woman had fallen off a tram together, at Eccleshill on February 18th. Asked if he had any money on him, Wardell produced three £1 notes and two 10s notes, explaining that he had made some spindles for a Mr Anderson and been paid £7. The superintendent asked if there might be any more cash at Wardell's house, to which he replied that there was a wallet there which contained perhaps a further £12.

Wardell was taken to his home at 30 Howard Street where he produced the wallet and handed it over to Superintendent Petty. There was indeed £12 in £1 notes in the wallet and the notes were crisp and new. Various documents were also discovered, which Wardell admitted he had written himself. These, of course, were later used for handwriting comparisons, both with the note found in the door of no. 23 by the removal men and also with the Goodson letters.

Superintendent Petty took Wardell back to the police station and left in cuistody while he returned with other officers to Howard Street. A large number of items were removed from the house, including a three-legged stool, a brown carpet, blankets, bedspreads, tablecloths, curtains, an oil painting, candlesticks, a teapot, a decanter and even two books on Abyssinia. Similar items had been reported as missing from 23 Sunderland Road and if identified, would provide a direct link between Wardell and the murder house.

Back at the police station, Superintendent Petty showed the articles to Wardell, who claimed that he had started dealing in such items and had bought these from a Miss Hudson. Told that he would be charged with killing Mrs Reaney, Wardell cried, "I did not. I should not have come here if I had done this. You would have had to fetch me from as far as possible."

Wardell's first appearance at the Bradford police court took place on February 28th. Only evidence of arrest was given, the police adding that they believed Wardell to be a native of Whitley Bay and pointing out how closely he resembled the description of the wanted man published in the newspapers. Wardell, naively perhaps, asked the magistrates for bail. The request was refused and he was remanded in custody until March 7th, with further appearances following on March 14th and March 21st, during which Wardell was represented by Mr H.A. Demaine. In due course, though, the body of evidence appeared to be strong enough to support a charge of murder and Wardell was committed for trial.

The trial opened on May 8th, 1924, before Mr Justice Avory. Wardell was defended by Mr C.J. Frankland while the case for the prosecution was led by Mr C.F. Lowenthal, assisted by Mr C. Paley Scott and Mr Frank Beverley.

Some of the early witnesses proved a direct link between Wardell and the dead woman. James John Froome was a cashier at the Leeds branch of the Bank of England. He told the court that on February 13th, in the course of his daily duties, he had cashed a cheque for £7,500 for John Charles who was a messenger for the Midland Bank at Market Street, Bradford. Mr Charles was given £5,000 in £1 notes and £2,500 in 10s notes and the bank, as a matter of record, kept details of the serial numbers of new banknotes. The £1 notes had been a batch whose serial numbers began C141 and ran to C150.

Back at the Midland Bank, those new £1 notes were handed over to John Edward Wilman, the chief cashier, who testified that the notes had been locked away in the safe and bundles had been removed from time to time over the next few days. On February 16th, another of the cashiers, Benjamin Hugh Busfield, had given a bundle of the new £1 notes to William Tordoff who was the cashier at the Oak Lane branch. That bundle contained £100 in £1 notes and Mr Busfield, although he did not note the numbers, swore that it had come from the original consignment of £5,000.

William Tordoff testified that he had collected the £100 bundle on February 16th and on the same day had cashed a cheque for £30 for one of his customers, Mrs Reaney, who had held an account at his branch since October 9th, 1919. In addition, four days later, Mrs Reaney cashed a further cheque for £125, of which £100 was paid out as a bundle of new £1 notes.

None of these three gentlemen could state what serial numbers the notes paid out to Mrs Reaney bore, but they could say that she must have received some notes from that original bundle of 5,000 new notes bearing serial numbers from C141 to C150. When the police had searched the murder house they had, of course, found a large number of £1 notes and some of these began with the number C144. Notes bearing that same serial number were found in Wardell's wallet and when a complete list was presented to the court, the inference was obvious. The note which bore number C144 728739 was in Wardell's possession. Numbers 728740 to 728747 inclusive had not been found. Note number 728748 was Wardell's, 728749 was in Mrs Reaney's house, 728750 was found on Wardell and 728751 was missing. Continuing the list, 728752 was in Wardell's wallet, 728753 was missing, 728754 was Wardell's, 728755 to 728759 were found at Sunderland Road, and numbers 728760 to 728767 inclusive were in Wardell's possession.

Wardell, of course, had suggested that he had earned those £1 notes from a Mr Anderson who owned a large house at Thornton. Wardell had made a number of spindles for him and said that he had been paid with these new £1 notes. The prosecution now called Frank Wilman, who was the rates collector for Thornton. Mr Wilman was able to confirm that there was no one named Anderson who ran a business in the town.

The prisoner had also claimed to have owned two houses at Scarborough. Arthur Clayton was the head clerk for Messrs Bobb & Sons, a firm of solicitors based in York. For many years his firm had been concerned with the properties at 55 and 57 Prospect Road, Scarborough. The houses had first been purchased by a Mr William Taylor in 1877, and in 1890, along with other properties, had been mortgaged to one of the partners, William Henry Bobb. In 1907, Mr Taylor had died and the houses had passed to his widow. Since that date, Mrs Taylor had lived alone in number 55 and had derived an income from renting out number 57. At no stage had anyone named Wardell any claim on either property.

Evidence was now given that Wardell, contrary to what he had told the police, had at least some financial problems. James Jessop was the manager for George Taylor Financiers of 7 Bond Street, Bradford. On June 1st, 1922, Wardell had applied to him for a loan of £10. That loan had been granted on June 2nd and with the interest applied, Wardell was now indebted to him to the sum of £14. By September 25th of that year, the balance owing had been reduced to £7 but four days later, on September 29th, Wardell applied for a further loan of £7, which was granted. On June 7th, 1923, a request for a third loan, this time for £20, was made and this was also agreed. By December 1923, Wardell's account stood at £7, which was still owing at the present time.

There was also testimony that showed that Wardell was about to leave the district. In January, and on two occasions in February 1924, Wardell had placed advertisements in the *Bradford Daily Telegraph*, advertising furniture for sale. One of these appeared on February 2nd and another on February 11th. All gave the address at 30 Howard Street and callers were told that everything there was for sale.

Edith Jenkins lived at 12 Ebor Street, Bradford, and had seen an advertisement in January. Edith was looking for a carpet, and Wardell showed her one for which he was asking 25s. He explained the selling of his household goods by saying, "My wife has been ill and been away for a year. I am leaving to go south." Two days after her first visit, Edith had returned, paid £1 for the carpet and another 5s for some lino.

Lily Atkinson was a second-hand furniture dealer working from premises at 437 Manchester Road. In February she bought a large number of articles from Wardell but when she visited him again on February 22nd and again on the 23rd, he was not at home. Calling again on the 25th, at 3.30pm, she noticed that his face was bruised and he told her that he had fallen off a tramcar.

William Gladstone kept an apartment house at 40 Ashgrove in Bradford. He visited Wardell at Howard Street on February 2nd. Once again Wardell explained his actions by saying that his wife had been ill and he was moving south to be with her. Mr Gladstone picked out a number of articles for which a price of £2 12s 6d was agreed. This amount was paid over on February 8th and the articles taken away.

Solomon Cohen was a master tailor but also ran an apartment house at 13 Howard Street. He called on Wardell on February 11th and bought some items for £2. Wardell had explained that the house had been sold and he had to move on and did not want to take the furniture with him.

For once, Wardell was telling the truth, for his house had indeed been sold. Maude Atherton lived next door to Wardell at 32 Howard Street. She earned her living by taking in commercial travellers and was seeking to expand her business. Wardell had told her back in June 1923 that he was intending to move away from the district and Mrs Atherton thought his house would be an ideal extension to her trade.

In that same month of June, Maude Atherton made an offer for number 30 and bought it, subject to Wardell being allowed to stay as a tenant until he found a place in the south of England. Although Mrs Atherton tried to get vacant possession on more than one occasion, Wardell stalled her repeatedly, saying that he was unable to move until he saw his wife.

In early January, 1924, Wardell, now only a tenant of his home, paid the rent to Maude Atherton who again asked him when he was likely to leave. To this he had replied, "I am going to see my wife at Buxton and I will let you know." However, it was not until January 22nd that Maude next saw him. On that date he stopped her in the street and told her, "You can have your house in April because we have got a smaller one." April was quite a long time away and Mrs Atherton asked if he could not make it a little sooner. Wardell thought for a moment and then said, "Probably in a fortnight's time.

If I can't give you possession, you can start with the bedrooms." The same day, Wardell invited Maude to see if there was anything she wanted to buy from inside the house. She told him to put together whatever he wanted to get rid of and she would decide.

John Driver told the court about the circumstances in which he and his partner, Herbert Pickersgill, had found the body of Elizabeth Reaney. He went on to give details of his financial dealings over the purchase of the house. He had completed the purchase on February 18th and on that date had called at the offices of Greaves & Firth, Mrs Reaney's solicitors, with his clerk, Madge Lockwood. The various documents had been signed and then Driver had handed over £115 in banknotes and a cheque for £264 which was drawn on the Union Bank of Manchester, Halifax branch.

John Greaves was a senior partner in Greaves & Firth and he confirmed the evidence of Mr Driver. He also reported that his firm had acted for Mrs Reaney since the end of 1919 and gave details of various sums paid to her under her late husband's will. He had acted in the sale of Mrs Reaney's house and handed over to her the cash and cheque after the sale was completed.

What had happened to that cheque for £264 was made clear when Percy Wilcock gave his evidence. Wilcock was employed as a cashier at the Union Bank of Manchester at their Market Street, Bradford branch. On February 19th a woman had presented the cheque to him for payment. There was no doubt that it was the same cheque. It was payable to John Driver and had been endorsed by him. The back of the cheque bore a second signature, that of Elizabeth Reaney, and, of course, it was for the same amount, £264.

Percy Wilcock was also able to tell the court that his bank had held an account in the name of William Horsely Wardell since June 3rd, 1910. In the early days, an overdraft of £45 had been agreed, for which the bank held shares as security. These shares had been sold on July 5th, 1921, and the sum of £45 15s 5d credited to the account. That amount had been drawn soon afterwards and the account had been mostly dormant ever since.

The prosecution were alleging that Wardell had killed Mrs Reaney for the cash he knew she had somewhere in her house. That cash had subsequently been found by the police but the significance of the note to the removal men had not been missed. Surely it did not matter to Wardell when Mrs Reaney's body was discovered. If he had placed that note in the door, telling the removal men to come back on Monday, then he might have intended to return to the house in Sunderland Road to make another search. Evidence was now called to show that this was exactly what he had intended.

Mrs Reaney was last seen alive on the night of Friday, February 22nd and the following day had failed to admit the removal men. In all probability, then, she was battered to death on the Friday night. However, at 6.45pm on Sunday, February 24th, before the knowledge of the discovery of the body had become widespread, Constable George Hague noticed a man behaving suspiciously in Oak Lane. The man stopped in front of some hoardings and looked furtively around. Seeing the policeman, he crossed Oak Lane and headed off in the direction of Sunderland Road.

Hague followed into Sunderland Road but, looking down the street, could see no sign of the man. Then, a minute or so later, the man reappeared from the back of Sunderland Road. Constable Hague walked over to him and asked him if he lived in Sunderland Road. The man replied that he did not and when asked what he was doing at the back of the houses, denied that he had been there. Constable Hague said, "I have been watching you for some time and saw you go on the back of Sunderland Road, come back on Athol Road and down Garfield Avenue." Faced with this, the man claimed that he had been looking at some railway posters, adding that he was going to Brighton soon. As if to explain his actions he produced a half-empty bottle of whisky from his pocket and muttered, "I have had a drop of this. I don't know my way about in the district." Hague saw no reason to detain the man but asked for his name and address. The reply was, "William Wardell, 30 Howard Street."

It now became necessary to show the court that Mr Goodson and

William Wardell were one and the same. Gerald Francis Gurrin was a handwriting expert who had studied the subject for 20 years. He had examined a number of exhibits which included the Goodson letters, samples of Wardell's handwriting and also that of Elizabeth Reaney. Mr Gurrin stated that he was certain that the Goodson letters had been written by Wardell. As for the pencilled note in the door, asking the removal men to call back on the Monday, there were not enough words to say with any degree of certainty that it had been written by Wardell, but Mr Gurrin was able to say that it had probably not been written by Mrs Reaney.

It was known that the guest Mrs Reaney had been expecting on the night she died smoked Robin cigarettes. Eric Pullan was the manager of a grocer's shop at 65 Heaton Lane and Wardell was a regular customer there. Mr Pullan was able to say that Wardell always purchased Robin cigarettes.

Leonard Heseltine, Ben Pickles and Fred Mawson told the court of the events at the Peel Hotel on the night Wardell was arrested. In addition, Pickles pointed out that Wardell always seemed to have plenty of cash to spare. On one occasion, on February 18th, he had seen a wad of £1 notes in Wardell's wallet and yet he had still paid for a round with a £5 note. Heseltine was able to say that on the night of February 22nd, the night Mrs Reaney was expecting her visitor, he had left the Peel Hotel with Wardell at around 10.15pm. They had parted soon afterwards and the last he had seen of Wardell, he was heading up Longside Lane. That thoroughfare was on the way to Sunderland Road but Wardell was also in the habit of calling at a fish and chip shop at 57 Longside Lane. The prosecution called Elizabeth Reid who worked at that shop and she testified that although Wardell called on the Monday, Tuesday, Wednesday and Thursday nights of that week, he did not appear on the Friday.

Police evidence was given showing that a notebook found in Wardell's possession contained an entry which read, 'Mrs E. Reaney, 23 Sunderland Road, Bradford — Goodson. (Mr G. Goodson, c/o Timms, 7 Grand Arcade, Leeds.)' The prosecution called Ellen Maria

Westcott. She had known Wardell for 30 years, first becoming acquainted with him when he lived with his mother in Pickering. Wardell started paying attention to her and they even agreed to marry but for one reason or another, Wardell kept putting the wedding off.

On October 10th, 1908, a few months after his mother had died, Ellen and Wardell moved to Bradford. Two years later they moved to 30 Howard Street where Ellen kept them by renting out rooms. Wardell did little or no work and in due course Ellen grew tired of supporting him and left on December 8th, 1921. Ellen's evidence not only showed that Wardell was averse to earning his own living by honest means, but knowing him so well, she was also able to identify his handwriting on the documents which Mr Gurrin had used to compare with the Goodson letters.

When it became clear to him that his relationship with Ellen Westcott was floundering, Wardell had not wasted much time in seeking a replacement companion. Hylda Kidd testified that although she now lived in Sleaford, Lincolnshire, she had worked as a shop assistant in Bradford in 1921. On July 26th, she had first met Wardell and they began keeping company together. At Christmas, only two weeks after Ellen had moved out of Howard Street, Hylda moved in. This new relationship was shaky from the start and Hylda moved out, only to twice move back in. She finally left Wardell in January 1923. During the time they were together, Wardell never appeared to do any work but always seemed to have plenty of cash. He also had a habit of coming home with furniture and household goods which he said he had been given by a friend at Queensbury. Hylda identified various items, including a teapot, carpets, and curtains, as having come from this friend. In fact, all these items had previously been shown to have come from Elizabeth Reaney's home.

Medical evidence was given by Dr Alfred Hayes Smith, and Dr William Wrangham, two police surgeons. Both had visited the murder scene and the following day had worked together on the post-mortem. They detailed a large catalogue of injuries but stated that the cause of death was fracture of the skull and laceration of the brain caused by direct external violence. The time of death was given as some time between 11.00pm on February 22nd and 3.00am on February 23rd.

The jury retired at 12.45pm on May 10th and took just over an hour to decide that Wardell was guilty of murder. For the defence Mr Frankland confirmed that there would be an appeal, which was heard on June 2nd before the Lord Chief Justice, Sir Gordon Hewart, and Justices Roche and Swift. There were two factors which the defence wished to put forward.

The first argument was that the note found in the door at Sunderland Road was never shown to be in Wardell's hand. Even if it had been written by him, it did not necessarily connect him with the crime. The note had been written in blue chalk pencil and because no such pencil being found at the house it was held that Elizabeth Reaney could not have been its author. Since the trial, however, just such a pencil had been found in a handbag at the house, showing that it was indeed possible that Mrs Reaney could have written the note.

The second point was that in his summing up, the trial judge had made a good deal of the various pieces of circumstantial evidence which told against Wardell, but had paid little attention to facts which told in his favour. In due course, the judges held that, despite these factors, there was a wealth of evidence showing that Wardell was the man responsible for Elizabeth Reaney's death. The appeal was dismissed.

The night before his execution, Wardell's sleep was disturbed by a heavy thunderstorm over the city of Leeds. The following morning, Wednesday, June 18th, 1924, at 9.00am, William Horsely Wardell was hanged by Thomas Pierrepoint and William Willis. It was only the third execution of 1924.

Mr Justice Coleridge who took part in three of the earlier cases reported in this volume. (Hulton Getty)

The house at Sunderland Road, Bradford, where William Horsely Wardell brutally battered Elizabeth Reaney to death. See Chapter 11. (Yvonne Berger)

Mr Justice Avory, involved in four of the cases in this book. (Popperfoto)

Bradford Town Hall where many of the investigations began and where newly arrested criminals were taken by the police.

Lord Hewart, who was Lord Chief Justice from 1922 to 1940. (Popperfoto)

Emily Yeomans allegedly strangled by David Maskill Blake in Middleton woods. See Chapter 14.

Part of Briggate in Leeds. It was in this street that Blake used to go drinking with the man who proved to be the main prosecution witness at his trial, and where Kowalewski argued with the woman whose life he was to claim an hour later. See Chapters 14 and 23.

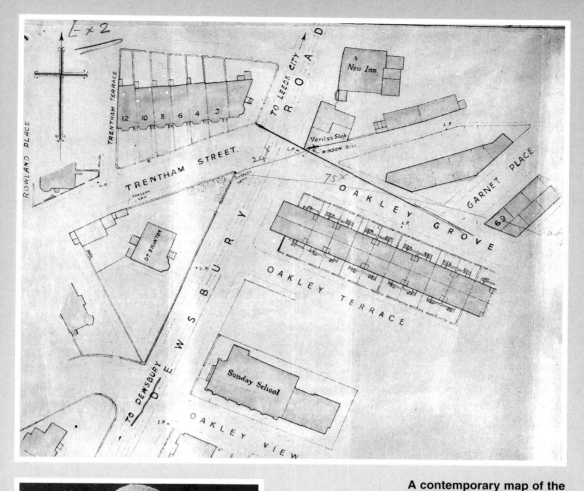

A contemporary map of the area around Dewsbury Road and Oakley Grove where Emily Yeomans met the man who killed her that same night. The butcher's shop from where three young boys witnessed the meeting is just below the 'New Inn' See Chapter 14. (Public Records Office)

Mr Justice Streatfeild who is mentioned in some of the cases in these pages, first as a barrister and later as a judge. (Popperfoto)

The Nag's Head pub at Clayton Heights at the time Jane Coulton met her death at the hands of Arthur Thompson. Note the broken glass in the door on the right-hand side of the picture. See Chapter 15. (Public Records Office)

Inside the kitchen at the Nag's Head. Thompson gained entrance through the window leaving spots of blood all over the sink and floor. See Chapter 15. (Public Records Office)

The Nag's Head as it is today. Jane Coulton's body was found in the room at the top of the rounded part of the building. See Chapter 15.

Leeds Town Hall. The main police station used to be in this building and many of those who were hanged would have been questioned there.

The body of Dr Dewar
lying in his driveway.
See Chapter 16.
(Public Record Office)

The driveway where
Thomas Eric
Richardson killed Dr
Dewar, as it is today.
The wrought-iron
gates have replaced
the wooden ones in
the previous picture.
See Chapter 16.
(Yvonne Berger)

CHAPTER TWELVE

MURDER AT THE PIGGERIES

FIFTY-five-year-old Alfred Gill was a successful greengrocer who not only had premises in 1260 Leeds Road, Bradford, but also had a horse and cart with which he toured the Manningham district on Fridays and Saturdays, selling his produce and providing a welcome service for local families.

Friday, December 11th, 1931, was one of the days that Gill was due to make his rounds and his wife, Louisa, saw him leave their home, at 68 Wheater Terrace, Bradford Lane, Thornbury, at about 9.00am. Before he left the house, Alfred had counted his money on the table and although Louisa had no idea precisely how much he was carrying, she did see quite a few banknotes and estimated that the total might be around £50. She also knew that on a average day trading from his cart, her husband usually took perhaps another £20, bringing the total cash he should return home with to around £70.

But by 8.00pm, some two hours after the time he usually arrived back at Wheater Terrace, Alfred Gill had still not returned home. Concerned, Louisa set off for the stables to see if he was there, but at the last minute she passed by and went on to the shop in Leeds Road. There was no sign of her husband so, reluctantly, she returned to Wheater Terrace to wait and to give her son his dinner.

By 10.30pm, Louisa's husband still had not arrived and so she and one of her sons, also named Alfred, went down to Tyersal, near Pudsey, where the family kept some pigs. Alfred Gill senior often took scraps from the shops down to feed the pigs and perhaps he had gone down there, fallen ill or had some kind of accident and been unable to summon help.

The piggeries were locked and the gate closed, although it was not padlocked. Alfred junior shouted for his father but as there was no reply and the place appeared to be secure, he and his mother returned yet again to their home in Thornbury. The hours ticked away and it was 12.45am on the Saturday when Louisa, young Alfred and his brother, William Gill, went back to the piggeries.

This time, with the aid of a lamp, they made a more careful search and there, in the third shed to the west of the entrance gates, the brothers made an awful discovery — their father, lying dead on his back behind a pile of rubbish with a box placed on top of his body. Louisa removed the box and she and William stayed at the scene while Alfred ran to fetch the police.

It was 12.57am when Detective Sergeant John Hillerby and Detective Constable Clapham arrived at police box number 76, which stood at the junction of Dick Lane and Holland Street, Tyersal. There they met up with Alfred Gill, who took the two officers back to the piggeries. By the time the three arrived, Louisa Gill's two daughters, Louisa and Clara, had also appeared on the scene so that now there were five members of the Gill family standing over the dead body of Mr Gill.

Having briefly returned to the police call box to confirm with headquarters that a body had been found, Sergeant Hillerby made a careful examination of the scene. Alfred Gill had been badly battered about the head and face and there was a great deal of blood on the front of his shirt and on his muffler. His brown overalls and a waistcoat were both open at the front and from the waistcoat hung a watch. The glass in the timepiece was missing and the watch, now broken, had stopped. The time of the attack appeared to be 6.13pm.

The attack upon Mr Gill had apparently not taken place at the spot where his body was found. There was a pool of blood at the eastern end of the piggeries and a trail led from there to the entrance gates. Close by the gates was a large iron hinge which had been thrown to one side. This, too, was bloodstained and looked as if it might have been used to batter Mr Gill. At 2.10am Superintendent George Bell arrived at the scene and took charge of the investigation.

It was, of course, still dark and another search was made using torches and lamps. In the pool of blood at the east side, Superintendent Bell found what looked like a human tooth. The trail of blood extended for 51ft to a spot between two of the pig sties where another, smaller, pool of blood could be seen. The boards of the building here were spattered with blood, but only to a height of one foot. The trail turned in a north-westerly direction and ran for another 79ft to the spot where the body now lay. Along the trail, five coins — three pennies and two halfpennies — were discovered. In the dead man's pockets, the police found just 1s 5d in coppers. Alfred Gill had been battered to death and the motive seemed to be robbery.

The investigation was only a couple of hours old when a name was given to the police. Louisa Gill told the officers of a young man named John Henry Roberts who often helped her husband when he went out hawking. Indeed, just a few days before Alfred had been killed, on Tuesday, December 8th, she had been with her husband at the piggeries when they had seen Roberts hanging around. Louisa had asked him what he was doing and Roberts had replied, "I'm killing time. I've been to my sisters. I've to meet my father and I'm having a walk around." Since it was known that John Roberts had stabled Alfred Gill's horse it was highly likely that Roberts had been the last person to see the dead man on the Friday, so it was decided to speak to him at his lodgings, 35 Chesham Street.

It was 5.00am when Superintendent Bell and Detective Superintendent Frederick Petty called at the house owned by George

Lewis Mather and his wife, Beatrice Bell Mather, at Chesham Street, and asked to speak to their lodger, John Henry Roberts. As soon as the officers saw Roberts in his bed, they realised that they almost certainly had found their killer, for he sported a bruised face and a badly swollen eye.

Superintendent Bell woke Roberts from his slumbers and, handing over a pair of brown trousers which lay on a chair by the bed, Bell told his suspect to dress. Roberts rose, pulled on the trousers and also put on a brown coat and waistcoat. Bell, meanwhile, searched the room and took a towel, a handkerchief and a pair of brown boots. It was at this time that Chief Superintendent Blacker arrived and it was he who told Roberts, "Alfred Gill has been found dead at the piggeries. You are the last person known to have been in his company and you took the horse from the piggeries to the stable in Napier Street. Do you care to give an account of your movements yesterday?" Roberts made a brief statement which Superintendent Bell wrote down. Roberts read over the documents and, after making a footnote, signed it before being taken to the police station.

The police had also noticed what appeared to be bloodstains on Roberts' clothing. There were stains on the leg of his trousers and also on his jacket sleeve. This area seemed to have been wiped but the liquid had soaked through to the lining beneath. These items were taken from Roberts and handed to Inspector Sharp for further examination. Roberts was searched and was found to be carrying just over £1 5s in copper and silver. He also had with him a notice for the recovery of a debt.

At 7.45am on December 12th, John Roberts was charged with murder and taken down to the cells. It was from there, at 12.30pm that day, that he asked to see Chief Superintendent Blacker. Roberts was taken back to Superintendent Bell's office where he was told to write down whatever he wished to say. Roberts said that he would prefer Mr Blacker to write it for him. Roberts then made a second, more detailed statement which he later signed.

Later that same morning the police returned to Roberts' lodgings and made a thorough search of the room. It was there, at 11.45am, that Detective Sergeant John Denoon stood on a chair to look behind a stack of Burling Tables stored on top of a partition. There he found a roll of bank notes bound together by a piece of rubber that looked as if it had been cut from an inner tube. In all there were 21 £1 notes plus 15 10s notes to give a total value of £28 10s. More significantly, some of the notes appeared to be bloodstained.

John Henry Roberts made a number of appearances at the police court, the first being on December 14th when he was represented by Mr Edward Cawthorn, a solicitor of Tyrrel Street, Bradford. The final court appearance took place on January 8th, 1932, when Roberts was sent to the assizes on a charge of murder.

The trial of John Henry Roberts opened on March 11th, 1932, before Mr Justice Humphreys. Roberts was defended by Mr J. Willoughby Jardine, while the case for the Crown was led by Mr Walter Hedley, assisted by Mr E.A. Hawke. The proceedings lasted for two days.

Alfred Gill, the dead man's son, explained to the court that he lived with his parents at Wheater Terrace. On the morning of December 11th he had left the house at 8.30am, even before his father had risen from his bed. He, too, was a greengrocer and it was 8.45pm by the time he finally returned home, to learn that his father had not come home and his mother concerned. After having a quick bite to eat, Alfred had gone around to the stable where he kept his own horse to see that it was bedded down for the night. He went back home but his father had still had not put in an appearance, so Alfred went to his father's stable, which was in the same street as his own, to see if the horse had been put away. His father's horse was there, sure enough, so once again, Alfred returned home. It was now 10.30pm and in order to placate his mother, he accompanied her in a search for his father.

Checking the piggeries some time later, Alfred found the gate closed and everything apparently in order. He had shouted for his father but having received no reply, went back to Wheater Terrace with his mother. Later, as there was still no sign of his father, Alfred went to his brother William's house at 160 Dick Lane and told him that their father was missing. It was 12.45am by the time they and Louisa went back to the piggeries, with a lamp. After finding his father's body, Alfred had run to the police call box and waited there until an officer arrived. Finally, Alfred was able to state that his father had a habit of binding his banknotes together by means of an old piece of inner tube, exactly like the one around the bundle found in Roberts' bedroom.

Beatrice Mather said that Roberts had come to lodge with her on December 1st, 1931. She did not provide him with food and his bedroom cost him 6s 6d per week. On the day in question, Roberts had left home at around 9.00am and had been wearing a brown suit at the time. Although Beatrice didn't actually see that it was Roberts, someone came into the house and went up to his room at 8.30pm before leaving again five minutes later. It was 11.30pm before Beatrice actually saw Roberts and by then he had changed his clothes and was wearing a black suit, together with an overcoat. Beatrice noticed that Roberts' left eye was swollen but she could not see clearly the extent of the injury because his hat was pulled down, partly obscuring his face. Finally she was able to confirm to the court that she had not hidden any money in Roberts' bedroom so the money found in the rubber band was not hers.

George Mather confirmed that when he saw Roberts on December 9th, there were no injuries on his face. When he came back into the house at 11.30pm on the 11th, though, there was some kind of injury but George also referred to the fact that Roberts kept his head lowered and his face was partly hidden by his black bowler hat. Early the following morning, the police had called at his house and George was present as Roberts was being spoken to. During the interview, he could clearly see that his house guest had grazed one side of his face and when the police asked Roberts how he came by these injuries, George heard him reply, "When I was in the stable the cart shaft slipped and caught me in the eye." George, too, was able to swear that the money hidden in Roberts' room had not been put there by him.

Bert Edward Ward was a clerk for Josiah Huggins, a trade protection agent of Drewton Street, Bradford. He informed the court that on June 3rd, 1931, he had applied to Roberts for repayment of the sum of £1 13s 6d which was owed to Messrs J.G. Graves Ltd, a general merchants of Sheffield. He had received no reply to that letter and, as a consequence, had taken proceedings for the recovery of the debt at the Bradford County Court on June 12th. Roberts had not been present at the hearing which took place on July 21st and, consequently, judgement had been made that Roberts pay off the debt at 2s per month. No payments had been made to the court and so a final notice had been sent to Roberts on December 7th. This notice was found on the accused when he was searched at the police station and plainly showed that he had some severe financial problems. This was confirmed by the evidence of Henry William Wainwright who was a clerk at the Ministry of Labour in Bradford. His records showed that Roberts was unemployed from November 13th, 1930, to December 11th, 1931 inclusive and was drawing unemployment benefit of 15s 3d per week. The last payment had been made to him on December 11th.

James Doran had known the murdered man all his life and had often done odd jobs for him and occasionally had helped him with his rounds on Fridays and Saturdays. He, too, was able to say that Mr Gill had a habit of holding his banknotes inside a rubber band but he was able to go further than the dead man's son. Doran was able to identify the piece of rubber found around the notes in Roberts' room as the same one Alfred Gill had had around his money, for he had helped Gill when he had made the band. Doran held on to the inner tube while Gill cut it off. He had seen the band many times since and could pick it out by its colour and uneven markings.

Josiah Knight was a grocer who had known the dead man for more than two and a half years. Gill always called on him on a Friday afternoon and December 11th was no different. On that day, Gill called at some time between 2.30pm and 3.00pm and he had with him a young man who was wearing a brown suit. Although he could not be absolutely sure, Knight believed that this man was Roberts.

William Betts was a hawker of firewood and had known Alfred Gill for 30 years. At 4.55pm on December 11th, Betts was passing the piggeries at Tyersal and saw Gill's horse and cart standing near the entrance gates. Gill himself was in the process of opening the gates. Betts passed again at 7.30pm. By then the gates were closed and there was no one about.

George Maurice Read had also known Gill for 30 years. He knew that Gill had two horses stabled at the Napier Inn yard and some-times was there late at night. Read had last seen Gill at the yard at 8.30pm on December 9th. On the 11th, Read was at the stables at 6.30pm and at that time, Gill's horse was not in its place. Shortly after this, though, Roberts came in with Gill's horse. Read remarked that Roberts must have had a quiet day if he had finished so early and Roberts replied, "Yes, one or two people have removed and others were out." Read asked after Gill and Roberts told him that he had gone home for his tea.

Mr Arvester Little was the manager at a pawnbroker's shop in Mount Street, Bradford. He testified that on December 7th, Roberts' brother had pledged a dark suit for 20s. On December 11th, at 7.30pm, the accused man came into his shop and redeemed that suit for £1 0s 5d. This, of course, explained how Roberts could change his clothing after he had killed Alfred Gill.

William Harrison worked as a waiter at the Ring o' Bells Hotel in Bradford and he stated that Roberts came in some time between 7.15pm and 7.45pm on December 11th. He took a seat near the bar and ordered a half-pint of beer. Roberts called Harrison over and handed him half-a-crown, saying, "Give this to her when she comes in." Harrison knew that Roberts was referring to a lady friend of his who Harrison knew by sight. Roberts asked Harrison to tell his young lady that he would be back in at about 9.00pm.

The lady, Mary Ellen Eyres, came in at some time before 8.15pm and Harrison duly gave her the money and the message. She, in turn, went out of the Ring o' Bells soon afterwards and left her own message for Roberts. Soon afterwards, at 9.00pm, Roberts came in wearing his best clothes, a dark suit, overcoat and bowler hat. Harrison told him that Mary had gone on to a different pub where he should go to meet her. Roberts left to find her.

Mary Eyres who lived at 25 Jermyn Street, Church Bank, had first met Roberts in the Ring o' Bells towards the end of September 1931. She had met him perhaps five or six times between then and December 11th. On the 9th of that month, they went to Tennyson's Picture House and arranged to meet up again at the bottom of Jermyn Street at 7.30pm on December 11th.

Roberts did not turn up for that arranged meeting and so Mary went in to the Ring o' Bells where she got the message from William Harrison. She stayed there for perhaps 15 minutes before going on to the Wharfe Hotel, higher up the same street, after leaving her message for Roberts.

It was just after 9.00pm when Roberts joined her in the Wharfe Hotel. She noticed that his left eye was badly swollen and asked him what had happened. Roberts replied, "I was taking the horse out of the cart when the shaft flew up and hit me in the eye."

The couple stayed at the Wharfe until 10.00pm. Roberts had paid for all the drinks and later paid for their supper at an eating house in Bolton Road. After this, he walked her home and they parted at the bottom of Jermyn Street where Roberts handed her two 10s notes.

Dr Peter Lindsay Sutherland was the pathologist for the West Riding of Yorkshire and had examined the body of Alfred Gill at the piggeries. Gill was lying on his back in an open shed. His right leg and thigh partly overlapped his left leg and his face and hands were covered in blood. Gill's clothing, especially on the left side, was saturated with blood. Later that day, Dr Sutherland performed a post-mortem which revealed an irregular wound on Gill's upper lip, which completely penetrated the lip. Gill's nose was twisted to the right and the bones had been separated from their attachments. His right eyeball was haemorrhagic and pulpy and two teeth had been knocked out and subsequently swallowed as they were found in Gill's stomach. A total of 16 wounds were detected on Gill's scalp and all were of the same general size and character suggesting they had been made with the same weapon. There were two depressed fractures of the skull, one behind the left ear and the second slightly further forward. The base of the skull was also fractured.

Dr Sutherland found 6–8oz of blood in the dead man's stomach which had come from the mouth injuries. This showed that death must have taken place some time after the facial injuries had been inflicted. The actual cause of death was shock due to a fracture of the base and vault of the skull.

The doctor had also examined Roberts at the police station and reported that the young man was suffering from a swollen eyelid and abrasions over the bridge of his nose and over his left eyebrow. There was also a slight abrasion to the back of his left wrist. In summation, Dr Sutherland was able to say that the weapon that had been used on Gill was a heavy, blunt instrument. The hinge found at the scene of the crime could have caused some but not all of the injuries. A heavy brick might also have been used.

Dr John Henry Ryffel, a Fellow of the Institute of Chemistry and a clinical chemist to Guy's Hospital in London, had examined various articles handed to him by the police including two hammers found at the piggeries, the hinge and some of Roberts' clothing. He had found no trace of blood on either of the hammers but had found blood and wool fibres on the hinge, although there was no hair or skin on that particular item as he would have expected to find had it been used to batter Alfred Gill to death. Dr Ryffel was able to confirm that the stains on Roberts' brown suit were human blood and of the same type as Alfred Gill's.

The time came for Roberts' statements to be read out and for him to give his own account of the events of December 11th. According to that testimony, Roberts had indeed killed Alfred Gill, but he had been sorely provoked. After going back with Gill to the piggeries, Gill had asked him to feed the animals and in so doing, Roberts had accidentally spilled some of the swill. Gill over-reacted to this and swore at Roberts. In his turn, Roberts struck out at Gill who picked up a hammer and hit Roberts. A struggle followed during which Roberts took up a large brick and repeatedly battered Gill about the head. Roberts denied that he had gone to the piggeries with the intention of robbing Alfred Gill and he picked up the roll of banknotes from the ground only after the struggle was over. Roberts was saying that he had killed in self-defence and he was therefore guilty of manslaughter only.

It was on the final day of the trial that the jury stated that they wished to ask a question. Roberts had claimed that it had been the spilling of the pig's food that started the argument between him and Gill. The jury now wanted to know if the police had found any evidence of food being spilled. Superintendent Bell was recalled to the stand and stated that no such traces had been found.

For the defence, Mr Willoughby Jardine pointed out to the jury that the parallel grazes found on Roberts' face would not have been caused by a fist. Therefore, at some stage, Alfred Gill must have used some sort of weapon. In his summing up, though, Mr Justice Humphreys clarified the definition of just what might be termed reasonable force. If Roberts had struck out in self-defence and the jury were satisfied that this was the case, then manslaughter was a possible verdict. If, however, they came to believe that having got the better of his man, Roberts had hit him again and again with a brick while he was unconscious or otherwise incapacitated, then this was murder. It took the jury just over half an hour to decide that this was indeed the case and Roberts was sentenced to death.

Roberts' appeal was heard on April 13th, before the Lord Chief Justice, Sir Gordon Hewart, and Justices Avory and Hawke. Roberts' defence team reiterated that this was a case of manslaughter and complained that in his summing up, Mr Justice Humphreys had not properly directed the jury on the law with regard to provocation. Giving their verdict, the judges stated that in his second statement, Roberts had admitted striking Gill after he had made an insinuation regarding his parentage. Gill had been knocked out and was incapable of fighting back, but Roberts dragged him across the yard and put him into the shed where he would finally be discovered. At this point, Gill recovered somewhat and cried out, "Jack, don't!" But by his own admission, Roberts had hit him again because he was still so angry. There was no sign of pig feed spilled on the floor and so the provocation itself must be in doubt. In addition, it had long been decided in law that a man, even though he was provoked, who went on to kill by means of repeated and cruel blows, was still guilty of murder. The appeal was dismissed.

The dates of no fewer than three executions were now set. The first of these took place on April 27th, at Hull, when George Emanuel Michael, a West Indian, was hanged for the murder of Theresa Hemstock. The following morning, at 9.00am, 23-year-old John Henry Roberts was hanged at Leeds, alongside Thomas Riley, who had murdered Elizabeth Castle at Lepton, Huddersfield. The hangman was Thomas Pierrepoint and since it was a double execution, he had two assistants, Thomas Phillips and Alfred Allen. The inquest on both men was conducted by the city coroner, Mr J.H. Milner and in both cases, the usual verdict of death by judicial hanging was returned.

CHAPTER THIRTEEN

A MAN WITH A TEMPER

OUIS Hamilton had known Maud Hay for several years and in due course they started walking out together. When Maud found herself pregnant, Louis agreed to stand by her and the couple were married on July 1st, 1933. Just a few weeks after the wedding had taken place, a healthy child was born.

The Hamiltons started their married life by living at 128 Garnett Street, Bradford, a house owned by Louis' sister, Beatrice, and her husband, Walter Thackray. At the end of November, 1933, the Hamiltons left that address and went to live with Louis' mother at 16 Ireton Street, Lidget Green, also in Bradford, although the baby, then only four months old, was left with his sister. The relationship between Louis and his new wife had deteriorated, though, and on December 22nd, Maud Hamilton returned to her mother's house at 39 Jermyn Street, Stott Hill, Bradford.

The next night, December 23rd, Louis Hamilton called at Jermyn Street at 11.30pm wanting to speak to his wife. Maud had been to the theatre and when she returned, Louis demanded, "Where have you been?" He grabbed her and shook her violently, pulled her hair and kicked out at her. At one stage, Walter Hay, Maud's brother, tried to intervene but Louis grabbed him by the throat and might have done him a serious injury had he not managed to struggle free and run out of the house. Maud's mother, Miranda Bolton, screamed as she witnessed the attack on her son and daughter and then also ran out of the house as Louis dragged his wife off up the street.

Maud Hamilton did not return to her mother's house until 4.00am on Christmas Eve. She had obviously been subjected to further abuse for she bore three marks on her throat and another on the palm of her hand. Such a state of affairs could not be allowed to continue and so, the same day, Maud went to court and swore out a summons for assault against her husband.

On December 25th, Louis was back at Jermyn Street. Once again it was during the evening and again Louis demanded that his wife come out to speak to him. Maud refused to see her husband and, reluctantly, Louis walked away. It had hardly been the happiest of Christmas Days for any of them.

It was 12.05pm on December 26th when Constable Frederick Percy Grimes visited Ireton Street and served a summons on Louis Hamilton, who was ordered to appear in court on December 29th. Explaining that it was about the recent attack on his wife, the officer heard Hamilton say, "Oh, that's her game is it?" as he took the document. A woman who was present in the room asked Hamilton if he had assaulted his wife and Louis replied, "Yes, she's been asking for it."

On the afternoon of December 26th, Miranda Bolton went to visit her brother. She returned home to Jermyn Street some time after 3.00pm but did not go into her own house at number 39. Instead, Miranda called at number 58, a house owned by Mrs Clara Rhodes. She found Maud waiting for her there in an extremely frightened state.

Clara Rhodes told Miranda that Louis Hamilton had called at number 39 at about 2.00pm. At the time, Clara was not in her own house, but was visiting Elizabeth Thornton who lived at number 41. Clara clearly heard Hamilton shout, "Do you want to see me Maud?" There was a few moments silence before he continued, "Open the door, I want to show you something or do you want me to knock the door in?" After another couple of minutes, Hamilton, realising he was not going to gain admittance, had walked away. Clara dashed across to number 29 and collected Maud and Walter and took them to her home. After seeing that Maud was settled, Clara sent Walter for a policeman.

Even while this story was being told, Walter Hay returned to Clara's house with Constable Ira Holmes. The policeman timed his arrival there at 3.17pm. He took down the details of Maud's story, tried his best to calm her and explained that he would report the matter to his superiors who would no doubt pay another call on Louis Hamilton.

Once Constable Holmes had left Clara's house, she, Miranda Bolton, Walter Hay and, of course, Maud Hamilton walked to Elizabeth Thornton's house at 41 Jermyn Street. As the group sat quietly, Clara Rhodes and Maud saw Louis Hamilton emerge from the outside toilet at the back of number 39 and this so unnerved Maud that she rose to leave. However, as she opened the front door, Hamilton was upon her. He grabbed hold of his wife, shouted, "Get in there," and pushed her into her mother's house, number 39.

The sound of terrible screams came from inside Miranda Bolton's house but despite her best efforts, Clara Rhodes could not get in. There were a number of people about and a number of men dashed forward to offer their assistance. The front door was broken open and Clara Rhodes was the first person inside. To her horror she saw that Louis Hamilton was standing to one side, a long, narrow knife in his right hand, blood dripping from the blade. Maud was sitting on a chair, her face and chin covered in blood and there was a terrible rattling noise caused by the wound in her throat.

Louis Hamilton was dragged outside and some of the men, angered by what they had seen, began hitting and kicking him in a passageway near the house. He was rescued by some of the more controlled members of the crowd and taken to another house nearby, where he was held pending the arrival of the police.

The first police officer on the scene was Constable Victor William

Malt, who had been on duty in Barkerend Road when a man approached him and told him what had taken place. Malt went to number 39, saw that Maud was still breathing, and then to number 42 where Hamilton had been taken. Malt cautioned Hamilton who replied, "I quite realise what I've done. Take me back to see." Constable Malt did as he was asked and took Hamilton to see his wife, who was still alive. Having seen what he had done, Hamilton averted his eyes and murmured, "Take me away from it all." Malt handed Hamilton over to another officer who had just arrived, Constable Samuel Savage, and it was he who escorted the prisoner to the Town Hall.

Maud Hamilton arrived at the Royal Infirmary at 4.45pm and was pronounced dead on arrival by the resident surgical officer, Dr Leslie Bonthron Patrick. Back at the Town Hall, Hamilton was informed that he would be charged with murder. In reply he said, "I am not going to be awkward, but what is in there," at which point he indicated Constable Malt's notebook, "is true." Hamilton was searched and found to be carrying a pawn ticket, three and a half pence in copper and the summons for assault which he had received earlier that day.

There were a number of appearances at the Bradford City police court, where Hamilton was defended by Mr James A. Lee, while the case for the Director of Public Prosecutions was put by Mr E.G. Robey. The final hearing lasted two days, January 16th and 17th, and at the end, all of the evidence having been considered, Hamilton was sent for trial.

The case of the Crown versus Louis Hamilton was heard at Leeds on March 15th, 1934, before Mr Commissioner Joy and an all-male jury. The prosecution was led by Mr Walter Hedley assisted by Mr H.B.H. Hylton-Foster. Hamilton's defence lay in the hands of Mr J. Willoughby Jardine and Dr E.C. Chappell.

Many of the people who had been in Jermyn Street at the time of the attack were called to describe what they had seen. John O'Hara, who lived at number 23, had seen Hamilton being manhandled by the crowd, after the crime had taken place. O'Hara was the man who had rescued Hamilton and escorted him to Elizabeth Charlesworth's house and watched over him until Constable Malt arrived to take him into custody. O'Hara had accompanied Hamilton to the Town Hall, where Hamilton had asked him to tell his sister what had happened, gave him her address, but then added, "Don't tell my mother."

James Judge had been with John O'Hara when they saw Hamilton being attacked down the passageway. He heard someone shout, "He's killed his wife. He's cut her throat." Judge helped O'Hara to rescue Hamilton and as they were escorting him to safety, Hamilton turned to him and said, "Have I killed her? Is she dead?"

Richard Monaghan, who lived at 83 Jermyn Street, had rushed across to 39 when he heard the screams coming from within and saw Clara Rhodes trying to get in. He kicked open the door and followed Clara into the house. Monaghan said that when he first saw the accused man, he had a dazed look upon his face as if he did not know where he was. Once he had seen that he could offer no further assistance, Monaghan had run to fetch a policeman.

Mary Ann McDonald of number 52, was also one of the first people into the house after Richard Monaghan had kicked the door open. She, too, said that Hamilton looked to be somewhat dazed. This was also confirmed by Elizabeth Charlesworth who pulled Hamilton out into the yard, fearful that he might renew his attack on Maud. Finally, James Duffy described how, ten minutes after the attack, he had picked up the bloodstained knife from the passageway and later handed it over to the police. Presumably, Louis Hamilton had dropped this after he was attacked by members of the crowd.

Elizabeth Thornton, the woman in whose house Maud had sheltered before she was attacked, told the court that after seeing Hamilton drag Maud towards her mother's house, she had screamed as loud as she could to attract attention. She, too, went into number 39 after the door had been broken down and saw Maud, 'laid as if she were quite dead'. Hamilton was standing near a table, just a few feet away, and since he still had the knife in his hand he was pushed outside by some of the other people there.

Evidence was given of the history of Louis Hamilton's abuse of his wife. Arthur Joseph Ball was an inspector for the Society for the Prevention of Cruelty to Children. On October 1st, Maud had visited his office and complained that her husband had hit her while she had her baby in her arms. Mr Ball went to see Hamilton, who apologised for his behaviour and promised not to repeat it. A few days later, Hamilton and his wife returned together to Mr Ball's office. Maud told him that she wanted a separation but Hamilton cried and begged her to stay with him. Arthur Ball told the court that in his opinion, Maud had treated her husband in a taunting manner.

Sarah Duffy, whose husband James had already given evidence, referred to the incident which had taken place on December 23rd. It was 11.30pm when Miranda Bolton came to her house looking frightened and told her that Hamilton was causing problems. Sarah returned to number 39 with Miranda and saw Hamilton there. He turned to Sarah and demanded to know what she wanted. Sarah told him that he should not carry on the way he had been doing but Hamilton countered with a threat to kill his wife and himself before morning. As Sarah watched, Hamilton pulled his wife to the floor by her hair and kicked her twice while she was lying on the floor.

Louis Hamilton had been employed as a slaughterman at a company named Hazelton, Shackleton & Brown, and one of his fellow workers was John Leach. He said that Hamilton had two knives which he used in his work and Leach identified the one produced in court as belonging to the accused. The knife was also identified by Beatrice Thackeray, Hamilton's married sister with whom he and Maud had once lodged. Beatrice said that after her brother had moved out, the knife was left behind in a cupboard. Hamilton visited her from time to time, the last occasion she saw him being on December 22nd.

The knife was certainly still in the cupboard after that date but some time between 6.00pm and 7.00pm on December 26th she had noticed that it was missing.

The inference was that Hamilton had made a special trip to his sister's home to pick up a knife that he knew he had left there, and on the very day that he cut his wife's throat. This plainly showed premeditation. Beatrice, however, was also able to give evidence which assisted the defence. She stated that Maud seemed to show no interest in her child and had only visited once since she had moved out, leaving the baby behind. Beatrice told the court, "The poor little thing would have been dead if it had not been for me looking after it." She went on to tell the court that Louis had visited the baby many times and was deeply concerned about his wife's apparent lack of interest. The unhappy marriage had completely changed his character. Previously he had been a very happy man, but now he was sullen and morose.

Walter Thackeray, Beatrice's husband, confirmed that Hamilton had indeed called at their house at 2.50pm on December 26th, while his wife was out. Hamilton went back out within a few minutes and returned later with a pint of beer which they shared. While they were enjoying their beer, Hamilton showed Walter the summons which had been served on him and said, "I have just received this. My wife has sent it. We have had a quarrel." Hamilton had left at around 3.30pm and in Walter Thackeray's opinion, was quite sober. Finally, Walter confirmed that at one stage, Hamilton had been left on his own while Walter went to the toilet, so he had had the opportunity to take the knife from the cupboard without being seen.

Both Constable Malt and Constable Savage testified that Hamilton smelled slightly of drink when they saw him, after the attack on Maud. Detective Inspector Thomas Rushworth added that he had visited the scene of the crime and been given the knife by Constable Malt. James Duffy showed him the exact spot where he had picked up the knife and Rushworth noted that there were a few drops of blood around there. Back at the Town Hall, Rushworth had interviewed Hamilton and noted that his overcoat, trousers, shoes and three handkerchiefs were all bloodstained.

Dr Ralph Rimmer was the chief police surgeon for the district and had performed the post-mortem on the dead woman. He described a deep cut across Maud's neck, going from left to right for a distance of five inches. All the soft structures had been cut through including the carotid arteries on both sides of the throat. There were multiple small cuts on Maud's left hand and one long cut on the right, across all four fingers and extending down to the bone, showing that she had made some attempt to protect herself. The cause of death was haemorrhage from the throat wound and Dr Rimmer also told the court that Maud had been pregnant when she died.

With so many witnesses to what had taken place, the only possible defence was that Hamilton had not been responsible for his actions at the time he cut Maud's throat. A number of people had already referred to Hamilton being dazed afterwards. However, he had been examined at the Town Hall by Dr R.W. Pritchard who described him as being perfectly calm. Dr Pritchard found no evidence for suspecting that Hamilton was epileptic, even though it was true that Hamilton's father had suffered from that illness.

Dr Francis H. Brisby, the medical officer at Leeds prison, had examined Hamilton and he also stated that the accused was perfectly sane and there was no evidence of any nervous disorder. As a result of all this evidence, the jury took only 12 minutes to return their guilty verdict but added a strong recommendation to mercy.

On March 26th, Hamilton's solicitor, Mr Lee, announced that although it had been carefully considered, they had decided not to appeal. Instead, an attempt would be made to secure a reprieve on medical grounds. A petition was opened and public opinion was such that by March 27th, 111 applications for copies of that petition had been received from towns such as Sheffield, Huddersfield, Halifax, Middlesbrough, Hull, Dewsbury and Barnsley.

Eventually, more than 30,000 people signed the petition,

including two Bradford Members of Parliament, Joseph Hepworth and George Eady. The Lord Mayor, Captain A. W. Brown, played an active part in trying to secure a reprieve and even visited the Home Office on March 29th to state his case in person. In the event, it all came to nothing. On April 4th, a letter was received by the Under-Sheriff of Yorkshire, Mr B. Dodsworth. From the Home Office, it stated that the matter had been carefully considered but that the Home Secretary had seen no reason to interfere with the sentence. Captain Brown was interviewed by the local newspaper and commented, "I cannot but express my profound regret at this decision."

At 9.00am on Friday, April 6th, 1934, Louis Hamilton was hanged at Leeds by Thomas Pierrepoint, who was assisted by Alfred Allen. Despite all the efforts made to save his life, barely a dozen people had gathered outside the prison at the appointed hour.

CHAPTER FOURTEEN

MAN NUMBER ONE

EMILY Yeomans was a 23-year-old waitress who lived with her uncle, Joseph Adams, at 69 Garnet Place, off Dewsbury Road, Leeds, and worked at the Lyon's Cafe in County Arcade. By all accounts, Emily was a happy young woman whose love was dancing. Quiet and shy, she was not known to have a regular boyfriend.

On Tuesday, October 16th, 1934, Emily came home from work at about 4.20pm and when her uncle arrived a few minutes later, she told him that she was going out that night. The couple sat down to a snack of tea and currant bread, chatting to each other about what they had been doing during the day. Later, Emily wrote a letter to her mother, who still lived in Emily's home town of Barrow-in-Furness.

It was 7.50pm when Emily walked out of 69 Garnet Place. Joseph left at the same time and as Emily walked eastwards down Oakley Grove, he turned the other way. They walked away from each other in opposite directions, Joseph turning at one stage and waving to Emily as she apparently met up with a male friend on the corner of Dewsbury Road and Trentham Street. As Joseph watched, they walked off together, the man on the inside close to the buildings and Emily on the outside nearest to the road, the couple soon vanishing out of sight behind the buildings in Dewsbury Road.

It was some time between 10.00pm and 10.15pm when Joseph Adams arrived back home. Emily was still not there but there was nothing unusual in that. Indeed, only a few nights before, Emily had not come in until 2.30am. Joseph went to bed and slept soundly but when he rose the following morning and saw that Emily's room was still empty, he grew concerned and considered whether or not he should contact the police.

George Newton, who lived at Fulham Street, Leeds, was an elderly man but, weather permitting, he still enjoyed his daily walk through Middleton Woods. A man used to rising early, by 8.00am, George was already pacing through the autumnal glades, enjoying the crisp morning air. It was 8.30am, by the time he turned off the main track and headed off up a narrow pathway where he found a woman's glove. George Newton hated litter in 'his' woods and picked up the offending item. But as he walked a little further, he saw a young woman to whom the glove had apparently belonged, for she wore its twin on her right hand while her left was bare. At first, George thought the woman was asleep or ill and he gently shook her shoulder to rouse her. Only then did he see that there was a pink chiffon scarf knotted tightly around her throat and blood around her mouth. Police officers called to the scene soon located the dead woman's handbag which gave her name and address. Emily Yeomans had been found.

It was not long before several important witnesses came forward. Joseph Adams, who had collapsed when he identified his niece's body, told the police of the man he had seen walking off with Emily. This had also been witnessed by three young boys who were sitting on a window sill at Verity's butcher's shop on the corner of Dewsbury Road and Oakley Grove. Albert Deighton Bethall, Lawrence Trilk and Jeffrey Charles Sutton were all 14 years of age and at 7.50pm on October 16th, were idling away some time together when Emily Yeomans walked past them.

All three boys knew Emily, and indeed her uncle, quite well and after she had passed the group, Emily briefly vanished out of sight behind a bend in the line of houses before the boys saw her again, with a man, near Dr A.J. Swanton's gate, in Dewsbury Road. The boys said that the man was somewhat taller than Emily, who was herself 5ft 2ins, and they caught only a glimpse of his face as most of the time the man had his back to them. Between them, though, Albert, Lawrence and Jeffrey were able to provide the police officer in charge of the case, Detective Chief Inspector James Craig, with a basic description.

That description was released to the press on October 18th. It read, 'About 24 years of age, 5ft 6ins to 5ft 8ins in height, medium build, clean shaven, hair brushed well back and appeared to be greased. Wearing blue suit, no head-dress, no overcoat, of smart appearance.' The inquest on Emily opened on the same day, but was immediately adjourned until November 2nd.

It was also on October 18th that a distraught Joseph Adams received a telegram which he believed was from the killer. The telegram read, "We know all about it. How's man." This did not make sense to Joseph and he felt it might be from the killer, taunting him, but the police soon discovered that it came from Emily's family in Barrow and contained an error which was the fault of the Post Office. The last two words should have read, "How's Mam?"

Things progressed slowly. On October 19th, the police announced that Emily was, after all, a Yorkshire girl. Although she had spent much of her life in Barrow, she had been born in Pepper Road, Hunslet, and the family had moved to Barrow when she was still a baby. Chief Inspector Craig also stated that his officers did not believe there was any connection between this crime and another, still unsolved murder, that of Mary Learoyd, who was killed at Ilkley in 1929.

The body of Emily Yeomans was buried at Walney, Barrow-in-Furness, on the afternoon of Saturday, October 20th. The same day speculation was rife when police stated that, after the description had been published, a man had been detained, pending forensic examination of his clothing. This man, one who would play an important part in this case, would never be named by the police or the press and would consequently be referred to as Man Number One. He was someone who had been out with Emily on at least one occasion. Finally, after being held for almost 60 hours, he was released without charge, even though two of the witnesses had picked him out at an identity parade.

On October 22nd the police, believing that someone might be sheltering the killer, gave notice that a reward would be offered. In fact, there were two separate rewards. The Chief Constable of Leeds offered £50 for information leading to the man's conviction and £20 for information which led to the identity of the man with Emily in Dewsbury Road on the night she was last seen alive.

It was on Wednesday, October 24th that the case took a spectacular turn. Norah Menzies was the wife of the licensee of the Mulberry Tree Inn, Folly Lane, and one of her regular customers had been saying that he knew the identity of the man who had met Emily in Dewsbury Road. Acting on this information, Chief Inspector Craig, together with Detective Inspector Murgatroyd and Detective Sergeant Binns, called at 33 Lady Pit Lane and there took into custody 29-year-old David Maskill Blake. In due course, Blake, too, was placed in an identity parade but no one picked him out. It was true that there was forensic evidence which linked Blake to the crime but the same, it transpired, could be said for Man Number One.

When first questioned, Blake denied even knowing Emily Yeomans. It was only when faced with evidence that he had been out with her that he admitted that this was the case, but he still denied seeing her on the night she died. In due course, Blake made a lengthy statement to Chief Inspector Craig. That statement read, 'I am making this statement of my own free will. I have been cautioned by Chief Detective Inspector Craig, that anything I say now may be given in evidence.

'You will wonder why I never admitted that I knew Emily Yeomans at the time I was arrested on suspect of murder. The reason was why I am not sure of this date, Thursday or Friday, that I met Emily Yeomans coming from a dance at the hour of 2am, of which I knew she had gone. I walked up the street with her, that is in Dewsbury Road, and we stood round the corner talking and messing about for a matter of an hour and a quarter.

'I knew that she was living with her uncle, but I thought they called her Adams. We were messing about for an hour and a quarter and a policeman came down the road, stood about 30 or 40 yards away, and we packed up and said goodnight as she told her uncle she would not be long. I promised to meet her the following Thursday at nine o'clock at night. I was there at 9pm. She did not come and then I connected her with this murder. I am not the man who met her on Tuesday night, the night of the murder, and that is the truth, inspector.

'I have met her on several occasions and had drinks with her. I mean she had drinks with me. The reason I did not like saying anything was because of my previous convictions and reading about scientific microscopical inspections on her clothing knowing full well they were practically bound to be on mine. I think this is all I can say, inspector.

'Also, I am not the man that emerged from the woods on the Wednesday morning of the finding of the body.

'This statement had been read over by me, it has been made voluntarily and it is true.'

What was also true was that there were now two suspects in the case but other witnesses made statements which seemed to indicate that it was Blake and Blake alone who had been involved in the crime. For this reason, only Blake was charged with the murder of Emily Yeomans.

David Blake made his first appearance in the police court on October 26th. He was defended by Mr Alfred Masser and the proceedings lasted for only three or four minutes. Evidence was given that in answer to the charge, Blake had replied, "Never inspector. That is all I can say." Blake was remanded to November 1st.

Further appearances followed. Blake was back in court on November 1st, November 7th, November 14th and finally on November 19th when he was sent for trial at the next Leeds assizes. Evidence had been given that the digestion of the raisin skins Emily had eaten put the time of her death from two to four hours after she had consumed them. Since Joseph Adams had said that they had eaten the currant bread just before 5.00pm, this put the time of Emily's death somewhere before 9.00pm on October 16th. This, of course, would prove to be crucial later.

The trial of David Maskill Blake opened on December 12th, 1934, before Mr Justice Goddard and a jury of ten men and two women. Blake's defence lay in the hands of Mr C. Paley Scott and Mr H.B.H. Hylton-Foster while the prosecution case was led by Mr J. Willoughby Jardine and Mr G.H.B. Streatfeild. The hearing lasted until December 15th.

Joseph Adams, in addition to repeating details of the events of October 16th before Emily went out to meet the man who was almost certainly her killer, told of another encounter which had taken place on the previous Friday night. Emily had been on a late shift and so only got home from work at 7.00pm. By 7.50pm, she was out again, saying that she was going to a dance. Joseph went out with his cart, returned home and went to meet Emily near the Dewsbury Road police station. At 1.45am on October 13th he saw that she was with a man and another couple. Seeing that Emily was not alone, Joseph told her to 'hurry up' and went home to wait. Emily had come in some 45 minutes later.

George Newton explained how he had found the body and pointed out that Emily was lying not far from the tram lines which led to Leeds city centre. In fact, from close by the body, the tram lines could be seen and this made the evidence of two more witnesses quite significant.

Bert Foulds was a tram driver, working on the Leeds–Middleton route. At about 7.15am on the morning of October 17th, he saw a man who looked like the description subsequently released by the police. This man was standing in the woods, close to where Emily's body was found just over an hour later. Another tram driver on the same route had also passed close by at 7.00am and from his tram he saw a man emerge from the woods at a distance which he estimated was just a few yards from where Emily lay. These two sightings were, of course, well after the time of death determined by the medical evidence, but the police felt that the killer might have returned to the scene of his crime. Neither of these witnesses, though, had picked out Blake at his identity parade but Bert Foulds had picked out Man Number One at the earlier parade.

Albert Bethall, Lawrence Trilk and Jeffrey Sutton, the three lads on the butcher's window sill, had also attended those two identification parades. Their task was made all the more difficult since they had seen the man who met Emily only from the back and two of the boys failed to pick out anyone. After asking the men to turn around, though, Lawrence Trilk did point to a man who he thought most resembled the one he had seen. Once again, this was Man Number One.

John Thomas Yeoman, who was no relation to the dead woman, told a most curious story. He had been in Middleton woods with a friend of his at around 8.00pm on the evening of the murder. As they stood near a hut, close to the football fields near Middleton Park, they noticed a man and a woman together. They were on the grass and appeared to be struggling. The man was obviously engaged in some amorous pursuit for one of his hands was between the woman's legs and her light coloured panties could plainly be seen. Yeoman and his friend stood watching for a few moments until he accidentally trod on the man's foot. Immediately the man sprang up, faced Yeoman and demanded to know what he wanted. Seeing that he was angry, Yeoman backed away. At no stage had Yeoman seen the woman's face, but he caught a good sight of the man. Yeoman failed to pick anyone out at the two identification parades and it may be that he saw a courting couple who just happened to be in the woods at the same time.

The most damaging witness was undoubtedly Albert Schofield, a boot repairer of 6 Buckton Street, Leeds. Schofield had first become acquainted with Blake on August 25th, but the two men had soon become friends and had started going out together to various dance halls and clubs. Schofield was a member of the 43 Club situated in Rialto Yard, Briggate, and this was where Schofield's narrative of his and Blake's movements began.

According to Schofield, he and Blake had met in the 43 Club at around 3.20pm on October 11th. They had stayed there drinking, until some time between 7.00pm and 7.30pm when they had moved on to the Imperial Hotel at Beeston. They parted at closing time, 10.00pm. Blake, though, had apparently met someone else afterwards for when Schofield saw him again, on Saturday, October 13th, Blake explained that he had met a girl in Dewsbury Road. Blake went on to say that this girl worked in the Lyon's Cafe in town, her name was Yeomans and he had arranged to meet her again on the coming Tuesday.

Blake and Schofield met again a number of times in various public houses but the next meeting of significance was Tuesday, October 16th, the day Emily Yeomans met her death. The two men had met each other, by arrangement, at the corner of Boar Lane and Briggate at 3.20pm. From there they went to the 43 Club again, leaving at around 7.20pm. Outside they saw a woman they both knew, Mary Wilson. Schofield had walked on to Briggate alone while Blake spoke to Mary. Returning a few moments later he saw Blake playfully pick Mary up and spin her around, to which Schofield had shouted, "Nark it, you know where you are."

Mary Wilson left the two men at this time and Blake and Schofield walked on to Dewsbury Road. Blake now told his friend that he had arranged to meet a woman near the traffic lights, close to the Hunslet Road police station. However, when they reached these lights, Blake said, "No, further on," and they walked on to the bottom of Trentham Street where Blake said he had said he would wait. Schofield walked on alone, up Trentham Street. It was now around 7.50pm and Schofield watched with interest as a girl appeared from Oakley Grove, crossed to where Blake was waiting, and the couple strolled off down Dewsbury Road with Blake on the inside. Although he could not identify the girl, Schofield was telling the court that he had actually witnessed a meeting between Emily Yeomans and David Maskill Blake.

Blake was engaged to be married at this time and the date for that ceremony had been set for the next day. It was around 11.00am on Wednesday, October 17th that Schofield next saw Blake when he called at Schofield's shoe repair shop, and reminded him that he had agreed to be Blake's best man. He also mentioned that when he had met the girl the previous night, she had wanted to go to the pictures but since he didn't have any money, they were unable to. Blake had tried to catch Schofield up but couldn't find him. The discussion ended when Schofield told Blake that he would see him later at the registry office.

According to Schofield, he next saw Blake outside the registry office whereupon Blake produced a copy of the *Evening Post*, and pointed out a headline which referred to the murder of Emily Yeomans. Blake had said, "Didn't I tell you I had met a girl named Yeomans who worked at Lyons?" Schofield said that indeed he had and Blake continued, "Look at that," and handed over the newspaper for Schofield to read.

The wedding ceremony took place without incident and Schofield next saw Blake on October 18th, when they went to the 43 Club again. Schofield left the club at 5.00pm, Blake remaining behind. That evening, at about 8.00pm, Schofield saw Blake again, this time in the Varieties Bar. Blake was with two women at the time.

On October 19th, the two friends met in the Mulberry Inn and by now the description of the wanted man had been published and Schofield remarked that it fitted Blake well. The following Monday, October 22nd, they were back in the Mulberry Inn and Blake, speaking about the reward offered for information had said to Schofield, "Now's your chance to get twenty quid. We'll see if you are a pal or not." He had replied, "I'll nothing to do with it," and said that he held no idea that his friend might be the killer.

This statement appears to have been a lie because Schofield had been talking of his suspicions in the pubs he frequented and this had come to the attention of the police. They had come for Schofield on Wednesday, October 24th, and only then had he told them of the things he had seen and Blake's possible involvement in the crime. Under cross examination at the trial, though, Schofield had to admit to Mr Paley Scott that he, too, was not the most honest of men. On October 11th, he had stolen a car from Cemetery Road, driven out to the country and later abandoned the vehicle in Westwood Lane, Headingley.

As if Schofield's damning testimony against Blake was not enough, the prosecution now called Arthur Jubb who lived in Duncombe Street, off Park Lane. At a time between 11.00pm and 11.30pm on October 18th, Arthur Jubb was walking down Bond Street when he saw Blake and asked him if he could change a half-crown piece for him. Blake said he couldn't but the two men fell into conversation and went for a walk together. Eventually Jubb invited Blake back to his house for a cup of tea. It was there that Blake picked up the evening newspaper and began reading about the murder.

Jubb told Blake to make himself comfortable and take off his coat. As he did so, something rattled inside Blake's pocket and he took out a tube of cream and a compact containing face powder. Blake asked Jubb if he wanted these items for his wife and Jubb replied that she didn't use such things but Blake put them on the mantelpiece anyway and told Jubb he could do what he wanted with them.

At one stage, Jubb saw that Blake's trousers were ripped on one leg and he claimed that Blake told him that he had torn them on some barbed wire on the Tuesday. It was not until 8.15am on October 19th that Blake left, taking with him a envelope bearing Jubb's address which he had handed over in case Blake ever wanted to call again. That envelope was found on Blake when he was arrested and when the police spoke to Jubb, he handed over the cream and powder which he said had remained untouched on the mantelpiece until that time.

It was that face compact which was to prove significant. The paper lid had a small tear in it and no fewer than five women who worked at the cafe with Emily Yeomans said that her compact had just such a tear. Eva Ogier had known Emily for 11 months, and had been out dancing with her. She told the court that the box of powder Emily used had just such a tear as the one produced in court. Eva also told the police of a man she had seen out with Emily and stated positively that this was not David Blake. Eva was never called to any identification parade and it may well be that the man she saw out with Emily was Man Number One, although there is no proof of this.

Irene Walker and Mary Halton were two more waitresses and both reported the same tear, Mary going so far as to say she believed it to be the same box that Emily had possessed. However, both these witnesses also admitted under cross examination that they believed Emily's box to be somewhat dirtier and more battered than the one shown to them in court. Irene Walker further admitted that she had never heard Emily refer to a man named Blake, but she had spoken to her about Man Number One, the first man the police had picked up. Indeed, it had been Irene who first introduced this man to Emily, not being aware at the time that he was a married man. Finally, Margaret Longe and Alice Watts also agreed that Emily's compact had been torn just like the one they now saw. However, none of these witnesses ever reported seeing Emily with a tube of face cream and, of course, just such a tube had also been left by Blake at Jubb's house.

All these witnesses had proved to be dangerous to Blake. Between them they had put him in Dewsbury Road at a time someone fitting his description had met Emily and shown that he apparently had with him property he might have taken from her dead body. Other witnesses, at least in part, backed up some of what had been said.

Mary Wilson confirmed that she had seen Schofield and Blake at the 43 Club on October 16th and that she had left with them some time after 7.00pm. Janet Bussfield had been in the Varieties Bar on October 18th and had seen Blake with a woman she knew, Gladys Brook. They were there together until closing time at 10.00pm. This later statement, of course, contradicted Blake's claim that he had gone to meet Emily on the Thursday night, even though he knew she was already dead.

Gladys Brook herself also gave evidence which showed that Blake could not have gone to a supposed meeting with Emily on Thursday when she said that she had met Blake in the 43 Club at 4.30pm on October 18th. They were in each other's company at that club until 7.30pm when they went to the Varieties Bar, staying there until closing time. From the bar they went to a fish restaurant and had a supper of fish and chips, saying their goodnights at about 10.30pm.

The time had come to call the medical and forensic evidence. Dr Cyril Robert Manley, the city analyst, had examined the contents of the powder compact. One of Emily's fellow waitresses had once given Emily some of her own powder when she complained that the brand she was using was too light. In an attempt to show that the compact handed in by Arthur Jubb was indeed one taken from Emily, Dr Manley tested the contents, hoping to show that it was a mixture of two individual types. Curiously, he found only 30 grains of face powder which he was unable to test accurately. The remaining 170 grains of 'powder' in the compact turned out to be pure boracic acid. It was never explained how this substance had got into the compact, or who might have put it there.

Dr Hoyland Smith, the police surgeon, had examined Emily's body at the secne of the crime and later performed the post-mortem with Dr Cyril John Polson. Dr Smith testified that when she was found, Emily's skirt had been pushed up at the back and opened up the front, except for the top hook. There was bloodstaining in the genital region and although her underclothing was in place, there was evidence of penetration although no semen was found in the vagina. The pink scarf had been wound four times around Emily's throat and the cause of death was asphyxia due to strangulation.

Dr Gerald Roche Lynch was the senior analyst to the Home Office and on October 22nd he had been given the dead woman's clothes by Chief Inspector Craig. Three days later, on October 25th, he was also given several items of male clothing including a coat, a waistcoat and a pair of trousers. Dr Lynch said that he had found blood on the man's trousers, on the lining behind the fly. There were also smears of blood in the pocket lining, consistent with a bloodstained hand being put into that pocket. Finally, Dr Lynch found evidence of semen staining on the trousers, close to the fly buttons.

Of even more interest was the evidence given by Professor Frederick G. Tryhorn of University College, Hull. On October 19th, Professor Tryhorn received Emily's coat from Chief Inspector Craig. He also received her brown skirt and other items of her clothing. On the coat was a short hair, two inches in length, which was a human pubic hair. There was also a fibre which turned out to be from some navy blue worsted material.

The professor testified that the hair could have come from Blake and the fibres matched his navy blue suit which had a small triangular tear on the trousers. This tear, incidentally, could have been caused by barbed wire and there was some of this wire close to where Emily had been found. However, Professor Tryhorn had also examined clothes taken from Man Number One. His suit was brown, so the navy blue fibre could not have come from that garment, but samples of his hair had also been taken and the hair found on Emily's coat could equally have come from Man Number One.

Professor Tryhorn continued by saying that in addition to the fibres and hair mentioned already, he had also found some red wool fibres on Emily's skirt and some small fragments of feather on her jersey. At the time of the attack upon her, Emily was wearing a red jumper. Those fibres could have come from her own jumper, but

Man Number One also had a red jumper and they could have come from that. Finally, on Man Number One's trousers, Professor Tryhorn found small pieces of feather which matched those found on Emily.

Before outlining the evidence of the various defence witnesses, something should be said about the relationship between David Blake and Jean, his new wife. Until her marriage, Jean's surname had been Whitehead and she lived at 1 Buckton Place, off Cemetery Road, Holbeck. She had a baby who was now seven months old and Blake had never denied that he was the father. Jean's family, though, had not approved of the match and a good deal of animosity existed between Blake and the Whiteheads.

Thomas Whitehead, Jane's brother, testified that on August 25th Blake had been involved in an argument at Buckton Place. A fight had broken out which ended with Blake having to be admitted to hospital for treatment to a head wound after Thomas Whitehead had struck him with a poker. This was confirmed by Charles Edward Gomersal, who had been at the house, had seen the fight and at one stage had become involved himself. Confirmation of the hospital treatment was also given by Eleanor Thomas, the nurse who attended Blake. Before Blake was seen, he was asked to remove his clothing and as Eleanor treated him, she noticed that the bundle of clothing he carried was navy blue. This perhaps explained the presence of blood on Blake's blue suit.

Right up to the moment of his arrest, Blake had lived with his married sister, Florence, and her husband, Albert Norman Bousfield, at 33 Lady Pit Lane. Space there was at a premium so even after Blake and Jean had married, she continued to live with her family at Buckton Place and Blake resided at the Bousfield home, although Jean was a regular and welcome visitor.

Albert Bousfield returned home from work at 6.00pm on October 16th, the day of the murder. He had a bite to eat and then went to sleep on the settee in the living room while his wife busied herself upstairs with the household chores. At the time he settled down, Blake was certainly not in the house. It was no later than 7.00pm.

At about 8.00pm, or perhaps a little later, Florence Bousfield, who was still upstairs, heard Blake calling her from downstairs. He was asking if she knew where he might find a razor blade. Florence confirmed that she did not actually see her brother at this time but she knew his voice and swore that he was home then.

By the time Albert woke at 9.00pm, Blake was not there. Some 25 minutes later, Jean came in and within three minutes, Blake followed her into the house. The newlyweds went out again and Blake came back alone at about 10.25pm. Further, the very next day, Wednesday, October 17th, Florence had noticed that Jean had left behind her powder compact and a tube of face cream. She pointed these out to her brother and he picked them up and put them into his coat pocket.

The Bousfields were also able to give other information which helped Blake's defence. Both confirmed that on the night he had been involved in the fight with Thomas Whitehead, he had been wearing his blue suit. Both were also able to state that on October 14th, Blake had been on a friend's motorcycle when he had been involved in an accident. As a result of that, Blake had injured one of his hands and had also torn his trousers.

Jean Blake confirmed that she had arranged to meet her husband in Vicar Lane at 9.00pm on the night of October 16th, but she had not finished work until 9.20pm and when she saw that Blake was not at the meeting place, simply assumed that he had already gone home to Lady Pit Lane. She caught a tram there and Blake came in a few minutes later. That night, she left her make up compact and a tube of face cream on the sideboard.

The time came for David Blake to step into the witness box and give evidence on his own behalf. Blake admitted that he had first met Emily Yeomans about three weeks before she died and had been out with her three or four times since then. They had first met at the junction of Meadow Road and Dewsbury Road, at around

11.45pm and had last seen her on Friday, October 12th. On that occasion she had told him that she was going to a dance. He did not like dancing but arranged to see her afterwards. They met at about 1.20am and were together for about an hour.

Blake agreed that he had arranged to meet Emily again, but this was not on the Tuesday, but Thursday, October 18th, and confirmed that the arrangement was to wait at the crossing on Hunslet Hall Road. He denied that at any time he had told Schofield that he was seeing a girl named Yeomans. He had said that her name was Emily but he did not know her surname. He knew she lived with her uncle and thought she had the same name. Blake thought that Emily's surname was Adams.

On the day in question, October 16th, Blake said he had met Schofield and they had been to the 43 Club together. While there he told his friend that he had arranged to meet Jean in Vicar Lane at 9.00pm, so could not stay too long. They left the club at 7.30pm and far from walking down Dewsbury Road to meet Emily, he had climbed on to a tram at Hunslet Hall Road.

It was just after 8.00pm when he arrived at Lady Pit Lane, a time confirmed by his sister, and saw his brother-in-law asleep on the sofa. Blake shouted upstairs to Florence and asked her for a razor blade. He shaved and washed and went to meet his wife. Boarding another tram, Blake alighted at Boar Lane corner and walked to Vicar Lane to wait for Jean. After being there for 15 minutes he became convinced that he had missed his wife but just in case, chose to walk home along the tram route. If she passed him, she would see him and know he was on his way.

After a few minutes, a tram passed him and he saw Jean was on it. Blake ran after the tram but could not catch it and so waited at the nearest stop and caught the next one. That was how he got to Lady Pit Lane just after Jean. Blake went on to deny that he had been obsessed with the murder and although he had a copy of a newspaper carrying a report of the crime, he had bought this for the racing results. Only later did he see the crime headlined and this so surprised him that he pointed it out to Schofield outside the registry office.

Blake claimed that he had not said to Schofield, "Now's your chance to get that £20." It was Schofield who was talking incessantly about the crime and claiming that Blake was involved and at one stage he had lost his temper and said, "Well if you think I have anything to do with her, go to the police and tell them, if you think you can get the £20."

There was, however, one shaky moment for the defence. Under cross examination, Blake had to admit that he had gone to 'meet' Emily on the Thursday, already knowing that she was dead. Asked to explain this Blake shouted, "A man is not in his right senses when he is charged with murder. There's no one in court who realises what it is like." He went on to say that he had lied about this when interviewed by the police because he did not want his wife to know that he had been out with Gladys Brook.

Having heard all the testimony, the jury took just 75 minutes to decide that Blake was guilty and he was sentenced to death. Only now could it be revealed that Blake had something of a history of crime. At Christmas, 1929 a young girl, visiting her sister in Castleford, missed her last bus and set off to walk home. On the way she met two girls who had a man with them and he offered to escort her home. On the way, that man battered and almost choked her, taking from her a gold necklace. That man was Blake and for that offence he received a sentence of three years imprisonment.

Even before this, while serving in India with the King's Own Yorkshire Light Infantry, Blake had been involved in several offences which culminated in the rape and assault of an old native woman. Blake was charged with others and was sentenced to prison but this was subsequently quashed on a technicality. All this seemed to confirm that the police had indeed got the right man.

Blake's appeal was heard on January 21st, 1935 before the Lord Chief Justice, and Justices Avory and Swift. Here it was stated that Emily Yeomans had been killed some time between 8.00pm and

9.00pm, at a distance of some 2,000 yards from where Blake lived and there was testimony that he was at home soon after 8.00pm. There were other problems with the evidence which also had to be considered. Two of Emily's workmates had failed to identify the powder compact as the one which Emily had owned. One of the tramcar drivers and one of the young boys who had seen Emily meet a man, had made positive identifications of Man Number One and forensic evidence also linked him to the crime. In addition, there was doubt over the evidence given by Schofield. He had claimed that he had seen Blake and a woman walk off together, yet if his story was true and he had been there, he would have been unable to see down Dewsbury Road from the far end of Trentham Street. In short, there was sufficient evidence to suggest that the prosecution had failed to prove their case beyond a reasonable doubt.

In giving their judgement, the judges stated that there were a number of suspicious circumstances to Blake's behaviour, including the fact that when first interviewed he had denied even knowing Emily. In addition, if the jury accepted Schofield's evidence then there was no doubt that Blake was the man who met Emily on the night she died and this, together with other evidence which linked him to the crime, was more than enough to demonstrate his guilt. The appeal failed.

It is, of course, the duty of the prosecution to prove their case beyond a reasonable doubt. No one had to prove that Blake was innocent. It may well be true that he was responsible for the death of Emily Yeomans but another man had been suspected at an early stage in the investigation, forensic evidence had linked him to the dead woman and the evidence Schofield had given was suspect. None of these considerations, though, would save the life of David Blake.

On Thursday, February 7th, 1935, despite a petition carrying over 10,000 signatures pleading for a reprieve, David Maskill Blake was hanged at Leeds by Thomas Pierrepoint and Alfred Allen. His sister, Florence Bousfield, was outside the prison gates, along with 1,000 others, to witness a service conducted by the Salvation Army. It was the day before Blake's 30th birthday.

Man Number One has never been named. It is perhaps time that he was. During his cross examination of Chief Inspector Craig, Mr Paley Scott handed him a piece of paper on which he had written a name and asked Mr Craig to confirm that this was the identity of Man Number One. That confirmation was given and the piece of paper, Exhibit 23, was entered into evidence. Today that piece of paper is preserved in the Public Record Office in London and shows that Man Number One was a gentleman named Joseph Talbot.

CHAPTER FIFTEEN

THE PUB WITH NO BEER

HILDA Grange lived at 3 Back Lane, Clayton Heights, Bradford, and her house adjoined the yard of the Nag's Head Inn which was run by her close friend, 69–year–old Jane Coulton.

It was autumn 1944 and although Allied troops were now fighting their way across the battered continent of Europe, the war with Germany would last for another six months. In England, many things were still rationed, or simply in short supply, and it was not uncommon for shops and stores to run out of certain items. Indeed, even public houses ran short of beer and towards the third week in September, Jane Coulton's pub ran dry, although she continued to open for her regulars who could still buy spirits and other liquors.

At 6.45am on Thursday, September 21st, 1944, Hilda Grange left her house by the back door. As she strolled past the back of the Nag's Head, something caught her eye. Looking across towards the pub, she saw that one of the downstairs windows appeared to be broken. She stepped through the open gates, walked up to the pub and saw that not only had the kitchen window been smashed, but so had a glass panel in the back door. Hilda shouted for Jane and when there was no reply, went over to her brother's house to get assistance.

Hilda and her brother returned to the pub but still there was no reply to their calls, so Hilda's brother climbed on to the window sill, pulled back the blackout material and peered into the kitchen. He saw that the light was still on and that some drawers in the dresser had been opened. Hilda, meanwhile, had tried the back door and found it unlocked. She stepped inside the hallway only to find pieces of broken glass from the door panel and a large stone which had probably been thrown through the panel in order to break it. It was obvious that something seriously wrong and without further delay the pair contacted the police.

It was 7.05am when Frank Thorpe, a war reserve constable in the Bradford City force, arrived at the rear of the Nag's Head. He, too, entered by the unlocked back door and having checked the downstairs rooms, proceeded upstairs where he found a small fox terrier dog. Although it was barking furiously, the animal did not appear to be aggressive and made no move to attack Thorpe who began searching the three bedrooms. In the second bedroom, he saw drawers thrown open in a dressing table, as if someone had conducted a hasty search. It was in the third bedroom, though, the one at the front of the pub, that Constable Thorpe found the body of Jane Coulton lying in her bed.

By 7.30am Detective Sergeant Albert Hustler had arrived at the scene. He was admitted by the front door, which was opened by Constable Thorpe. Sergeant Hustler inspected the rooms and noted that there were footmarks on the draining board of the kitchen sink. There were also some spots of blood on the sink and at various locations around the kitchen floor. Upstairs, in the bedroom where Jane Coulton lay, there were more blood spots on the counterpane, close to her face and yet there was no sign that Jane herself had shed any blood. It was likely therefore that the person who had gained entry by smashing the kitchen window had cut himself in the process and dropped blood as he moved about the premises.

Jane Coulton was beyond all help. A stocking had been tied tightly around her neck and there were also signs of bruising on her face. Underneath the pillow on which her head lay, Sergeant Hustler found a purse and a cash bag. There was money in the purse, but the cash bag was empty. The thief, though, had not discovered all the bar takings. In the same bedroom, Hustler found some locked drawers and when these were opened later by a locksmith, £119 10s 3d was found inside.

Signs on the bar door showed that someone had tried to force it open, possibly believing that there was further cash to be found there. There could be little doubt that someone had broken into the pub to steal the takings and had struck Jane Coulton after she had disturbed the burglar. The intruder had strangled her and tried to find the money kept on the premises. He had managed to take some cash, but had missed the money in the locked drawers. Later still, relatives and friends of Mrs Coulton also gave details of jewellery which seemed to be missing, so the thief had obviously taken more than just cash. The question was, of course, who was responsible?

Two days after the discovery of Jane Coulton's body, a name was suggested to the police. Leo Fretwell was a lieutenant in the General Service Corps and on September 23rd, he received a letter from one of his men who had gone AWOL. This soldier had been due to attend an adjourned hearing regarding his conduct during a brawl in Manningham Lane, Bradford. The soldier had not appeared at the hearing on September 22nd and now Lieutenant Fretwell had received a letter, postmarked Bradford, 5.15am on September 21st, the day of the murder.

The letter had come from Lance-Corporal Arthur Thompson, serial number 2940127, and the return address was, 'Somewhere in England.' Addressed to the CO at the General Service Corps headquarters in Valley Lane Parade, Bradford, it read, 'Dear Sir, with regard to a charge I was to appear before you today on. I wish to say that whatever happened I was fully responsible for and any other persons are not to blame. For I attacked three soldiers in Manningham Lane and whatever they did was done in self defence.

'I was drunk and fully determined to kill them for no reason, other than I'm just a fighting nature. I got the worse of it and I'm just leaving. Yours sincerely, A Thompson.' The letter had been written on YMCA paper.

It could, of course, have been pure coincidence that a soldier, who by his own admission was violent, had been in Bradford some hours after Jane Coulton was killed and had now gone absent without leave, but the matter deserved further investigation.

Inquiries into Arthur Thompson's recent movements showed that at the beginning of September he had received facial injuries in the fracas in Manningham Lane. As a result he had been admitted to Bradford's Westwood Hospital, from where he had been discharged on September 18th. When other men, still in that hospital, were interviewed they revealed some interesting information which only went to confirm that Thompson may well have been involved in the killing of Jane Coulton.

Thomas Thomson was in the Royal Scots Fusiliers and had been a patient at Westwood since August. When Arthur Thompson had been admitted, he had been put on to Thomson's ward and the two had become friends. Neither man was confined to the ward and had been out drinking together on many occasions. The public house they most often went to was none other than the Nag's Head. Thomson, though, was able to give the police some even more relevant information. Arthur Thompson had confessed to him that he needed £18 to pay off his lodgings and had told him that he might break into some place to get the money.

William Lillycrapp was a private in the York and Lancaster Regiment and had been in Westwood since September 1st. He also came to know Thompson and had once lent him 3s. The debt had been repaid soon afterwards but despite this, at some time between 2.00am and 2.30am on September 21st, while he had been lying in bed awake, Lillycrapp had seen Thompson enter the ward, place 11s on his locker and explain this action by saying, "I owe you that." Thompson asked where another soldier was. Lillycrapp pointed out the right bed and Thompson went over to him and woke him.

This second soldier was Trooper Laurence Heys of the Royal

Armoured Corps. He had been in Westwood for some time, since July 1st in fact, and was another friend of Thompson's. In the early hours of September 21st, he was sound asleep when Thompson gently shook him awake and handed him another 11s which he again said he owed. Heys told the police that Thompson had never borrowed a penny from him, although he had given him cigarettes from time to time. Before Heys could protest that Thompson did not owe him any money, Thompson grasped his hand, shook it vigorously and said that he was going.

There had been another witness to Thompson's early morning visit to his old ward at Westwood Hospital. Jamesine Dickson was a nurse on duty on that ward on the morning of September 21st. It was around 2.00am when Thompson came in and went to Lillycrapp's bed. Because Dickson was busy at the time she did not hear any of the conversation that followed, but she did hear the clink of coins. She saw Thompson walk quietly over to Heys' bed and wake him up. Not wanting her patients disturbed, she went over to Thompson and asked him not to wake any of the men. As she arrived at Heys' bedside, Dickson saw cash being handed over. Thompson moved to leave the ward but stopped and tried to press some money into her hand, asking her to 'buy some cigarettes for the boys', but she laughed and pushed him away.

It was a simple matter to determine what had happened to Thompson after he left the ward where Jamesine Dickson was on duty. Frederick Coldwell was an ambulance driver and at 1.45am on September 21st, he took a road accident victim to the Westwood Hospital. Some 20 minutes or so later, Coldwell had noticed a young soldier wandering about in the hospital and later still, at 2.40am, saw the same soldier who was by now walking down Great Horton Road. The soldier flagged the ambulance down and asked Coldwell for a lift into Leeds. Coldwell asked the soldier if he was looking for a bed for the night and having ascertained that he was, dropped him off near the Town Hall at Bradford, giving him directions to the YMCA. The soldier's description fitted that of Arthur Thompson and, of course, there were already links with the YMCA since the letter to his commanding officer had been written on paper from that establishment.

George Thompson Smith was a part-time voluntary worker at the YMCA. He told the police that at around 3.00am, or perhaps a little later, a soldier had come in and asked him for paper so that he could write a letter. Having been given paper and an envelope, the soldier left at 4.00am to post the letter, saying that it must be at his barracks before noon. The man came back to the YMCA soon afterwards and when Smith left, at 4.30am, he was still there. Once again, the description fitted Arthur Thompson.

Evidence was now presented which indicated that Thompson might have made for Halifax. John Clayton earned his living as a taxi driver and at 4.30am on September 21st he was at the rank outside Forster Square railway station in Bradford when a soldier climbed into his cab and said, "Halifax." Clayton explained that he did not have enough petrol to make such a journey, whereupon the soldier had asked him to drive as far as he could. Still reluctant, Clayton told the man that he should go to the offices of Ryburn United Transport, once they were open, as they would probably take him for free, or at least very cheaply. The soldier offered no argument and the last time Clayton saw him, he was walking off towards Well Street.

The investigation now moved towards Halifax and here another witness was found who seemed to confirm that Arthur Thompson was moving westwards. Hilda Halstead was a bus conductress and on September 21st had been serving on the route from Halifax to Blackshaw Head. Her bus had picked up a soldier who looked dirty and was wearing full battledress and a forage cap. He handed Hilda a shilling saying, "As far as you go," adding that he was only going along for the ride. He alighted at the terminus.

Other inquiries in this location now produced a farmer, Thomas Edmondson, who had land at Hebden Bridge. At 7.30am on September 21st a soldier passed his farm. The man was wearing khaki and, seeing Edmondson, asked him if he had a good overcoat for sale for which he would pay £2. Edmondson said that the only thing he had available was an old coat which the soldier could have for nothing. The soldier took the coat and handed over 2s anyway, saying that he was making for Manchester. He went on to explain that he had 'jumped it' and was going to take a few days' leave. Thomas Edmondson took this to mean that the man had gone AWOL. The last time Edmondson saw the man he was wearing the overcoat and striding purposefully towards Burnley.

This, however, was not the end of this particular incident. The farmer's son, Allan Edmondson, saw the man walking away from his father's farm. The soldier could not see Allan and after he had gone 400-500 yards, Allan saw the soldier stop, remove the coat and drop it over a low wall. A couple of hours later, Allan Edmondson retrieved the coat and gave it back to his father.

Constance Patricia Corello helped her father at his gentleman's outfitters which he ran from 4-6 Sandygate, Burnley. On September 21st, a soldier, wearing battledress, came into the shop and asked for an overcoat. Eventually the man purchased not just a coat, but also a grey suit, paying £4 10s for the lot. The soldier changed into his new clothes and left behind his uniform, together with his cap, saying that he would call back for them later. The man never returned and Miss Corello still had the clothing which she handed over to the police.

At first, it appeared that this proved that the soldier in question was not in fact Arthur Thompson, for the name and serial number inside the cap was that of Private Farquhar Fraser of the General Service Corps, number 10682865. This soldier was quickly traced and interviewed and confirmed that in early September he had gone to the quarter-master to complain about his cap being too large. By coincidence, there was another soldier there at the same time, complaining that his cap was too small. The ever resourceful quarter-master had told the two men to exchange headgear. When Private Fraser's cap was inspected, it was found to contain Thompson's name and serial number. There could now be little doubt that the soldier the police were tracking across Yorkshire and Lancashire was none other than Arthur Thompson.

There had, however, been another sighting of Thompson in Burnley. George Ormerod was the licensee of the Barrack Tavern in that town and at 1.00pm a man had come into his bar and ordered a pint of mild, Thompson's usual drink. The two men fell into conversation about the war and the stranger said that he was a discharged soldier who was on his way to Preston. After a few minutes, a regular customer came in. The man, a gentleman named Nixon, was shown a five-stone diamond ring and asked, "Do you known anything about diamonds?" The discharged soldier said he had bought the ring the day before, for £18, and was now looking to sell it. Nixon said that he knew nothing about jewellery but tried the ring on his pint glass to see if the diamonds were real. A ring containing five diamonds in a cluster was one of the items missing from Jane Coulton's pub.

Since Thompson was now apparently trying to sell the items he had taken from the murder scene, it was reasonable to assume that he would eventually approach a jeweller. He had said he was going to Preston but no one in that town reported anyone trying to sell items that were on the police list. However, once the net was spread a little wider, John Sculthorpe, a watchmaker of 58 Market Street, Lancaster, came forward.

Mr Sculthorpe reported that some time between 2.30pm and 3.00pm on September 22nd, a man had come in to his shop, explaining that he was a bullion dealer from Southport. The man wanted to buy a wrist watch and Mr Sculthorpe showed him two. The customer finally picked out a ten-carat Elgin watch but rather than pay cash, sought to do a trade. A ring was produced and Mr Scultorpe agreed to take it, but only pending the man's return with cash. When he did so, the ring would be returned. The man had not returned and so Mr Sculthorpe still had the ring. Once this was produced, it was seen to be one taken from the Nag's Head.

Then Daisy Phyllis Rouse, who worked at her husband's jewellery shop in Morecambe, told police that at 3.30pm on September 23rd, a gentleman had entered her shop and offered an Elgin watch for sale. He said he wanted £5 cash for it but eventually settled for £4 10s. The watch was the one picked up in Lancaster the day before, in exchange for a diamond ring.

The village of Overton is less than three miles from Heysham which is itself just south of Morecambe. It was 2.30pm on September 24th, when a man walked into the Globe Hotel and ordered a drink. George Slater, the licensee, pulled the pint for his customer and asked what had brought him there on such a cold day. The man said that he had come from the Cumberland Hotel, Morecambe, and had been staying there all week. He went on to volunteer the information that he had just had a £10 each- way bet on a horse called Teheran, which had won him £60. The man seemed to be unkempt and behaving suspiciously so when he went to the toilet, Slater telephoned the police and described his unusual customer in detail.

The man returned to his pint and finished it, staying in the Globe for a total of perhaps 30 minutes. Just as he was about to leave, Sergeant Sidney Wood and Constable Charles Benjamin Towndrow of the Lancashire Constabulary walked in the door. As they entered, the man rose to leave, even going so far as to bid them, "Good afternoon." He was asked for his identity card.

A card was produced, bearing the name Kidd, but it had been signed R.Reid, in pencil. Asked his name, the man said it was Robert Reid whereupon he was asked for further identification. An Army medical card was handed over and this gave the name R.N. Reid of 47 Harrington Street, Preston. An Army discharge certificate was also produced, this time giving the name Robert Noel Ried (*sic*). The two officers now asked 'Mr Reid' to accompany them to the police station.

Wood and Towndrow had driven to the Globe in a police car and on the way to the station, their passenger repeatedly asked for the windows to be opened. Permission was refused as was a request to stop so that their prisoner could relieve himself. Mr Reid became heated and threatened to sue for wrongful arrest once all this was sorted out.

Back at the police station the car was garaged and Mr Reid was questioned briefly, after which he was placed in the cells. Only when he was taken down to the cells by Constable Towndrow did Mr Reid say, "Tell the sergeant I am Arthur Thompson and I have deserted from my unit." At last, the search was over.

As soon as details of the arrest had been sent to Bradford, Detective Chief Inspector Thomas Rushworth drove to Morecambe to interview Thompson. In that interview Thompson claimed that his only offence was a military one, going absent without leave. As for the money found on him, this had come from some items he had raffled in pubs along Manchester Road in Bradford. He had managed to get rid of some boots, cigarettes and chocolate which raised more than £10. After enjoying some fish and chips, he had gone to the Westwood Hospital where he gave some money to his friends. He admitted getting a lift in the ambulance, and going to the YMCA where he wrote the letter to his commanding officer. Later he caught a train to Burnley from where he travelled on to Preston, Lancaster and Morecambe. The various identification cards had been his, but he had altered them to the name Reid. He was certainly not responsible for the death of Jane Coulton.

The final link in the chain of evidence came on September 25th. The car used to take Thompson to the police station had not been out of the police garage again until the morning of the 25th, a Monday, when Sergeant Wood climbed into the vehicle. As Wood checked over the car he noticed that the foot mat in the back was out of place. Going to straighten it, Wood noticed something underneath the mat and, pulling it back, he found two rings and two brooches. These were shown to have been Mrs Coulton's property and Arthur Thompson was now charged with murder.

The trial of 34-year-old Arthur Thompson opened on December

6th, 1944, before Mr Justice Oliver. The case for the prosecution was led by Mr G.H.B. Streatfeild, assisted by Mr Myles Archibald, while Thompson's defence lay in the hands of Mr J. Stanley Snowdon, aided by Mr Eric Greenwood. The jury originally consisted of ten men and two women but Thompson, through his barrister, objected to the presence of females on the jury and both were replaced by men. The proceedings lasted for three days.

Further evidence was given of Thompson's movements after his flight from Bradford. John Clayton, the Bradford taxi driver, George Smith from the YMCA, Hilda Halstead, the bus conductress, Thomas Edmondson, the farmer from Hebden Bridge, John Sculthorpe, the watchmaker from Lancaster, Daisy Rouse from Morecambe, and George Ormerod of the Barrack Tavern in Burnley, all told the court that they had picked out Thompson at identity parades.

Doreen Knight of 55 Edward Street, Morecambe, testified that she took in lodgers and had a bed and breakfast sign in her window to attract passing trade. On the morning of September 22nd, Thompson had called at her house saying that he wanted a room for just one night, for which she told him the charge would be 6s. The following morning, Thompson left after breakfast but returned at 4.00pm to tell her that he had changed his mind and wanted the room for the week. In the meantime, however, she had taken in another guest and had to tell him that the room had been let.

Thompson was a native of Bootle and in 1942 had lodged at 21 Tennyson Street, a house owned by Letitia Waring. She gave evidence that Thompson had remained with her until August, 1944 when he was called up. At the time he left, he owed her not £18, but £20 for his lodgings and other money she had lent him. He had promised her that he would send her 10s a week from his Army pay. Letitia never saw any of the money but received three letters from Thompson over the period in question.

One of these letters, postmarked September 19th, read, 'Dear Ma, received your welcome letter alright, and was glad to hear you are all very well. Sorry to hear Jim's not doing so much. Sorry about having disappointed you about the money I owe you, and I don't feel like offering explanations or excuses, but will repay you as soon as I can. I have been here five weeks now and have only had £2 15s the whole time. As soon as my records get through from the other regiment I was in I'll get all my back pay from the time I joined up. I also am entitled to about £10 refund from the Income Tax, which I shall be able to get next time I'm in Liverpool.

'Tell Jim it was nice to hear the fellows were asking after me. I was made a lance-corporal two weeks ago and have been in hospital since. Some fellows got me down and kicked my face and head. I wasn't supposed to have been out so I will lose my stripe when I leave hospital and I've got a little reckoning to do with three fellows who put me here.

'I hope I'll be able to come and see you soon. I wish the war would finish. I'm getting a bit fed up here having to do this and that, get in by such a time. It was a bit of fun at first but it's beginning to wear off a bit now. Well, please remember me to all. Yours sincerely, Arthur.'

Another letter, written just before his arrest, was put forward by the prosecution as proof that Thompson was admitting that he had committed some terrible crime and was now contemplating suicide. In one part it read, '... You will know everything I done by now, but you'll never know how much I hate and despise myself for it.'

'From where I am writing now I can see. I look out of the window and can see everything that God made that was beautiful. The sea, the hills in the far distant (*sic*). The cry of the seagulls. The restless waves that soon I shall be lying beneght (*sic*). Do not have any regrets for any memories you may have of me...'

Three people were called to identify the jewellery found in the police car and the single piece exchanged for the watch in Lancaster. Jane Elizabeth Summerfield had worked as a cleaner for Jane Coulton for a number of years. She was able to say that the two brooches found were identical to those she had often seen her employer wearing.

Harriet Catherine Whitaker lived at 45 Highgate Road, Clayton Heights, and had known the dead woman for more than five years. She explained that since the pub had run out of beer, on September 17th, Jane had not bothered to open up to the general public at all. On the night of September 20th, Jane had called on Harriet at her home, where they had stayed together until 8.30pm. Jane had returned home but about 25 minutes afterwards, by arrangement, Harriet had been admitted to the pub where she stayed until 9.45pm when Jane dropped the latch and locked up for the night. Harriet was able to state that she had, at various times, seen Jane wearing all the jewellery produced in court and was able to identify the five-stone diamond ring, another diamond ring, an opal ring and the two brooches. Finally, Edith Scarborough, who had been Jane's step-daughter, and who now lived in Haworth, was also able to give evidence that the rings and brooches were Jane's.

The final proof that it had indeed been Thompson who broke into the Nag's Head was given by the medical and forensic testimony. Dr Ralph Rimmer was the police surgeon who had examined Jane's body at the scene. On the fold of her left ear, Dr Rimmer had found a small amount of blood which did not belong to the dead woman. On September 25th, he had examined Thompson and found small cuts near the ends of his fingers on his right hand. These were consistent with the kinds of cuts one might obtain from broken glass. He had taken a blood sample from Thompson and this had proven to be group 'A'.

Lewis Charles Nickolls of the North Eastern Forensic Science Laboratory at Wakefield had also visited the murder scene and had taken samples of blood from the window frame, pieces of broken glass, sink top, kitchen floor and the counterpane on the bed. All this blood was group 'A' but the dead woman was group 'B'.

Some of the history of Arthur Thompson was now given by Dr Francis H. Brisby, the medical officer of Armley jail. He stated that Thompson's medical records showed that his paternal grandmother had died in a mental hospital. Thompson had first joined the Army when he was 15 and had served initially for five years. In 1932, the prisoner had contracted syphilis and at the end of 1936 had suffered a severe head injury which necessitated a spell in hospital. In August 1944, he was called up and at the beginning of September, had been admitted to hospital suffering from facial injuries after a fight.

While he had been in prison awaiting trial, Thompson had been given an encephalogram which suggested that there had been traumatic damage to the left side of his brain. Dr Brisby's conclusion was that Thompson was a most unstable type and since he had admitted that on the night of September 20th, he had consumed around 15 pints of beer, this would have exacerbated his condition.

Thompson went into the dock to give evidence on his own behalf. He denied again that he was responsible for the murder although he admitted that he had said he was thinking of breaking into a house to get some money. Thompson explained away the jewellery by saying that up to 1938, he had been a dealer in such items. He had purchased these items from a man named 'Buck', who he had once met in Chichester and met up with again in Bradford a couple of days before the murder. Thompson had hidden these items in the police car but only because he had read about the murder after he left Bradford and realised that 'Buck' must have committed the crime and the items could link him with it.

A final witness for the defence was Betty Foster, another nurse at Westwood. Blood had been found on Thompson's battledress when it had been retrieved from the shop where he left it. The prosecution suggested that this blood was shed by him when he broke into the Nag's Head but nurse Foster testified that on September 18th, Thompson had reported bloodstains on his tunic and she had tried to clean them off with methylated spirits.

The jury had little trouble in finding Thompson guilty. Before he was sentenced to death, he exclaimed, "I am not guilty. There are better men and braver men than me who have gone to their deaths every day for civilisation and justice. What does it matter one more?"

Thompson's appeal was heard on January 15th, 1945, and dismissed. Soon afterwards, the death sentence was confirmed and on Wednesday, January 31st, 1945, Arthur Thompson was hanged at Leeds by Thomas Pierrepoint who was assisted by Herbert Harris. It was already the fifth execution in an English prison that year.

CHAPTER SIXTEEN

BAD MEDICINE

JUST before 1.00am on Sunday, April 29th, 1945, Dennis Wilson, a railway fireman who lived at Back Lane, Beeston, was walking home from a late shift at the Holbeck Engine sheds when he passed down Beeston Road. Suddenly, a pale-faced young man wearing a light raincoat ran past him. Dennis Wilson caught only a glimpse of the running man and would be unable to positively identify him but would put his height at around 5ft 6ins or perhaps even a little taller.

Some 15 minutes later, Joseph Edward Charles Freshwater, another railway worker, walked up Cemetery Road towards Beeston and his home at 17 Sunnyview Terrace. As Mr Freshwater strode past the entrance to number 176 Beeston Road, he saw a car in the driveway and that the gates to the drive were partly open. There was nothing unusual in this. He knew that the house belonged to Dr David Walker Dewar, a well known and respected medical man who often left his car parked on the driveway overnight. Joseph Freshwater also noticed an object, which he assumed was a sack, lying by the side of the car.

It was not until 8.10am, that another worker, William Ernest Whitaker, also walked past the end of the small driveway of Dr Dewar's house. He also saw the car and the object, which at first he thought was someone working under the vehicle. The man's position seemed strange, though, so Whitaker walked into the drive and then saw that the figure was lying in a pool of blood. He knocked frantically on the front door of number 176 but got no reply and so dashed to the nearest telephone box, called the police and returned to Beeston Road to await their arrival.

The prostrate figure on the driveway of 176 Beeston Road was that of 42-year-old Dr David Dewar and when the police surgeon, Dr Hoyland Smith, arrived, he pronounced that life was extinct. Dr Dewar's head was a mass of wounds and a subsequent post-mortem revealed that someone had struck the doctor nine or ten times with a sharp, heavy instrument, such as an axe. The cause of death was given as a compound fracture of the skull and laceration of the brain.

The police officer in charge of the investigation was Detective Superintendent James Craig and his early inquiries revealed some dark secrets in the history of Dr Dewar. Although an outwardly respectable physician, Dewar also had a habit of visiting late night drinking establishments, gambling at dog tracks and was known to be extremely fond of the company of ladies, even though he was a married man. In due course, one of those ladies was revealed to be Mrs Laura Walker, who lived at 3 Lady Pit Crescent, Leeds, and whose husband was serving abroad in the armed forces.

Before Laura Walker married, her surname had been Broadley and Dr Dewar had been her family's physician for many years, in fact ever since he had first moved to Leeds in 1931. In 1942, Dr Dewar had become friendly with his patient and he and Laura had started seeing each other socially. He would often take her out in his car, they began visiting public houses together and soon became lovers. Eventually, the relationship cooled and Dr Dewar stopped seeing Laura. However, when interviewed by Superintendent Craig, she admitted that about two weeks earlier, Dewar had contacted her once more and they had started seeing each other again.

The inquest on Dr David Walker Dewar opened on May 1st 1945, before the deputy coroner, Dr A.J. Swanton. Evidence of identification was given by John Dewar, the dead man's brother, and details of the various wounds was given by Dr Hoyland Smith. Superintendent Craig told the court that his investigation was far from complete and the proceedings were adjourned until May 15th. When the inquest reopened, Superintendent Craig explained once again that as yet, no arrest had been made, and once again an adjournment was made, this time until May 30th.

Laura Walker was interviewed a number of times and eventually told Superintendent Craig of another man she had also been seeing at the same time as she had been going out with Dr Dewar. She said that she had not mentioned him before as she had never thought he had anything to do with the attack on Dewar, but he had now confessed to her that he was responsible. The name she gave the police was that of 27-year-old Thomas Eric Richardson. So it was that at 12.40pm on May 21st, Superintendent Craig, accompanied by Detective Inspector Thirkill, called on Richardson at his home in Harlech Avenue, off Dewsbury Road.

Thomas Richardson eventually made a voluntary statement to the police. It read, 'For the past two years I have been friendly with Laura Walker of Lady Pit Crescent, Leeds. She is the wife of Private A.B. Walker, who I knew when I was at school.

'I saw her a few times prior to April 28th, 1945, and promised to see her in Tempest Road at seven that evening, which was Saturday. I knew she was friendly with Dr Dewar, who has a surgery in Beeston Road, but I have never met him, although he has been pointed out to me.

'When I met her on this evening she told me she was going to meet Dr Dewar, so I asked her if she would see me later, but she said she could only give me an idea when she would be back, but she did say round about 12.30am.

'I was very annoyed and grieved and I left her and went home. I went to town and had two or three halves of beer at the Hope Inn and the Templar and returned home again. I talked to my father and then I went to bed.

'I was very ill with a carbuncle on my neck and everything was whizzing round in my head. I could see Laura's face in front of me, and I began to have nightmares. I knew I had to have the carbuncle dressed and I got up and did it. I could see Laura's face all night and I don't know what I was doing.

'Laura had told me to go down to the house at 12.30am when she came back with the doctor as she was to dress my carbuncle which she had done before for me, but I was in such a state of mind, I can't say now whether I went to her house or not at that time. All I have is a faint recollection of waking up in the morning. During my friendship with Laura I have complained to her of her association with the doctor and we have had words about it.

'Two days after the murder of Dr Dewar I saw Laura and asked her whether the police had discussed me with her, and I have seen her several times since as regards this. She told me on each occasion that she had not mentioned my name to them. I could not understand why Laura was keeping company with the doctor and it made me very unfriendly towards him.

'When she left me on the night of April 28th I was very bitter, and I might have said things which I don't remember now. I don't think I have actually asked Laura to keep me out of it, but she has mentioned it to me that the police had not mentioned my name.

'If I have killed Dr Dewar I have no recollection of what I was doing as I was ill and my mind was in such a state. This statement has been read over to me and it is a true statement.'

At no stage in that statement had he admitted that he was responsible for Dr Dewar's death, but he had confessed to feeling animosity towards him, confirmed that he knew his movements on the night he was attacked, and this, together with other circumstantial evidence, led Superintendent Craig to charge Thomas Richardson with murder.

Richardson's first appearance before the magistrates followed on May 22nd when he was remanded to May 30th. A second remand followed, this time to June 8th, and after the evidence had been heard, Richardson was sent for trial at the next Leeds assizes.

The trial of Thomas Eric Richardson, who since his arrest had turned 28, opened on July 16th before Mr Justice Hallett and a jury of ten men and two women. The proceedings lasted for three days and Richardson was defended by Mr C.B. Fenwick and Mr Rudolph Lyons. The prosecution case was led by Mr G.H.B. Streatfeild, who was assisted by Mr Myles Archibald.

One of the most important witness was, of course, Laura Walker. After giving some details of the history of her relationships with Dr Dewar and Richardson, she went on to tell the court of the events of the night of Saturday, April 28th, 1945. On her way to meet Dewar, she had seen Richardson in the street and after telling him where she was going, he begged her to stay with him. Laura explained to him that she and Dewar were only going to visit some friends and pointed out that she expected to be home at around 12.30am and Richardson was welcome to return at that time if he wanted to see her.

Laura met Dewar as arranged and went with him on his rounds, staying in the car while he attended his patients. Dewar finished working and took Laura on to the Spring Hill Tavern where they arrived at some time between 10.15pm and 10.30pm. They spent the next couple of hours drinking with some friends and finally left the tavern at about 12.30am. Dewar drove Laura back home and dropped her off outside her house at about 12.45am.

Laura Walker now made herself some supper and it was not until 1.20am that Richardson appeared. He apologised for being late, saying that he had been in bed asleep. Laura dressed the carbuncle on his neck and it was not until 5.00am that he left. She next saw Richardson at 2.00pm on April 30th when she went to his work to ask him if he had heard the news about Dr Dewar being killed. Richardson replied that he had seen some reports in the newspaper. The couple did not meet again until May 2nd when they had lunch together in the Lonsdale cafe, but on that occasion they did not speak about the crime.

Two weeks after this, Laura saw Richardson again. She was with a sailor in the Imperial Hotel on Cemetery Road, enjoying a drink in the bar, when Richardson came in, took her to one side and demanded to know the identity of her companion. She told him that the sailor was a friend and was staying with her for a while, at which point Richardson became angry and demanded that she throw the man out of her house. Laura refused and when Richardson asked when he might see her again, and she said she was unable to make any definite plans, he threatened to beat up the sailor in front of her. Eventually she managed to calm Richardson and he left the bar when she asked him to.

The following day she saw Richardson in Malvern Road and he said that he knew the identity of Dr Dewar's killer but was not willing to tell her. She would not accept that and eventually Richardson admitted that he was the murderer, saying, "Yes, I done it." As a result of that conversation, the next time Laura was interviewed by Superintendent Craig, she told him what Richardson had said.

Cross examining her, Richardson's defence tried to suggest that what he had actually said was, "Would you think any more of me if I had to say I had done it?" Laura, though, was not to be moved and insisted that Richardson had confessed to being the killer.

Thomas Richardson worked for Thackrays Ltd, a firm of surgical instrument makers. He was on permanent day shift and had not worked on Sundays for over a year, yet on Sunday, April 29th, the day Dr Dewar was killed in the early hours, Richardson went to Thackrays' factory in Viaduct Road, Leeds.

Leonard Rollitt was responsible for ensuring that the factory premises were secure. On Saturday, April 28th, he had locked up at 12.30pm as usual and deposited the keys with the National Fire Service station, which was next door. This routine was well known to all the factory employees, including Richardson, but Mr Rollitt confirmed that no one was authorised to collect the keys without his permission. And he had not given permission to Richardson.

William Walker was one of the firemen who worked at the NFS station and he reported that at 8.45am on April 29th, Richardson called at the station and asked for the keys to Thackrays. He explained that he had inadvertently left his pay packet on a bench and needed to get in to collect it. The keys were handed over and Richardson returned them after 15 minutes.

At the rear of the factory ran the River Aire and this was inaccessible from any point along Viaduct Road, but could be reached by going through the factory. The prosecution was suggesting that Richardson had gained access to the factory in order to dispose of the murder weapon in the river, although after his arrest, the river was dragged for 200 yards either side of the factory and no axe or similar weapon was discovered.

It may have been that if Richardson had dumped the weapon here, he might only have been reconnoitring the area on his first visit, for Fred Jones testified that Richardson returned to the factory later the same night. Jones had authority to collect the factory keys and did so at 8.30pm on that Sunday so that he could begin his shift. Just before he picked up the keys, he saw Richardson waiting in the street. The young man said he had returned for his lighter and admitted to Jones that he had already been in once, to look for his wages. Richardson told Jones that he had used his lighter to search for his wages and had left it behind. Jones let Richardson into the factory for a second time and some three minutes later he reappeared, saying that he had found the lighter which he showed to Jones before leaving.

Dr Hoyland Smith repeated the medical evidence he had given at the inquest and the magistrates' court but went into more detail about the way Dr Dewar had been attacked. The first blow seemed to have been delivered from behind while the doctor was standing, but blood splashes and other evidence showed that the remaining blows had rained down on Dewar while he was lying on the ground. It appeared that the assailant had lain in wait, probably behind the open garage door, and attacked Dr Dewar as he got out of his car.

There was some dispute over just what Richardson had admitted in front of the police. Both Superintendent Craig and Inspector

Thirkill claimed that as they arrived at Richardson's home he had greeted them with, "I've been expecting you." Later, at the police station, he had said, "I know you have got me well tied up. I did it. If you let me see Laura for one minute, I will make a statement." After being allowed to see Laura, Richardson made the written statement already referred to and when asked about the murder weapon, had said, "It was an axe. It is either at the works or in the river. I can remember seeing the water when I threw it in."

Under cross examination, Superintendent Craig admitted that he had questioned Richardson for about an hour and only afterwards had he written down the statements which appeared to be relevant. There was no verbatim record of what had actually been said but both Superintendent Craig and Inspector Thirkill denied that any pressure had been brought to bear on the accused. As a matter of course, all Richardson's clothing had been tested and no trace of blood had been found on any of the items. In addition, Craig told the court that it had been established that during the war Richardson had served in the Home Guard and had been transferred from the artillery section to the infantry and eventually discharged on account of dizziness. Richardson also had a history of fits.

Some of this was backed up by Dr Francis H. Brisby, the medical officer at Armley jail. Two days after his arrest, Richardson had suffered some kind of seizure while he was at exercise. His jaw was clenched, there was froth around his mouth and his arms grew stiff. This seemed to be indicative of epilepsy, although some of the more classic symptoms were absent. After this attack, Richardson had been transferred to Brixton prison in London so that he could be properly examined. Doctors there had determined that he was not epileptic.

In his defence, Richardson said that he had suffered from dizziness for the past year. He agreed that on the night of April 28th, he had met Laura Walker at about 7.00pm, after which he went for a few drinks before getting home at around 10.30pm. He went to bed and his next recollection was waking up at 8.00am the following morning. He did not go back to see Laura that night and his statements to the police were either not true or had been obtained under duress.

In the event, on July 18th, the jury retired and having considered the evidence, returned a verdict that Richardson was guilty, although they added a strong recommendation to mercy. An appeal was entered and this was heard on August 22nd. There were two main grounds, misdirection and misplacement of evidence, but these were divided into a number of points including that the judge had misdirected the jury by saying that there was no possibility of any mistake by a police officer in regard to Richardson's statement, that there was misdirection as to the proof of insanity and that the judge had admitted evidence of threats against a sailor even though the prosecution had considered it inadmissible. The prosecution had relied on what Richardson had allegedly said to Laura Walker, a verbal admission to the police and a written statement which in itself was no admission of guilt. In effect, the judge had made the jury's deliberation a vote of confidence in the two police officers concerned in the case.

The appeal court judges considered that there had been no misdirection, however, and that there was more than enough evidence to prove Richardson's guilt. The appeal was dismissed and when the Home Office announced that there would be no reprieve despite the recommendation of the jury, the death sentence was confirmed.

At 9.00am on Friday, September 7th, 1945, Thomas Eric Richardson was hanged at Leeds by Thomas Pierrepoint who was assisted by Herbert Harris. Only a handful of people had gathered outside the prison to read the formal notice when it was pinned to the gates. Three days later, on September 10th, details of Dr Dewar's will were published. He left property worth £4,186.

Lord Goddard. Appointed Lord Chief Justice in January 1946. He served until September 30th, 1958. (Universal Pictorial Press and Agency)

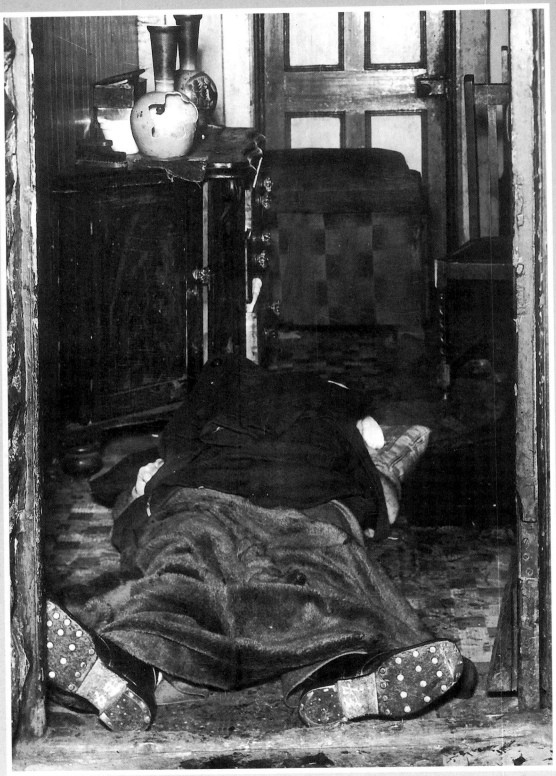

The body of Samuel Hammond Gray lying on his living room floor after he had been shot by William Batty. See Chapter 17. (Public Record Office)

The old court at Bradford City Hall. Many of the Bradford men who ended their lives at the end of a rope faced the magistrates here before being sent to the assizes.

Sir H.B.H. Hylton-Foster who served as a barrister in many of the famous cases which fill these pages. (Popperfoto)

enthing a tall but I want to tell all about I did on
saturday.

The first time I meet the Dr he gave me a ride to
the ring road and the seconde time he gave me aride
he start meesing about with me and I told him to stop
it and he did not so I stop the car my self and
I got out and walke and then he came up after me
and told me he was sorry.

and on saturday he gave me aride he told me he
would take back to camp but he did not he told me
he had a call to make but he did not so he start
fooing about and then he pull me back in the car
I had abit of came to get away from him and the
the gun went off in my hand I did not mean to
shoot hime I am sorry for what has been done.

Albert Sabin

The short statement written out by Albert Sabin admitting that he shot Dr Macleod, though he claimed it was an accident. See Chapter 18. (Public Record Office)

Vicar Lane, Leeds. This thoroughfare is mentioned in three chapters in this book and in three separate public houses there, Blake, Sabin and Kowalewski were well-known. See Chapters 14, 18 and 23. (Yorkshire Evening Post).

Albion Street where Walter Sharpe killed Abraham Levine. Note the shattered nameplate to the right of the doorway and the small bullet hole above the display window in the shop to the left. Mr Levine was attacked inside the jeweller's shop in the middle. See Chapter 20. (Public Records Office)

Inside Levine's shop at 132 Albion Street, Leeds. See Chapter 20. (Public Records Office)

Leeds Infirmary. It was to here that Gertrude Briggs was rushed in an attempt to save her life, and where Abraham Levine was taken after being shot by Walter Sharpe. See Chapters 19 and 20.

The Quarry Hill Flats complex where Czelsaw Kowalewski killed Doris Allen. See Chapter 23.

Robert William Moore who killed a business rival and buried his body in a shallow grave at Fewston. See Chapter 22. (Mirror Syndication)

The house where Edward Lindsay Reid killed his fellow lodger, Arthur White. See Chapter 24. (Yvonne Berger)

Claremont, Bradford. Arthur White's body fell from the small window right at the top of the house. The fire escape was not there at the time. See Chapter 24.

CHAPTER SEVENTEEN

THE KILLER NAMED 'NOBODY'

IN 1941, Samuel Hammond Gray, who was then 29 years old, answered the call of his country and joined the Army. Almost as soon as he had completed his basic training he was sent overseas and found himself fighting the Japanese in Burma.

Back home, his wife Nellie saw no reason why her social life should suffer. After all, thousands of other women still went out to dances and enjoyed themselves. And like so many of those women, it was perhaps inevitable that eventually she would meet someone else. And so she did, in 1942.

The object of Nellie Gray's affections was 23-year-old William Batty. They started walking out together, visiting public houses and soon Batty found himself invited to Nellie's house at 45 Prince Street, Dudley Hill, Bradford. The couple became lovers although Nellie had never pretended to be anything other than a married woman.

Batty, though, was a jealous man and had often said that he hated the idea that one day Samuel Gray would return to claim his rightful place as Nellie's husband. Still, that might be years away and it was time to live for the moment. Batty apparently put such thoughts to the back of his mind, although on one occasion he showed Nellie a gun which he said he had bought in Leeds. He gave her the feeling that when Samuel Gray returned, he might use the weapon to make Nellie Gray his own.

The relationship between Nellie and Batty continued for three years. Then, on August 9th, 1945, she received a telegram from her husband. He was coming home and, indeed, would arrive the next day. At first Batty appeared to take the news reasonably, announcing that it was his intention to talk over the situation with Samuel when he arrived. But then he added, "If he won't let you go, I'll shoot him."

On Saturday, August 11th, Samuel Gray arrived back at the house in Bradford which he had last seen some four years earlier, and that evening he was enjoying a cup of tea when there was a knock on the door. Nellie answered it but from where he sat, Samuel could not see the caller, although he heard a man's voice ask, "Where is the next-door neighbour, Margaret?"

The caller was none other than Batty, who, as he said these words to Nellie, made a gesture with his hand, beckoning her to come outside and talk to him. Nellie, though, closed the door in Batty's face. She had not even returned to the settee when there was a loud noise outside. Samuel Gray, who had spent years on active service, knew exactly what it was. Someone had just fired a gun.

All this took some explaining but when a letter from Batty arrived on August 14th, Nellie showed it to Samuel and told him about the relationship she had enjoyed while he had been in the Far East. However, she had decided to stay with her husband and William Batty was firmly in the past. Now fully aware of what had been going on, and of Batty's threats, Samuel Gray determined that if the young man returned, he would answer the door himself.

At 9.10pm on August 14th, Margaret Ripley, a friend of Nellie's who lived at 47 Prince Street, called at the Gray household. She, Nellie and Samuel were together in the small living room when, at some time around 10.30pm, there was a knock on the door. It was Samuel who answered it and this time the open door shielded the caller from the view of both Nellie and Mrs Ripley. Once the person had spoken, though, neither woman had any doubt about who it was.

"Is Nellie in?" asked Batty, to which Samuel demanded, "Who are you? What do you want?" There was a pause of no more than a couple of seconds before Batty answered, "I am nobody." and with that, a shot rang out and Samuel Gray fell backwards into the room. This was immediately followed by the sound of someone running down the passageway which led to Nellie's door, and escaping into the street. Margaret Ripley dashed for help but it was too late. Samuel Gray was already dead.

The first police officer on the scene was Sergeant William Ryall. He was on duty at the Cutler Heights police station when he received a call and went to 45 Prince Street. He arrived there at 11.07pm and found Samuel Gray lying on the floor, his wife applying cold compresses to his head. Other neighbours had come to help but Sergeant Ryall made a brief examination of the body and saw that a bullet had entered the stomach about three inches above his navel. Soon afterwards, Dr George Reginald Granton arrived and pronounced life extinct. Later still, as the dead man was being moved, underneath where Samuel had been lying Sergeant Ryall found a bullet which had apparently passed completely through his body. A neighbour found a cartridge case outside and this was handed over to Ryall who began taking the details from the witnesses.

Knowing who they were looking for, two police officers, Detective Constable Stanley Metcalfe and Constable Croydon, went to 65 Ireton Street where Batty lived with his mother. Armed with a search warrant, the officers went over the house, especially Batty's bedroom, but could find no sign of either the wanted man, or the gun he had used. They left at 12.15am on August 15th but positioned themselves nearby and watched the house, hoping that sooner or later, Batty would put in an appearance.

Only five minutes after the police had left 65 Ireton Street, Batty knocked on the door of number 33, a house occupied by Florence

Heavysides. She was a close friend of Batty's mother and the latter often stayed with Florence until the small hours of the morning. As Florence opened the door, Batty asked, "Is my mam here?" Florence replied, "She has gone on home. She went at 9.45." Batty headed off towards his mother's house.

As Batty knocked on his mother's door, Constable Metcalfe listened carefully. The door was opened by Mrs Batty who told her son, "The police are looking for you, they've been here and searched all over the house." At this Batty said, "If they come again, tell 'em you haven't seen me." But as he turned to leave he was confronted by the two officers who cautioned him and told him that they were taking him to the police station. In reply to the caution, Batty said, "I can tell you where I have been tonight. I know nothing about it." Later that morning, Batty was charged with murder.

William Batty made his first appearance before the magistrates later that day, Wednesday, August 15th. As usual, only evidence of arrest was given and for the police Detective Superintendent Thomas Rushworth asked for a formal remand until August 23rd. Batty appeared calm in court, and no objection having been made, the remand was granted, as was legal aid for Batty's defence.

Further remands followed and it was not until November 29th, 1945, that the trial finally opened at Leeds, before Mr Justice Lynskey. Batty was defended by Mr C.B. Fenwick while the case for the prosecution was put by Mr G.H.B. Streatfeild.

Nellie Gray told the court of the events leading up to the shooting of her husband on August 14th. Referring to the letter which she had received that morning and which she had shown to her husband, Nellie testified that Batty had written, 'Dear Nellie. Please give me a straightforward answer as to how we stand for it is sending me mad just sitting here studying. Has all this just been a bit of fun to pass your time away, for if it has, well, you have the pleasure of knowing you have broken my heart. So, please give me an answer or come and see me at my mother's or else I will blow my brains out. I don't want to live without you."

Even before her husband's return, Nellie Gray had tried to break off the relationship with Batty but he had always said he would not allow her to. In July, a month before the shooting, Batty had shown her a revolver and 50 rounds of ammunition, saying that he had bought them in Leeds. It was for this reason that she had not wanted Batty and her husband to meet. She knew there would be trouble if they did.

Margaret Ripley testified that although she had not seen the man who knocked on the door of 45 Prince Street on the night of August 14th, she had recognised his voice and knew that it was Batty. She had seen him at Nellie Gray's house many times before and had spoken to him on numerous occasions. Margaret also told how after the shooting, Nellie had rushed out of the house and she had followed. They had not seen the assailant and returned to give what aid they could to the dying man.

There were many other people in Prince Street that evening and they, too, gave details of what they had seen. Fred Mitchell lived at 63 Prince Street and he walked down the street some time before 10.30pm on August 14th. At the top of the street, he saw a young man leaning against the wall. Soon afterwards, Mitchell saw Agnes Feather, a neighbour of his who lived at number 57. They walked down Prince Street together and upon arriving at their homes, heard that there had been a shooting at number 45. Fred and Agnes went to Nellie Gray's house and saw Samuel lying on the floor. He was still alive at the time, moaning and groaning, and having heard from Nellie what had happened, Fred and Agnes returned to the top of the street to see if they could find Batty, who Agnes knew well. He had gone by then, but Fred Mitchell found a cartridge case in Prince Street, about five yards from Nellie's front door.

Much of Fred Mitchell's evidence was confirmed by Agnes Feather. She had been to the cinema and estimated that it was around 10.30pm when she met Fred Mitchell at the top end of Prince Street. At the time, Batty was still leaning on the wall but he had gone by the time they returned to look for him.

Elsie May Sefton and her husband, James Arthur Sefton, had also been to the pictures that night and they lived at 37 Prince Street. It was just after 10.30pm when they turned into Prince Street from Tong Street and as they did, they heard what sounded like a shot. Both Elsie and James saw Batty, a man they knew, running up Prince Street. He passed close to them and had his right hand thrust deep into his jacket pocket.

Batty was apparently not standing alone at the top end of Prince Street, for Harry Kaye, John Lavery and Jack Gallagher all stated that they had been in conversation together at the same location when they saw Batty walk up Prince Street, stop near them and lean on the wall for three or four minutes before strolling back down Prince Street. None of the three friends had heard the shot and were unaware anything had happened until Fred Mitchell asked them if they had seen Batty.

The final person to see Batty in Prince Street on that fateful night was Reuben Fearnley. He was yet another picturegoer and at around 10.30pm, as he walked down Prince Street, Batty was walking towards him. Reuben saw Batty turn into the passageway which led to number 45. Mr Fearnley had not known Batty before but he, along with most of the witnesses already referred to, later picked out Batty at an identification parade.

Albert Edward Leeming, a milk roundsman, gave details of Batty's movements immediately before the shooting had taken place. Leeming spent the evening of August 14th in the Cross Keys Hotel on Rooley Lane and he was playing dominoes with Batty until 10.00pm, closing time. Leeming said that when they left the pub, Batty appeared to be perfectly sober.

Batty had, of course, also paid a visit to 45 Prince Street on August 11th, three days before the shooting. Alice Spilsbury, who lived at 20 Prince Street, gave evidence of a curious incident on that evening. Her house was directly opposite number 45 and as she arrived home at 11.10pm on the 11th, she saw a young man sitting on her wall. At first she thought it might be her brother but as she drew nearer to her home, she saw that it was Batty.

Somewhat nervous, Alice backed away a little, whereupon Batty said, "Will you go through the passage opposite and tell Mrs Gray that there's someone wanting her?" Alice refused, told Batty to get off her wall and went inside her home. Looking out a few minutes later, she saw that Batty had gone and so she went to visit a friend who lived further up the street. However, as she left her home she saw that Batty had only moved across to the opposite side of the street. She saw him put his hand into his right-hand coat pocket and pull something out. Almost immediately there was a flash and a loud report which at first Alice thought might be a firework but soon realised had been a shot. Terrified, she ran to her friend's house at number 15 and was afraid to come out until 1.20am the next morning. Even then, Batty had not given up and gone home, for as she hastened to her house, Alice saw him lying in a doorway opposite number 15.

Dr Ralph Rimmer, the chief police surgeon, had examined the body of Samuel Gray at the scene and later performed a post-mortem. The body bore two wounds. The first of these was a small circular wound in the upper part of the abdomen midway between the navel and the breastbone. This proved to be an entry wound caused by a bullet which had passed through the body and caused the second injury, an exit wound, at the back. Samuel Gray's abdomen was filled with free blood and the bullet had passed through the stomach, aorta and the body of the 11th dorsal vertebrae, damaging the spinal cord. Early the next morning, Dr Rimmer had also examined Batty at the police station and was able to say that although he had taken some alcohol, he was not under the influence of drink.

Lewis Charles Nickolls, the director of the North Eastern Forensic Science Laboratory at Wakefield, had examined two cartridge cases and testified that they had been fired from the same weapon. Further, having seen the powder burns around Samuel Gray's stomach wound, Mr Nickolls was able to state that the shot had been fired from a distance of less than one and a half inches.

Batty went into the witness box to give his version of events. He claimed that on August 14th, he had gone to Prince Street to see Nellie but her husband had opened the door and shouted, "I know who you are and what you want." Gray produced a gun which he pointed at his visitor. Batty, fearful for his life, grabbed at the gun and in the brief struggle that followed, it went off accidently. As Gray fell, Batty saw that he was holding the gun and ran off, throwing it over a railway embankment on the way home.

On November 30th the jury retired and after an absence of just 25 minutes returned a guilty verdict. Asked if he had anything to say, Batty replied, "I protected my life just to forfeit my life."

In fact, this was not the first time that William Batty had seen the inside of a courtroom. He had a long criminal record beginning with the minor offence of riding a bicycle without a rear red light, in Wetherby, for which he was fined 5s on September 27th, 1934. Batty progressed through many other offences including stealing a watch, for which he was bound over, and taking a car, for which the prosecution offered no evidence. His first period of imprisonment came on April 5th, 1938 when he received three years Borstal training for stealing and breaking into a warehouse. A further month's imprisonment followed on May 20th, 1940 when he was charged at York with taking a car without consent. On January 7th, 1941, Batty received ten months' hard labour for breaking into a store and larceny. Finally, on April 12th, 1943, he was given three years for housebreaking and theft. In all, he had made 16 previous court appearances before facing his trial for murder.

Batty's appeal was heard, and dismissed, on December 21st. On Tuesday, January 8th, 1946, William Batty, still only 27 years old, was hanged at Leeds by Thomas Pierrepoint and Harry Allen. Only half a dozen people waited outside the prison to read the notices of execution.

CHAPTER EIGHTEEN

THE BODY IN THE DITCH

SOME time after 3.15pm on Saturday, September 21st, 1946, Harry Philpott, who lived at 43 Wide Lane, Morley, was walking past the offices of the disued Topcliffe Colliery, accompanied by two young boys, when he saw what looked like a pool of blood. Investigating further, he found that a trail of blood led around the side of the offices.

His curiosity aroused, he continued to follow the trail and found a penknife. A few yards further on he found a gun and decided that it was time to call the police. The boys set off to do just that while Harry Philpott continued his search. The trail of blood eventually led to a ditch and there, at the bottom, Philpott saw the body of a man, lying on his right side. Philpott touched nothing and stood guard until the police arrived.

One of the first officers on the scene was Constable Timothy Heaver. He arrived at Topcliffe Colliery at 3.32pm and by 3.45pm had found a set of car tyre tracks which gave the appearance of a vehicle having been turned around and accelerated away rapidly. Constable Heaver also discovered other bloodstains including some on tufts of grass which looked as if they had been used by someone to wipe their hands. Amongst a pile of personal items found by Constable Heaver were a pair of spectacles, a pouch and two white handkerchiefs which had 'N. Macleod' embroidered on them.

The gun was examined. This, too, was bloodstained and still held three live cartridges. The other three chambers held expended cartridges, implying that three shots had been fired. At the edge of the ditch where the body lay, Heaver also found a propelling pencil. The constable was present when Dr John Owen Schofield arrived and confirmed that the man was dead. The body was taken to the mortuary where Constable Heaver removed the clothing. In the pockets of the trousers, he discovered the sum of £8 in cash.

The body of the dead man was officially identified on September 22nd when Robert Macarthur, who lived in Middlesex, stated that this was his brother-in-law, 52-year-old Dr Neil Macleod. In fact, the police were already aware of the man's identity, for Dr Macleod was a well-respected local man and one of the senior police officers on the case, Detective Superintendent Charles Frederick Marson, had known him for many years.

One of the first ports of call for the police was Dr Macleod's surgery at 25 Park Square, Leeds. Here the receptionist, Kathleen Maude Hewson, told them that Dr Macleod had only three patients on that Saturday and, after he had seen them, he had left the premises just before 2.00pm. This was confirmed by another doctor, Rhoda Hicks Butler Adamson, who had consulting rooms next door to Macleod, at number 24. She told officers that it was around 1.45pm when she left her rooms and, by coincidence, Macleod was leaving at the same time. They fell into conversation and it was not until a few minutes before 2.00pm, that they finally parted and Macleod climbed into his car. Dr Adamson walked to her own car and as she was unlocking the door, she saw a young man in battledress dash from the south side of Park Square to the passenger door of Dr Macleod's car. The soldier put his foot on the sill of the car as if he was about to climb in and she saw that he was talking to Dr Macleod, although she could not hear their conversation. After a minute or so, as Rhoda Adamson drove off, she looked in her rear-view mirror and saw that the soldier, a man with corn coloured hair, had finally climbed into the passenger seat of Dr Macleod's car. Her impression was that Dr Macleod was not pleased to see his visitor and at one stage, the two men had appeared to be arguing.

It now became a pressing matter to trace Dr Macleod's car, a Ford V8, bearing the registration number BDN 114. A description was circulated to all police officers and it was Sergeant John Stanley Metcalfe who was the first to spot the vehicle. He was in Church Lane, Pudsey, at 11.52pm when he saw a soldier stop the car, get out and talk to two men on the pavement. The driver walked towards Chapletown. Metcalfe followed him but was unable to catch up with the man.

World War Two had ended just over a year earlier but a soldier in full battledress was still a common sight on the streets of Britain. Dr Macleod had been seen with a soldier, and a soldier was now driving his car. It was logical to assume that if the police questioned all the soldiers in the area, they might obtain the breakthrough they needed. Luckily there were relatively few places in Leeds where soldiers were now stationed and this made the police's task that much easier. It was for this reason that officers including Detective Inspector John Edington and Detective Superintendent Marson, visited Tingley Hall, which was then being used as a prisoner-of-war hostel.

It was at Tingley Hall that a search revealed a hat, raincoat, briefcase and a case book all hidden underneath blankets in a storeroom. This, together with interviews with the guards and some of the prisoners, led the police to 21-year-old Private Albert Sabin, a hostel guard whose home address was Brookfield Road, Langley, Birmingham.

Back at Morley police station, Sabin was interviewed by Superintendent Marson and Inspector Edington. He was cautioned for a second time, told that Dr Macleod had been found dead, that property apparently belonging to the dead man had been found in a storeroom at Tingley Hall and that he had been seen taking these items to the storeroom. Sabin was asked to explain his possession of these items and without hesitation, replied, "Yes, I killed him. I'll tell you all about it."

Inspector Edington asked Sabin if he wished to make a statement and when he replied in the affirmative, handed over paper and a pen with which to write it out. At this Sabin said, "You write it down. I am a poor writer." Edington took down Sabin's words and later, satisfied that it was correct, Sabin signed it.

In this first statement, Sabin said, "As I was riding along I made up my mind to have some money off him. As we got near Tingley crossroads, the gun went off. I do not remember firing three times. I pulled him out of the car and dragged him towards a ditch. I took £20 out of his pocket. I am sorry I did it. Nobody else had a hand in it." Sabin also told Inspector Edington that he always carried a gun with him and patted his breast pocket to show where it was usually kept.

Albert Sabin made his first appearance in court on September 23rd, where the presiding magistrate was the Mayor of Morley, Alderman T. Redick. Here, some brief details of Dr Macleod's career and past life were given. A native of Skye, he had been a consultant at Leeds since 1938. Before this he had been a naval surgeon, had served in World War One and had been present at the Battle of Jutland, the greatest sea battle of the war. Dr Macleod had left behind a wife, Mary Elizabeth, and two sons aged seven and 11. After hearing evidence of arrest, Sabin was remanded in custody until October 14th. On that date, a further remand followed, this time until October 22nd and it was on that date when he was sent for trial.

The trial opened on December 5th, 1946, before Mr Justice Henn-Collins and a jury of eight men and four women. The Crown case was led by Mr C.B. Fenwick, assisted by Mr G.W. Wrangham. Sabin was defended by Mr C. Paley Scott and Mr A.M. Hurwitz and the trial lasted for two days.

Some of the early witnesses helped to pinpoint the exact time of the attack on Dr Macleod. Joseph Taberner was acting as a relief bus driver on the Dewsbury-Leeds route on September 21st. His bus left Dewsbury at 2.30pm and it would be around 2.45pm when it stopped at the Tingley cross roads to let some passengers off. Taberner saw a car turn right into Topcliffe Pit Lane, without signalling. Although he could not see the occupants clearly, Taberner described the vehicle as a dark saloon car.

William Alcock Smith was the foreman at Topcliffe Farm and he was in the yard there between 2.30pm and 3.20pm. During that time he heard shots which appeared to come from the direction of the disused colliery. This apparently was nothing unusual. People were often over that way, shooting at rabbits or birds, so Smith took no further action at the time.

It was the evidence of Leonard Drake which enabled the time of the attack to be placed squarely between 2.30pm and 2.55pm. Drake walked down Topcliffe Pit Lane a number of times on September 21st. The first was between 1.30pm and 2.00pm, the second at 2.30pm, and on neither occasion did Drake see anything unusual. When he walked down for a third time, though, at 2.55pm, he saw a pool of blood on the edge of the road and a pair of spectacles lying in that pool. Drake picked up the glasses and walking a little further, saw two handkerchiefs and a box of matches. Feeling uneasy, Drake put the glasses down by the handkerchiefs and walked on to Mr Brook's shop in Thorpe Lane. On the way back home, Drake met Derek Brown and Stanley Beman, the two youths who had been with Harry Philpott, and together all three called the police before returning to Topcliffe Pit Lane.

Horace Wood was a corporal in the Pioneer Corps and one of the three guards, along with Sabin and Corporal Morris, stationed at Tingley Hall. He told the court that he had been at the hostel for five months. Sabin had arrived one week later and they had been quite friendly ever since, often going out for drinks together.

A few weeks after Sabin had arrived at Tingley Hall, Wood had been checking the blankets when he found a revolver, similar to the one now produced in court. Sabin had told Wood that this weapon belonged to him. It was loaded at the time and Wood ordered Sabin to make sure it was unloaded in future. About a month after this incident, Sabin told him that his father had just bought a new car and as a result had given him the old one. This was an old American type and was still at his uncle's farm near Birmingham.

At the end of August, Wood had been in the headquarters room when Sabin made a telephone call and told Wood that he had asked a friend to bring the car up to him and expected him on the Sunday night. Although Sabin waited for it to arrive, it never did. Next morning, Sabin told Wood that his friend who had been bringing the car had picked up two young ladies at the White Bear but had been involved in an accident. An old lady had been killed and the car was now in Timms' garage which was under the arches at the back of the Queen's Hotel.

One day in mid-September, Sabin returned to the hostel driving a Morris Eight which he said had been lent to him by Mr Timms since his own car was still not quite ready. About a week later, on September 20th, Sabin had asked Wood if he could have permission to collect his own car the following day. Wood agreed and on September 21st, Sabin left the hostel at 12.25pm, saying that he would not be long.

At 1.15pm, Sabin telephoned the hostel to tell Wood that he had the car and would be back soon. He finally arrived at some time after 2.30pm, driving a Ford V8 which skidded into some bushes as Sabin drove it into the camp. Wood and Morris helped Sabin get the car out, after which Wood went for a haircut. He returned to the hostel and he, Sabin and Morris all went back out to look at the car. At the time, Morris remarked that there was blood on the right side of Sabin's trousers and that he appeared to be limping. Sabin claimed that another car had knocked him as he was getting into the Ford, but when Wood offered to take a look at the injury, Sabin declined.

Continuing his inspection of the car, Wood noticed some items on the back seat, including a grey trilby hat, a coat and a briefcase. Sabin claimed that the hat and coat were his but the briefcase belonged to someone who had driven the car to the garage and he would return it later. Soon afterwards, Sabin produced £20 which he asked Wood to count and left behind with the corporal for safekeeping while he changed his trousers, throwing the bloodstained ones on to his bed. When the police arrived at the hostel, Wood still held £17 of that cash for Sabin, which he handed over to the police.

Ronald Alfred Morris was a lance-corporal and the other guard at the hostel. He confirmed much of the evidence given by Corporal Wood but said he had also noticed some blood on the running board of the car on the driver's side. When Morris pointed this out to Sabin, he claimed that it was his and must have come from his leg injury. Later still, Sabin had taken the car to a garage for a quote on fixing the radiator, and had returned to say it would take half an hour. That night, Wood had gone out and Sabin had arranged to pick him up from Leeds. Soon after 10.40pm, Sabin had driven out of the hostel, saying he was going to pick Wood up but returned alone at 12.20am to announce that he had been unable to do so as the car had 'gone wrong' and he had been forced to leave it at a garage for repair.

John Booth was employed at the Tingley Crossroads garage, an establishment owned by Messrs F. & H. Tinker. He testified that at 3.30pm on September 21st, he had attended to a Ford V8 saloon car whose radiator had been pierced by a fan. Booth told Sabin the car would take about half an hour and at that, the customer asked him to get the vehicle ready for a journey as he intended to go to Cardiff on holiday. After the repair was complete, Booth put five and a half gallons of petrol in the tank and took ration coupons for seven units, noticing that they were somewhat unusual in that they carried no numbers. Booth also stated that as he was working on the car, he noticed bloodstains on the driver's seat and also on the floor of the vehicle.

John Allen Atkinson was standing near a tailor's shop in Church Lane, Pudsey, at 11.45pm on September 21st when a blue saloon car, coming from the direction of Leeds, stopped about ten yards from where he was. The driver, a soldier, climbed out and asked Atkinson if he knew of a garage in the area. Atkinson gave the man directions and watched him walk off. Only a minute or so later, Sergeant

Metcalfe appeared and asked him about the soldier. Atkinson was unable to give much of a description.

The next sighting of Sabin that night was by Lawrence Hutson, a taxi proprietor, who picked Sabin up in Greenside, Pudsey, at 12.15am. Sabin asked to be taken to the White Bear at Tingley cross roads and on the journey, mentioned that he was a guard at the prisoner-of-war camp.

It was not only the British soldiers at Tingley camp who gave evidence against Albert Sabin. Some of the prisoners, too, had seen things which helped the prosecution case. Four prisoners gave evidence through an interpreter, Alfred Loehner.

Karl Heinz Muhl had seen Sabin with a revolver which looked like the one used to kill Dr Macleod. Muhl had also helped to push the Ford V8 out of the hedge on September 21st and he had previously heard Sabin boast that he owned an American car. Muhl saw blood not only on Sabin's trousers but also on the driver's seat of the car as he pushed it backwards. Later, it was Muhl who helped Sabin inspect the car engine and commented that the radiator hose was broken and in need of repair. Shortly afterwards, in the hostel office, Muhl saw Sabin draw a bloodstained handkerchief from his pocket and throw it on to the fire. He asked Muhl to wash the bloodstained trousers but the PoW had simply put them into a basin to soak.

After taking the car out to have the radiator hose repaired, Sabin returned to the hostel and Muhl saw him remove the briefcase and other items from the back seat and hide them underneath some blankets in a cupboard. The prisoners at the camp were allowed into town, provided they had permission, of course, and when Karl Muhl asked Sabin if he could go out, Sabin agreed but added, "If anyone asks you about a motor car, say you haven't seen anything."

Heinz Wagner, another prisoner, had seen the revolver several times. He was also called over to help push the car out of the bushes at Tingley Hall and not only saw the bloodstains, but also found a bullet at the back of the running board. Wagner handed this over to a fellow prisoner, Kurt Gockert. At 9.00pm that evening, as Wagner passed the washhouse, he saw Sabin scrubbing the trousers which had been left soaking in a basin.

Kurt Gockert gave evidence that after receiving the bullet from Wagner, he had handed it to Corporal Wood who put it on a shelf. This had later been found by Ronald Morris who threw it on to the fire in the office. Finally, Ewald Schalm testified that on September 25th he had found 27 petrol coupons hidden behind a fire bucket in the yard at Tingley Hall. These were handed to the camp leader and, in Schalm's presence, he later handed these over to the police.

Those petrol coupons were now referred to by Irene Pickles, a typist at the offices of the Ministry of Fuel and Power in Leeds. On May 31st, 1946, she had issued a number of petrol coupons to Dr Macleod and she identified the coupons exchanged at the garage and those found by Schalm as part of that batch. Another link was provided by Kathleen Townsend, Dr Macleod's secretary, who identified the items found hidden in the cupboard at the hostel as belonging to her employer.

Two of the prisoners–of–war had referred to a spent bullet which was subsequently thrown on to the fire by Ronald Morris. Detective Inspector George William Towell told the court that during the early hours of September 22nd, he had recovered some ashes from the fire grate at the camp and subsequently found a bullet which had been examined by Dr James Brierley Firth of the North Western Forensic Science Laboratory.

Chief Inspector George Joseph Woolcoot referred to searching the grounds of Tingley Hall and finding, near a tool shed, a glucose tin in which were 62 live rounds of .38 ammunition, a bandage and four white handkerchiefs, three of which were marked 'Macleod'. He had also tried to trace any garage in the district which was named Timms but had failed to do so.

Dr Peter Linsay Sutherland had examined the body of Dr Macleod at the scene of the crime. He testified that upon his initial viewing he had noted that the front left loop of the doctor's braces were unfastened. The dead man's shirt was extensively torn and stained with dirt which would be explained by Sabin's admission that he had dragged the body to the spot where it was found. Dr Sutherland later conducted a post-mortem at the mortuary in Morley. He noted a bullet wound on the left tip of the nose. There were also wounds in the neck and the chest, but it had been the head wound which had proved fatal. The cause of death was given as haemorrhage and laceration of the brain, coupled with an injury to the left lung, caused by the bullets. Dr Sutherland also stated that there had been some seminal emission and that this was common in cases of sudden death but under cross examination he agreed that this could have taken place prior to death.

Dr Firth had also examined the dead man's wounds and he was able to say that in some cases the gun had been held more than six inches from Dr Macleod but that there were powder marks on the entry wound in the neck. This was the bullet which had passed up into Macleod's brain and, according to Dr Firth, this had been fired from about three inches. Further, at least one shot had been fired while Macleod was sitting in a normal position in the driver's seat of his car. Finally, Dr Firth had compared a bullet removed from the body with the one found in the ashes at Tingley Hall and confirmed that both had been fired from the same gun, a .38 Smith and Wesson double action revolver.

In his original statement, Sabin had claimed that he had gone to see Dr Macleod with the express idea of taking money from him. However, in a second statement and now again in court, Sabin told a somewhat different version of the events of September 21st.

Sabin now claimed that he had met Dr Macleod once before when he had given him a lift back to camp. Walking back towards the camp from Leeds, a car had pulled up in front of him and the doctor had asked Sabin where he was heading and offered to take him. On the way, Dr Macleod had tried to interfere with him and Sabin had expressed his displeasure, even knocking the car out of gear so that it would have to stop. He had climbed out of the car and started walking. Dr Macleod had apologised and offered to drive him to camp again but Sabin had refused.

On the day in question, Sabin had been drinking in the Town Hall Tavern in Leeds and was on his way to the Fisherman's Hut pub when he had been called over to the car by Dr Macleod. At first, Sabin had not recognised the doctor who asked him where he was going. Macleod said he was going in the same direction and again offered Sabin a lift. In due course, Sabin saw that Macleod was not heading for the Fisherman's Hut and thought he was taking him back to camp instead, until Macleod pulled into the area around Topcliffe Colliery where again sexual advances were made. Sabin had got out of the car, whereupon Macleod apologised and pulled him back into the vehicle. Sabin rolled over the footboards to get out again and lay on the ground as Dr Macleod came around the car, stood over him and told him to get up. No sooner had Sabin climbed to his feet than Macleod knocked him down again. A fight started and Macleod told Sabin to take off his tunic. As he did, the gun fell out and both men tried to grab it. Sabin seized the gun by the butt but Macleod had hold of the barrel and the weapon had gone off accidentally. Dr Macleod had been hit and it was now that Sabin dragged him to the ditch. He claimed that he did not remember firing again or taking the doctor's money and petrol coupons. As for the statements he made to the police, Sabin said he had no recollection of making them.

It was at best a weak story which did not agree with the findings of Dr Firth, and the jury had little trouble in finding Sabin guilty as charged. A subsequent appeal was heard on January 14th, when the defence claimed that if Sabin had been molested as he claimed, then the charge should have been reduced to manslaughter. Mr Paley Scott also wished to introduce new evidence that Dr Macleod had once admitted to having homosexual tendencies during a conversation in an officers' mess.

Giving the court's judgement, Lord Goddard, the Lord Chief Justice, stated that even if Dr Macleod had made advances, it would have no bearing on the case. Before the shooting, Sabin had bragged about having an American car and had gone out that day with a loaded gun and subsequently returned with just such a car. Lord Goddard added, "It was murder with the most sordid of all motives — robbery." The appeal was dismissed.

Still the drama in this case was not over. On the night before his execution, Sabin made a full confession to the murder of Dr Macleod in which he said that two other men were present and involved. As a result of this, and other information given by the condemned man, police officers visited the Robin Hood Hotel on Vicar Lane, Leeds, where they interviewed the landlord, Mr A. Holburn, his wife and a waiter.

There was no suggestion that any of those people had been incriminated by Sabin, but he had suggested that they might be able to assist the police trace the two men he had mentioned. In the event, they were unable to help and this line of inquiry came to an end.

On the morning of Thursday, January 30th, 1947, Albert Sabin was hanged at Leeds prison by Steve Wade, assisted by Harry Kirk. It was already the second execution of 1947, a year that saw a total of 12 men lose their lives on the gallows of English prisons.

CHAPTER NINETEEN

BEHIND CLOSED DOORS

I T IS said that behind every closed door there are secrets to be told and few of us really know what our neighbours might get up to. That could certainly be said about the household of Eric Charles Briggs.

It was 4.45am on the morning of Monday, February 10th, 1947, when Detective Superintendent James Craig and Detective Sergeant Staines knocked on the front door of 93 Caledonian Road, Leeds. A voice from inside asked who was there, the detectives identified themselves and asked if this was Mr Briggs. He confirmed that he was, but asked the officers to go around to the back of the house as he had lost the key to the front door and was unable to unlock it. A few moments later Craig and Staines were inside number 93 and talking to 40-year-old Eric Briggs, who at this early hour was still in his pyjamas. The officers noticed that Briggs' hands were heavily bloodstained.

Superintendent Craig asked Briggs if he knew the whereabouts of his wife. Briggs replied, "She'll still be at work I suppose." Briggs was asked where Mrs Briggs worked, what were her hours and what time would she normally be expected to return home. Briggs said that she worked as a plate washer at the Queen's Hotel, usually went to work at around 6.00pm and should have been home at some time between 1.00am and 2.00am. Briggs was asked where he had been the previous night and said that he had been at home. He had listened to the wireless until 10.30pm, after which he had gone to bed and had fallen asleep immediately. That was the last thing he could remember until the police had knocked him up. Only now did Superintendent Craig tell Briggs that his wife had been found dead and that he would be taken to the police station to answer further questions.

Eric Briggs' wife, Gertrude, had not been a happy woman. This had been her second marriage and she had brought her 12-year-old daughter Irene to the union. Irene had kept her father's name, Dugdale. Since the wedding, another daughter, Barbara, had been born but in addition, Irene had herself produced no fewer than four children, one of whom had died. So it was that Eric and Gertrude shared their home with two daughters and three grandchildren. In due course, however Gertrude Briggs had discovered that the man who had fathered Irene's four children, was none other than her own husband, Eric.

When questioned at the police station, Eric Briggs confessed that for some years he had been having sex with his stepdaughter Irene. He now claimed that they had gone to bed together at around 11.30pm on February 9th and had made love. Irene was menstruating at the time and the blood on his hands had come from his intimate fondling of her during the act. When the police questioned her, Irene Dugdale admitted that she had had sex with her stepfather that night and that she was having her period at the time, but she denied that he had touched her 'down there' with his hands. Faced with this, Briggs changed his story and admitted that he was indeed responsible for his wife's death.

After they had finished making love, Irene had returned to her own room and he had lain awake, thinking about the recent arguments he had had with Gertrude over his relationship with her daughter. When he heard a clock strike midnight, Briggs got up, dressed and went to Irene's bedroom door, telling her that he was going outside to the lavatory. Irene must have been asleep, for there was no reply. Briggs went out into the yard, but instead of going to the toilet he walked out of the yard door, along into Caledonian Street, down Willow Terrace Road, eventually arriving at Fenton Street where he hid himself in the doorway of Stroud's Garage. He knew that Gertrude would come home this way. All he had to do now, was wait.

It was not long before he saw his wife coming up Calverley Street and as she drew nearer to him, he whistled and called out, "Gertie." She was surprised to see him and asked, "What the hell are you doing?" Briggs did not answer her and she said something about him and Irene. Briggs could not recall exactly what Gertrude said, but it was something that upset him. His wife, though, was still not satisfied. She told Briggs that she had finished with him and was going on the streets to earn her living. He recalled saying something like, "Don't be a damned fool, come here." And he remembered grabbing Gertrude to pull her towards him. She said, "Don't, it is sticking in my neck. You are hurting me." At that everything seemed to go black and he noticed something sticky on his hands. Without waiting to see what he had done, he ran home, arriving there at about 12.40am. He went up to bed where he remained until the police arrived. On the strength of that statement, Briggs was charged with the murder of his wife.

Unfortunately for the police, what should have been an open-and-shut case was complicated by two factors. In the first place, Briggs claimed that his statement had been obtained under duress and he now wished to withdraw it; secondly, another man now confessed to killing Gertrude Briggs.

Dennis Wood was a 19-year-old private in the General Service Corps and lived at 25 Raynville Crescent, Wyther Park, Armley. Wood was serving at Lichfield in Staffordshire and on January 4th, he had assaulted Bridget Mary Theresa Russell. She had been returning home late at night when she heard footsteps behind her. Suddenly someone struck her in the back and then, as she turned around, hit her in the face several times. All Miss Russell could see was that her assailant had worn Army boots and a khaki overcoat. Her semi-conscious form was found an hour or so later and Bridget Russell was rushed to the Victoria Hospital, suffering from 21 stab wounds.

On February 8th, Wood was on leave in Leeds. In fact he spent that night in Hunslet where, at around 8.15pm, he met Elizabeth Donoghue in a public house in Camp Road. They left together at about 9.45pm when Wood said he would walk her home. As they reached Powell Street, he drew his bayonet and attacked Elizabeth.

Four days after this second attack, Dennis Wood, who had gone AWOL, gave himself up to Constable Stubbings who was on duty in Arundel Street, Sheffield. Wood readily admitted the attacks on Bridget Russell and Elizabeth Donoghue and said that he had also attacked a third woman, whose description and circumstances implied that this victim was Gertrude Briggs. After listening to Wood's detailed confession the police came to the conclusion that he was lying about a third attack. The weapon he had used in the other two cases, his bayonet, was the same one he claimed to have used to kill Gertrude Briggs but medical opinion was that the wounds could not have been inflicted by such a weapon. A bayonet would tend to leave rounded wounds, but Gertrude's were longer and thinner. It was also held that Wood had taken much of the detail in his confession from newspaper reports at the time, but this left two unanswered questions. Wood had described in detail what his 'third victim' was wearing. Such details had not been published but more important, there was Wood's description of Mrs Briggs' gait. Gertrude was bow-legged and very self-conscious of the fact. Again this was not mentioned in the newspapers, but Wood had said that his Leeds victim had a strange walk.

Despite these distractions, the police still felt that Briggs was the man who had killed Gertrude and proceeded accordingly. The magistrates agreed with their conclusions and Briggs was duly sent for trial at the assizes. The trial opened on May 8th, 1947, before Mr

Justice Pritchard and a jury of ten men and two women. The case for the Crown was led by Mr G.H.B. Streatfeild, assisted by Mr Norman Black, while Briggs was defended by Mr H.B.H. Hylton Foster and Mr A.M. Hurwitz. The proceedings lasted until May 13th.

One of the most important prosecution witnesses was John Christopher O'Connor. On February 24th, O'Connor had been serving a sentence of three months imprisonment for maintenance arrears. He, like Briggs, was held in Armley jail and during his stay there, he had got to know Briggs who told O'Connor that he was in prison for murdering his wife. Some time later, Briggs had confessed to O'Connor that he had committed the crime between Sunday night and Monday morning and had based his murder on a film he had seen. Briggs went on to say that he and Gertrude had argued on the Friday night, over the fact that he had been having sex with Irene. Finally, Briggs admitted that the weapon he had used was a hacksaw blade with a pointed end and told O'Connor that he had disposed of this weapon later.

Twenty-five-year-old Irene Dugdale admitted to the court that Briggs was the father of her three children and that she had given birth to a fourth which had died soon afterwards. She told the court that her mother had first met Briggs in 1932 and that Gertrude had known for some time about the relationship between her and her stepfather.

On February 9th, said Irene, Gertrude had left home at her usual time of 6.00pm. Later that night, she had sex with her stepfather, going to her own bed afterwards. By this time it was about 11.30pm and she had slept soundly until the police began hammering on the front door. Irene also explained that Briggs had been suffering from what appeared to be fits for some time and that during these attacks he would be unaware of what he was doing. On one occasion he had run down the street shouting, "Gertie, I want Gertie..." but had known nothing of this afterwards. He had also been involved in a car accident in January 1942 and ever since then had suffered from headaches. The fits had become more frequent and once he had tried to chase everyone out of the house.

Details were given of the movements of Gertrude Briggs on the night she met her death. Alfred Lewis also worked at the Queen's Hotel and he arrived for work at some time between 6.30pm and 6.45pm on February 9th. Although Gertrude was supposed to work until 1.00am, she left just after 12.15am. Alfred apparently ran a system whereby he covered for Gertrude, and some of her fellow workers, by clocking them off when he left. That was why Gertrude's card showed that she had left at 1.20am.

James Patrick Sweeney was a porter on the London, Midland & Scottish Railway and at 12.30am on February 10th, he was on his way home. Walking up Fenton Street, Sweeney heard some laboured breathing close to the junction of Fenton Street and Calverley Street. Looking around he saw a woman, half lying against the wall of a house. Realising that she was injured, Sweeney went to look for a policeman but before he had gone far, he encountered the next witness, Francis Miller. Sweeney and Miller returned to where the woman lay and having felt for a pulse, Miller ran to fetch the police.

Francis Miller agreed that it was about 12.35am when James Sweeney saw him in Woodhouse Lane and told him that a woman was lying hurt in Fenton Street. He went to Fenton Street with Sweeney and having seen that there was indeed someone needing urgent help, Miller dashed to a nearby telephone kiosk and rang the police.

Albert Edward Waters lived at 88 Fenton Street and was still in his front room at 12.30am on February 10th. Waters heard a cry at about that time, but looking out of his window, saw nothing to arouse his suspicions. Five or ten minutes later he looked out again and saw two men standing near his front wall. Going out to investigate, he saw Sweeney and Miller and the body of a woman lying against the wall between his house and the one next door.

Sergeant Ernest Cook Phillips was the first policeman on the scene. He arrived at 12.45am and saw Gertrude lying face down, her head against the wall between 88 and 86 and her legs pointing towards Woodhouse Lane. Her face was covered in blood and a pool of blood surrounded her head. Sergeant Phillips sent for the trolley to take Gertrude to the Infirmary which was only about 200 yards away from the spot.

Dr Yvonne Dales was on duty in the casualty department at Leeds General Infirmary and stated that Gertrude had been admitted at 1.15am. By that time she was already dead and Dr Dales put the time of death at 15 to 30 minutes earlier.

The post-mortem was carried out by Dr Peter Lindsay Sutherland and Dr Sinton. Dr Sutherland found no fewer than 41 small stab wounds in the front of Gertrude's neck and a further six at the side. Most of these wounds were superficial but a few at the front of the throat were deeper and had cut into the underlying tissues. The instrument used must have been long and narrow, with at least one cutting edge. The cause of death was shock and haemorrhage from those multiple stab wounds.

In addition to helping at the post-mortem, Dr Alastair Stuart Ritchie Sinton had also examined Briggs at the police station. Both of Briggs' hands appeared to have deposits of some material that seemed to be dried blood. These deposits were confined to the cuticles and Briggs had told him that he had no idea how it got there.

Dr Lewis Charles Nickolls of the North Eastern Science Laboratory at Wakefield had examined scrapings taken from beneath Briggs' fingernails and these had tested positive for human blood. Dr Nickolls had also examined a number of articles of clothing handed to him by the police. A mackintosh showed no obvious evidence of bloodstaining but there was a slight reaction for blood on both sleeves and on the lower part of the front and back. The front flap of a shirt had been extensively smeared with human blood and there were visible bloodstains on an overcoat. All of these items had been removed from Briggs' house.

Superintendent Craig told the court how Briggs had made a very telling statement when he had first seen him at Caledonian Road. Asked where his wife worked, Briggs had replied, "She worked at the Queen's Hotel." The use of the past tense was held to be highly significant.

It was unavoidable that Dennis Wood's name would come up in the trial of Eric Briggs. Detective Chief Inspector Thomas Bowman had been involved in the investigations of both Briggs and Wood and was ideally placed to give evidence.

Bowman outlined how initially, at the police station, Briggs had claimed he had picked up the blood on his hands from Irene. At that time he had also claimed that this had been the first time he and his stepdaughter had had sexual relations. It was not until he was faced with Irene's denial, that Briggs began to change his story.

Turning to the case against Wood, Chief Inspector Bowman determined that Wood had indeed been in Leeds at the time of the attack upon Gertrude Briggs. He had not left Leeds until 8.00am when he travelled to Pontefract. Referring to Wood's alleged confession, that statement said that Wood was near the Town Hall when he saw a woman walking on the right-hand side of the street. She passed a watchman's fire and he followed her, caught up with her and gripped her by the throat. The next thing he recalled was rushing past the Infirmary, his bayonet in his hand, dripping with blood.

According to Chief Inspector Bowman, most of Wood's evidence could be obtained from reports in various newspapers. Copies of the *Yorkshire Post* of February 11th and 12th, the *Yorkshire Evening Post* of February 10th, 11th and 12th and the *Yorkshire Evening News* of the same three dates gave much of this information. However, the chief inspector had to admit that none of these articles contained any reference to Gertrude being bow-legged, which Wood's statement did.

When Briggs went into the witness box to give evidence on his own behalf, he referred again to his accident in 1942 when he was knocked down by a car. He also related how on February 7th, he had gone to the Gaumont cinema with Irene where they had seen a film entitled *So Dark the Night*. In this, a French detective commits several murders without knowing that he has done so. Briggs was claiming that he had no knowledge of his wife's murder and if he was the man who had taken her life, it had been done in some sort of trance. As for his confession, this had been browbeaten out of him by the police.

In his summing up, the judge said that the jury were not trying Dennis Wood and they should consider seven questions in arriving at their verdict. Those questions were: First, what was the proper inference to be drawn from the conversation between Briggs and the police at Caledonian Road? Second, what inference could be drawn from the conversation at the police station? The third and fourth questions were what inference could be drawn from his verbal confession and his written one, again at the police station? Fifth, what could be determined from Briggs' conversation with his fellow convict O'Connor? Sixth, what was the significance of the blood on Briggs' overcoat and shirt? And finally, what could be taken from the story of Dennis Wood?

The jury retired at 3.30pm and eventually decided that Briggs was guilty as charged, whereupon he was sentenced to death by Mr Justice Pritchard. The following day, in the same courtroom, Dennis Wood was found guilty but insane of two attempted murders and was sentenced to be detained during His Majesty's pleasure.

Briggs' appeal was heard on June 4th. His defence referred again to the confession of Dennis Wood and Mr Hylton-Foster argued that, faced with the whole of the evidence, no reasonable jury could possibly convict either man as it was impossible to say with absolute certainty whether it was Briggs or Wood who had killed Gertrude Briggs. Giving the court's decision, Mr Justice Humphreys said that the statement Briggs had made to the police could not have been made by anyone apart from the murderer or an eye-witness. The appeal was dismissed.

At 9.00am on Friday, June 20th, 1947, Eric Charles Briggs was hanged at Leeds by Stephen Wade who was assisted by Harry Kirk. Only half a dozen people gathered outside the prison gates to read the notice of execution. It was the first execution attended by the prison governor, Captain S.C. Tunnicliffe, who had been appointed the previous month.

CHAPTER TWENTY

GANGSTERS

AT 10.15am on Wednesday, November 16th, 1949, Rhoda Silverman stepped inside an open doorway next to a bookshop, which led to the offices of Mr Saffman, her solicitor, in Albion Street, Leeds.

She was only a few feet into the doorway when she heard someone groaning and took a step backwards, just in time to see a man run across the road. Then, to Rhoda Silverman's horror, the man aimed a gun in her direction and fired a shot. She fled up the stairs to the sanctuary of her solicitor's office.

Miss Rene Ball worked in the office of the Tyne Solder Company on the second floor of the same building. At 10.15am she heard what she thought might be a car backfiring — but when she looked out of the window she saw a man run across the road and fire a revolver towards her side of the street. The man then turned and ran off up Albion Street towards the Marsden Monument. Along the way he was joined by a second man who also seemed to be carrying a gun. In the meantime, Rhoda Silverman had gone back outside and saw the two men running away at the top end of the street. Then, looking down, she saw that a bullet had indeed been fired at her. Mr Saffman's glass nameplate had been shattered and the pieces lay on the pavement at her feet.

There were a lot of people in the streets of Leeds at the time and many of them saw the two men running away from the scene of the shooting. Robert Smith was using one of the public telephone boxes outside the City of Leeds School and was looking down Albion Street when he heard two reports. He saw two young men running towards him and to his horror saw that both were carrying guns. He watched intently as the men ran past.

John Edward Millward was a clerk of works in the City Engineer's Department at Leeds and at 10.15am, or thereabouts, was walking across the car park at Merrion Street with a colleague. As they approached a footpath in Woodhouse Lane, they heard two shots. Looking in the direction from which the noise had come, Millward saw two men running across the top of Great George Street from the direction of the monument. Millward watched as the men passed the telephone kiosks where Robert Smith was making his call. Just after they had done so, the taller man passed a brightly plated gun to the smaller one, but Millward could see that he still had a dark coloured weapon in his other hand.

Millward had to dodge between the traffic, which slowed him down somewhat, but eventually he managed to get across the road and gave chase down Rossington Street, into Percival Street and on into Vernon Street. But as he turned into this last thoroughfare, another shot rang out and, realising that the men were warning him off, Millward held back as they ran into the main entrance of the Albert Hall.

Fred Bough was driving along Albion Street some time before 10.30am and as he passed the jeweller's at number 132 he saw a small knot of people gathered around a man who appeared to be bleeding from a wound in his face. Looking up the street, Bough saw two men running up Woodhouse Lane and decided to give chase. He saw the men disappear down Rossington Street but was unable to follow in his car so instead he drove around to the bottom of Vernon Street where he stopped the vehicle. As he stepped towards them, one of the men fired a shot in his direction. Bough took shelter behind his car and from this position of relative safety he saw them run into Cookridge Street and up the steps into the Albert Hall.

Another of those who had given chase was Charles Metcalfe. He was in Woodhouse Lane when he heard two bangs and saw two young men running past the pillar box at the top of Great George Street. Although Metcalfe saw that the men were armed, he ran after them along Rossington Street, into Percival Street and on into Vernon Street where another shot was fired. Metclafe, too, saw them enter the Albert Hall, but he had the foresight to go round to the back of the hall where, a couple of minutes later, he saw the pair drop down from a wall and land in Percival Street. The two were walking at a normal pace now and Metcalfe saw them stride into Portland Crescent, where he lost them.

One of the first police officers on the scene was Constable Lewis Armitage who went by car to the jeweller's at 132 Albion Street where he found the proprietor, Mr Abraham Harry Levine, collapsed on the floor at the customer's side of his small shop. Mr Levine had obviously been beaten and had a jagged wound over the bridge of his nose, a second over his left temple and was bleeding profusely. The most serious injury by far, however, was a bullet wound to his stomach.

Mr Levine was rushed to Leeds General Infirmary where, after being x-rayed, he was admitted to ward 22 and Dr Robert Aikman Hall, the surgical tutor at the Leeds School of Medicine, operated to remove a bullet from the wounded man's abdomen. The path of the bullet could plainly be seen, through the large bowel and two segments of the small bowel, but the bullet itself was too close to the spine for removal so Dr Hall merely repaired the damage to the intestine. The operation ended at 11.30am and Mr Levine was made as comfortable as possible. During the night, however, his condition deteriorated. At 4.00pm on Thursday, November 17th, he died and the Leeds police launched a murder inquiry.

It was not long before the police realised that there was almost certainly a connection between this crime and another which had taken place on the night of November 13th, or possibly during the early hours of November 14th, just a couple of days before the shooting of Abraham Levine. Linsley Brothers was a gunsmith's shop at 97 Albion Street, the same street as Levine's shop, and someone had broken in there and stolen a number of weapons. A stock check revealed that a .38 Colt, a .38 Webley, a .25 Webley & Scott Automatic and a .32 Webley were missing, along with a Webley & Scott air pistol, and a total of 52 rounds of ammunition which included eight rounds of cattle-killer cartridges, the type which had been used to kill Abraham Levine. Those rounds were slightly too long to fit the weapons stolen but whoever had shot the Leeds jeweller had filed off the nose of the bullet so that it could be used.

Descriptions of both men were widely circulated but it was a chance encounter in Lancashire that lead to the arrest of the two suspects. Detective Constable Gill Greenwood was cycling to duty at 8.50am on November 18th and as he passed down Cambridge Road, Southport, he saw two unkempt young men who seemed to be out of place. Constable Greenwood stopped his bicycle, identified himself as a police officer and asked the two what they were doing in the area.

Although they were unable to produce identity cards, they gave their names as Walter Sharpe and Gordon Lannen and said that they had come from Leeds on the previous Wednesday. Throughout this early exchange both men had kept their hands in their pockets and Greenwood, already suspecting that they might be the men his Leeds colleagues were looking for, asked to see what they were hiding. Lannen produced a handkerchief and some cigarettes but Sharpe had a Ronson cigarette lighter which appeared to be brand new. Sharpe explained that he had recently purchased this in Leeds but when asked where they had spent the two previous nights, Sharpe said that they had spent Wednesday in Liverpool and the Thursday in Southport.

Greenwood asked why they had left Leeds, to which Lannen replied that they had not been happy there. Satisfied that there were further questions to be answered, Greenwood told them that there had been two serious offences committed in Leeds recently, a theft of guns from a shop and the shooting of a jeweller a few days later. Since the two could not prove their identities, he was now asking them to accompany him to the police station. The two agreed and at the station both were searched. In the lining of Sharpe's jacket, officers found three rounds of .22 ammunition.

Sharpe and Lannen were questioned in separate rooms and in due course, it was Lannen who said, "Can I tell you something, sir? You know the shooting at Leeds? Well, we did it." Both men made verbal statements, admitting their part in the crime and later Lannen took officers to a point on the foreshore at the north end of the town. This was where he and Sharpe had burned the overcoats they had been wearing, and had thrown their guns into the river nearby. A pile of ashes was evident and the following day, near a bridge over the River Alt, the guns were recovered.

Neither Gordon Lannen nor Walter Sharpe had a previous record of violence. Until August 1949, both had been employed by a company at Roundhay which made surgical appliances. One day the manager had received a complaint that a silver cigarette case had been stolen from the foreman. A search revealed the case in Lannen's possession and for that offence he lost his job and faced a fine of 15s before the juvenile court. A few weeks later, Sharpe had also been dismissed but in his case it was for insubordination.

Gordon Lannen had been born at Worsborough, near Barnsley, on August 14th, 1932, which made him just 17 at the time of the shooting of Abraham Levine. Sharpe had been born in Holbeck on February 4th, 1930, making him 19 years old. The two had first met at the Middleton Council School after Lannen had moved to that location at the age of six, and was now living at Throstle Road, Middleton. Almost from the beginning, Sharpe had been a troublesome child, lacking the authority of a father since Mr Sharpe had died in 1943, from jaundice and malaria while serving in the Army in Italy. Walter was 13 at the time.

On November 18th, the same day that Sharpe and Lannen had been stopped by a vigilant Southport detective, Detective Inspector Harold Sydney Booth of the Leeds force received a telephone call from officers in Lancashire saying that they were holding two men who had admitted they were responsible for the shooting of Abraham Levine. Inspector Booth, together with Detective Inspector Andrew Leslie Renton, travelled to Southport to collect Sharpe and Lannen.

On the way back to Leeds, just as the car was passing through Clitheroe, Sharpe exclaimed, "Can I tell you about it, sir?" At this, Lannen also spoke, saying, "I would like to tell you as well." Inspector Booth ordered that the car be stopped and cautioned both men again. He explained that he would be more than happy to take statements there and then, or alternatively they could wait until they reached Leeds. Sharpe and Lannen both chose to wait and the car continued on its journey, finally arriving at Leeds police station at 7.35pm where both prisoners made written statements after which they were charged with murder.

The trial of Sharpe and Lannen opened at Leeds on March 9th, 1950, before Mr Justice Streatfeild. The case for the Crown was led by Mr Godfrey Russell Vick, assisted by Mr Carl Aarvold. Sharpe was defended by Mr G.R. Hinchcliffe while Lannen was represented by Mr Henry C. Scott. From the outset there was drama in the courtroom. Sharpe pleaded not guilty but to everyone's surprise and against the advice of his barrister, Lannen pleaded guilty. After some discussion with Mr Scott, the judge directed that a plea of not guilty be entered and the trial proper got under way.

Robert Smith and John Millward had both picked out Lannen from an identity parade, although neither had managed to identify Sharpe as the other man. Confirmation was given that two shots had been fired from the opposite side of Albion Street, both by Sharpe. One had shattered the solicitor's sign while the other had passed through a shop window. By Sharpe's own admission, these had been fired to warn people off as Lannen was still struggling with Mr Levine at the entrance to his shop.

Evidence was given first about the robbery from Linsley Brothers, the gunsmiths. Mrs Holly Stuart Mackie gave details of the weapons which had been stolen and identified the .38 Colt revolver as one of the missing items. This was confirmed by another of the employees, David Sampson, who also identified this weapon but confirmed that there was no safety catch on the gun and agreed that it might have gone off accidentally during a struggle. At this point the judge took up the gun, pulled the trigger and announced that it was not a particularly heavy pull.

Constable Alexander Caldwell, in response to a message from Constable Greenwood in Southport, had taken Sharpe and Lannen to the station in the police van. Before Greenwood had arrived to continue his questioning of the suspects, Caldwell had searched Lannen and found seven air pistol darts of the same type as those stolen from the gunsmith's shop in Leeds. Lannen said that he had had these for some time but in Constable Caldwell's opinion they looked brand new. Caldwell was present later as Lannen had said, "It's the Leeds murder you're on about. I was on the job but I didn't shoot him. He was shouting and we both hit him to keep him quiet. Then my pal shot him."

Sharpe's statement was also read out in court. In part this read, 'We made it up on Tuesday night to go round to Shapiro's shop in North Street the following morning. About ten o'clock we went to his shop. We didn't go in so we went round to Levine's shop in Albion Street.

'We took our revolvers out and Levine came round the corner and grabbed hold of Gordon. Gordon started hitting him with his gun butt. I grabbed hold of both and tried to push them round the counter. My revolver went off.'

Sharpe's statement continued by saying that he had gone outside the shop but turned around to see Levine still holding on to Lannen. Some people were moving towards the scene, apparently to offer assistance, so Sharpe fired a couple of shots, one to each side, so that they would back off and he and Lannen could make good their escape.

They had been chased for some distance but after they had finally shaken off their pursuers, they decided that they should get out of the city and the two friends now caught a bus to Liverpool where they stayed that night. The next day they caught a train to Southport where they were forced to sleep in a hut after disposing of the guns in the river. They had also burned their overcoats in case the police had a description of the clothes they had been wearing.

Other witnesses filled in some of the gaps in the narrative. John Naylor was a caretaker's assistant at the Albert Hall in Leeds and on November 24th, he had been guiding a delivery truck through the gates of the yard at the back when he found a cartridge case near the foot of the gate post.

Charles Sidebottom was another assistant caretaker and he found another cartridge case when he was shovelling coal at the Albert Hall on November 28th. Fourteen-year-old Walter Scarth had found three empty cartridge cases on a football pitch off Foundry Lane. Later he had handed these to his father, also named Walter, who had passed them on to the police.

Detective Sergeant John Marsden Barraclough had gone to Sharpe's house at 2 Brookland's Close, Seacroft, at 11.00am on November 18th. During a search of the premises he had found a locked suitcase under Sharpe's bed. When the locks were forced, Barraclough found a Webley & Scott .25 Automatic pistol and 41 rounds of ammunition.

Dr Lewis Charles Nickolls was the director of the North Eastern Forensic Science Laboratory in Bishop Garth, Wakefield. He had examined the various weapons and cartridge cases found and confirmed that the Webley & Scott Automatic had recently been fired, as had the .38 Colt. Two of the cartridges found had come from the Colt while the rest had been fired from the Webley & Scott. The shot that killed Abraham Levine, had been fired from the Colt.

Medical evidence was given by Dr Cyril John Polson who had performed the post-mortem on Mr Levine. He described injuries to the hairline and nose which could have been caused by blows from a gun butt. The bullet responsible for Abraham Levine's death had entered his body between the sixth and seventh ribs, fracturing the latter as it passed. The shot had passed in a downwards direction through the body, passing through the diaphragm down towards the lower end of the left kidney, finally coming to rest against the lower part of the spine. The cause of death was general peritonitis due to multiple perforations of the stomach, the small intestine and the large intestine.

For Lannen, Mr Scott had taken little part in the trial itself and at the close of the trial his speech explained that this was because his client was not disputing the basic facts of the case. However, Mr Scott went on to state that although he was armed with a loaded gun, Lannen had not fired a shot at Mr Levine. He admitted that he had used the gun to hit Levine, but this was only because he panicked when the shopkeeper moved forward and grabbed him.

Gordon Lannen was claiming that he had not fired the fatal bullet and was therefore not guilty of murder while Sharpe was saying that the shooting was accidental and was guilty of manslaughter only. The jury retired to consider their verdict at 12.15pm on March 10th and 20 minutes later, filed back into court to announce that both men were guilty of murder. Walter Sharpe was sentenced to death while Lannen, being only 17, was sentenced to be detained during His Majesty's pleasure.

There was no appeal, Sharpe instead hoping for a reprieve on account of his age. But the Home Office announced that there would be no commutation of the sentence. At 9.00am on Thursday, March 30th, 1950, Walter Sharpe, who had turned 20 less than eight weeks before, was hanged at Leeds by Stephen Wade and Harry Allen. A crowd of 50 people waited at the top of Gloucester Terrace, close by the prison, until the execution was over and were then allowed to the prison gates to read the notice confirming that the execution had been carried out. As they read, some of the women present burst into tears.

CHAPTER TWENTY-ONE

CONFLICTING EVIDENCE

AT 8.24am on July 9th, 1950, a man walking to work across waste land in Springfield Road, Leeds, came upon the body of a young woman. The woman had severe throat injuries and once a police surgeon had pronounced life extinct, the police began an investigation to identify the girl and find her killer.

The officer in charge of the case, Detective Superintendent Thomas Bowman, head of Leeds CID, found the first of those challenges fairly simple. Items found near the body, including a handbag, revealed that the victim was 19-year-old Ruth Massey, a tailoress who lived in Holbeck Lane, close to the spot where she had been found. Interviews with Ruth's friends and her sister-in-law, Miriam Massey, revealed that Ruth had been drinking in the Brougham Arms pub on the night of July 8th. At one stage Ruth, who was out with Miriam and a friend of theirs, fell into conversation with three men who they had never seen before. One thing led to another and just before closing time, Ruth had left the pub with one of those trio.

On the day after Ruth's body was discovered, Superintendent Bowman gave details of the man seen with her and asked members of the public who might have information to come forward and talk to him or his officers. The statement given to local newspapers read, 'The girl left a public house in the centre of the city about 9.50pm.

She was wearing a shabby lime green three-quarter length coat, blue and white spotted cotton dress, blue and white ankle-strap sandals, no headdress and no stockings. The police are anxious to trace any person who saw her after that time.'

In fact, the identity of the man who left the Brougham Arms with Ruth Massey had already been given to the police by other customers at the public house who knew not only Ruth, but also the man with her. This led officers to an address in Greystone Street, off Kirkstall Road, Leeds, where on July 9th they detained a 22-year-old linoleum hawker, Nicholas Persoulious Crosby. Crosby denied having anything to do with Ruth's death saying, "I didn't do it. I was not there." But bloodstains on his clothing, together with positive identifications from Miriam Massey and other witnesses, led to Crosby being charged with her murder on the morning of July 10th.

Crosby first appeared before the magistrates that same afternoon and was remanded to July 18th. Further remands followed and eventually, Crosby was sent for trial. Those proceedings opened at Leeds on November 27th before Mr Justice Finnemore and a jury of nine men and three woman. The Crown's case was led by Mr H.B.H. Hylton-Foster MP, who was assisted by Mr Alastair Sharp, while Crosby's defence lay in the hands of Mr H.R.B. Shepherd and Mr Henry C. Scott. The trial lasted a total of three days.

Witnesses were called who stated that they had seen Crosby talking to Ruth in the Brougham Arms and added that he seemed to be talking to her in a familiar manner considering that this was the first time they had met. Miriam Massey confirmed this and also said that as the couple left the pub together she had stopped Crosby and said, "Think on. Take her straight home."

It was plain that if Crosby was the killer, he had certainly not taken Ruth straight home for it was not until after 11.00pm, that two other witnesses saw a man and a woman together on the waste land where Ruth's body would subsequently be found. Mr Avison worked in Holbeck and it was 11.15pm when he saw a man who resembled Crosby walking across Holbeck Lane away from the scene of the crime. He could not positively identify Crosby as the man but was 'pretty sure' that it was him. The second sighting was made by Mr Naylor, who saw a couple making love close to the murder spot, although Naylor was unable to say if the man was indeed Nicholas Crosby.

It was when two blood relatives of Crosby's gave evidence that conflicting stories were told to the court. Gladys Crosby was the accused's 17-year-old cousin and Danny was his brother. Both lived with Crosby and his family at Greystone Street and they gave completely different accounts of the events of the night of July 8th, 1950.

Gladys claimed that it was nearly 1.00am on the morning of the 9th when her cousin finally arrived home. He looked rough, his hair was untidy and he walked straight past her without speaking and went into the kitchen. This was strange behaviour so Gladys followed Crosby into the kitchen and asked him what was bothering him. He said there was nothing on his mind but Gladys persisted until finally Crosby sat down on the arm of the chair and told Gladys that if anyone asked her about his movements on Saturday night, she was to say that she had seen him near Wakefield bus station and had travelled home with him and Danny.

Naturally, Gladys wanted to know why she had been asked to lie and Crosby explained that he had been with a girl and another man. They had had a few drinks together and both men had decided to walk the girl back to her home. Once they were close to her house, Crosby had walked on, leaving the other man to say goodnight to the girl. He had not gone far when he heard a scream so rushed back to see what had happened. To his horror, Crosby saw the girl lying on the ground with her throat cut and the man standing over her still brandishing a knife.

According to Crosby's account, he took the man home rather than go for help or call the police. Gladys, concerned that the girl involved in this story might be in desperate need of help, offered to return to the scene with Crosby but he claimed that he could not recall exactly where she was. Throughout their conversation, Danny

Crosby had been present in the room and heard everything his brother had said.

Danny, though, told a totally different story. Nicholas Crosby had arrived home not at 1.00am, but at a time much closer to 11.30pm on July 8th and had not even set foot into the kitchen that night. There had been no discussion about the death of a girl, no admission of any involvement and no request to tell lies if anyone asked about his movements.

Unfortunately for Nicholas Crosby's defence team, their client had been caught out in a number of deliberate lies and had constantly changed his story to fit the evidence. One example of this was the story he told regarding his ownership of a knife. When first interviewed, Crosby claimed that he had never had a knife. A friend of his, a Mr Meek, was called and he testified that on July 4th he had been drinking with Crosby in a pub when Crosby had produced a penknife with a two-inch blade and began hacking pieces out of the furniture. Meek asked Crosby what he was doing and he had replied, "It is a good sharp knife." Faced with this, Crosby now admitted that he had bought a small knife at Halifax some three weeks before July 8th but he had lost this about four days before Ruth's death.

Bloodstains had been found on Crosby's shirt and there was also a tear in the material. Crosby claimed that he had been in a fight and after it was over, he noticed that there was a small rip in his shirt and his face was bleeding.

Crosby tore off some of the material, wiped his face and threw it away. However, to counter this, the prosecution called Crosby's aunt who did his laundry for him. She testified that Crosby had given her the shirt to wash on July 1st and it had not been returned to him until July 7th. At that time, there were no stains on the garment and it was in one piece.

The post-mortem carried out on Ruth Massey's body showed that she had a wound slightly less than five inches long in her throat and this had cut through a main artery. In addition to this there was bruising on her face, lips and over her chin caused by the pressure of fingers over her mouth.

Crosby gave evidence on his own behalf. He explained that he had been out drinking with two friends and they had already been in two pubs by the time they got to the Brougham Arms. Three girls were there and although they did not know them, they began talking to them. By this time, Crosby had drunk at least eight pints and consequently he had no recollection of leaving the third pub in Ruth's company. He did not remember any conversation with his cousin Gladys and his next memory was waking up in bed the following morning. Indeed, at one point in his questioning, Mr Shepherd for the defence had asked Crosby if he had killed Ruth, to which Crosby had replied, "To be sure sir I don't know if I did. If I did, I don't remember."

Crosby said that it was true that he had made a statement to the police admitting that he had been with Ruth on the night that she died, but he had been pressurised into that. Inspector Booth had told him, "You will never go home. You will stay here until you die." The inspector had also said that he 'liked a lad to have a little chance', but he had none at all. Booth had continued, "You know we are not fools, you come clean and tell us and we can make it easy for you. We can make it easy or awkward." Inspector Booth denied all of these allegations. At no time had Crosby been threatened or cajoled and no inducements had been made to get him to make a statement.

The summing up by Mr Justice Finnemore took two hours. He covered every point of the evidence, beginning with Crosby's statements to the police. There could be no doubt that Crosby had made those statements in which he claimed that he had been befuddled with drink. The judge pointed out that drunkenness in itself was no answer to a criminal charge but stated that if they came to the conclusion that he was so drunk that he was incapable of forming the intention to kill or to inflict grievous bodily harm, then they must return a verdict of manslaughter. Moving on to the evidence given by Gladys Crosby, Mr Finnemore told the jury that if they accepted that evidence as true then it was very telling indeed, for Crosby gave details of the crime at a time when no one knew Ruth was dead, no one knew that her throat had been cut, and no one knew that she lay on waste land. The only persons who might conceivably have that information were the killer or someone who was there and witnessed the event. Further, if Crosby was a witness rather than the killer, why had he not summoned help.

Faced with this wealth of evidence, the jury returned after 55 minutes with a guilty verdict and Crosby was sentenced to death. A woman in the public gallery sobbed loudly as the words were uttered. Crosby did not appeal, preferring instead to hope for a reprieve, but on December 16th the Home Secretary announced that he had found no grounds to justify him recommending any interference in the sentence.

Under normal circumstances, Crosby would have faced his fate at Leeds prison but that establishment was undergoing structural alterations at the time, so the condemned man was moved to Strangeways jail in Manchester to await the appointed day. On Tuesday, December 19th, Nicholas Persoulious Crosby was hanged there by Albert Pierrepoint who was assisted by Syd Dernley. It was the 17th and last, execution in an English prison in 1950.

CHAPTER TWENTY-TWO

DOUBLE DEALING

ROBERT William Moore did not have the easiest of starts in life. Born in Canada, he and his mother had moved to England when he was just five years old. His father remained in Canada but soon after their arrival in this country, his wife received news that he had been killed in a fire in a block of flats and Mrs Moore was left to bring up her son alone. He was a sickly child who missed a good deal of education and when he finally left school he was still unable to read or write.

In 1944, Robert Moore joined the Army but 11 months later was discharged because of ill health. He married in 1950 and became the proud father of a son the following year. He tried various jobs, none of which lasted very long. Eventually Moore entered into a car-dealing partnership with a man called Thomas William Bramley. By then, it was March 1953.

By all accounts, the new business venture was quite successful and many of the deals that Moore did involved buying and selling from other dealers. One of these was 27-year-old Edward Watson whose address was Ringwood Crescent, Shadwell, Leeds, and it was on April 23rd that Moore purchased from Watson a 1935 Ford 10 for £55. Unfortunately, the deal soon turned sour.

Inspecting the car more closely, Moore discovered that it had a broken chassis, but when he pointed this out to Watson, he found that the dealer was unwilling to take the vehicle back or refund any of the money Moore had paid over. There was nothing else but to have the car repaired, which cost Moore a further £6, bringing his total outlay to £61. Things got even worse for Moore when he tried to sell the car on after it had been repaired. No one was interested and eventually the only person who made an offer was Watson. He ended up buying the Ford back, but for only £52. Robert Moore had lost £9 on the deal and the experience left a bad taste in his mouth.

Moore and Watson next met up at the Leeds Central Auction Mart on May 30th. They fell into conversation and it seemed that no animosity remained between them for they were friendly enough to each other. Indeed, towards the end of the auction, Moore even told Watson about a shooting brake he might be interested in. A man in Harrogate had this for sale and Moore said he would drive Watson out there to look at it. In the event, he ran out of petrol on the way and by the time this was sorted out it was too late to complete the journey so a new appointment was arranged for the following day, Sunday, May 31st, 1953.

Edward Watson did not return home that night and naturally his wife, Anita Watson, grew concerned. She made her own inquiries but when no trace of her husband could be found she took her worries to the police, reporting her husband missing on June 2nd, which, incidentally, was also Coronation Day.

At around 5.00pm, as the rest of the country reflected on events at Westminster Abbey earlier that day, Anita Watson, together with another car dealer, William Metcalfe, visited Moore at his home at Harlow Avenue, Harrogate, and asked him if he had any idea where Edward might be. Mrs Watson knew of the appointment her husband had made with Moore but when questioned on the matter, Moore said that Watson had never turned up for that meeting and consequently he had no idea of the whereabouts of the missing man.

On June 3rd, police officers investigating the disappearance of

Edward Watson found his car parked some 30 yards from Nash's garage, not far from where Robert Moore lived. That same day they also called on Moore whereupon he repeated his story of an appointment which Watson had failed to keep, adding at one stage, "He's done that trick on me before, ★★★★ him, but he won't do it again."

Unfortunately for Moore, the police had turned up some interesting facts on his recent movements. After speaking to William Metcalfe, the man who had accompanied Anita Watson to see Moore on June 2nd, they had discovered that Moore had paid a visit to Metcalfe's garage at 10.20am on May 31st, the day that Watson disappeared. Moore, though, had not wished to discuss cars at that meeting. Instead he had asked Metcalfe about a gun he owned and which he had heard might be for sale. The weapon, a .22 Winchester rifle, had been shown to Moore who had haggled about the price before buying the rifle for £15, together with cartridges, a silencer and a holdall. Yet another dealer, Eric Suffield, was present at those discussions and he had walked with Moore to his car. As Moore put the gun into the back of his vehicle, Suffield noticed a spade there. Suffield and Metcalfe watched as Moore drove off. By then it was around 10.30am.

Armed with this information, the police paid a second visit to Moore's home on June 5th. When asked about the gun by Detective Sergeant Wilby, Moore laughed and asked, "Do you think I have shot him?" He went on to make a detailed written statement, again refer-ring to his missed appointment with Watson, and there, for the time being, matters were allowed to rest. That evening, though, there was a dramatic development when Robert Moore was admitted to hos-pital after attempting to gas himself at a neighbour's house, making the attempt there because he did not have a shilling for his own meter. Moore recovered quickly and when the police interviewed again, he gasped, "I shot him. I have buried him at Fewston."

After being cautioned, Moore was taken to the police station where he made another statement. He said, "It's true. I've buried him in a wood near a reservoir with a wall on each side of the road. I knocked some stones off the top of the wall when I lifted him over, but put them back afterwards. I took £100 odd from his pockets before I buried him."

Asked why he had shot Watson, Moore replied, "He's been a proper ★★★★. He sold me a car which he said was right, but I found a broken chassis on one side and corrosion on the other. He told me it was my ★★★★★★ pigeon. I'd bought it. Then he cribbed it every time I put it in the sale and started it at a low figure."

Having admitted his guilt, Moore took officers to the place where he claimed he had buried the body of Edward Watson. It was difficult to locate the exact spot but finally Moore saw a tree where he had wiped dirt and mud from his spade. There, in a grave 3ft deep, officers found Edward Watson buried face down in a half-kneeling position. He had been shot five times in the upper part of his torso.

Robert Moore made his first appearance in court at Otley on June 6th and was remanded until June 12th. Moore was represented by Mr Ernest Wurzal and after other remands, including one on June 26th, he was sent for trial at Leeds. The case opened on November 23rd before Mr Justice Stable and a jury of ten men and two women. Moore was defended by Mr Rudolph Lyons and Mr E.J. Parris while the case for the prosecution was led by Mr G.R. Hinchcliffe assisted by Mr B. Gillis. The proceedings lasted for three days.

Thomas Bramley told the court of the deal which Moore had done with Watson which resulted in a net loss of £9. He also reported a conversation he had had with Moore after spotting a .22 carbine repeater in the back of his car some time after the beginning of June. Moore had stated that the gun was a, 'nice little shooter'.

Attempts were made to reconstruct Moore's movements on the day that Watson vanished, May 31st. It had already been shown that after buying the rifle from William Metcalfe, Moore had driven off at 10.30am. The next sighting was made by Edward Joseph Engert who knew Moore and saw him filling his car with petrol at a garage on the Knaresborough-Harrogate road at 12.50pm. Engert walked over to Moore and as they were talking, he noticed a spade in the back of Moore's car. The blade was heavily encrusted with soil and Engert asked if he was doing some gardening. Moore had replied, "Yes, I have to keep the weeds down." According to the prosecution, between those two sightings, Moore had met Watson, shot him, robbed him and buried him.

Mrs Darnbrook lived at Croft Farm, Killinghall, near Harrogate, and she was Moore's aunt. She told the court that her nephew had called at her home at 2.05pm on May 31st. Prior to this, on May 23rd, Moore had sold an Austin car for her and had told her he had received £253 10s in cash. This was confirmed by Christopher Lambert of the Central Auction Mart where the car was sold. On May 28th, Mrs Darnbrook had seen Moore and asked him for the money. He had told her that he did not have it with him but would be picking it up on Saturday, May 30th. When he called again, on May 31st, Moore had given her £249 and had stayed with her for a couple of hours. In his statement to the police, Moore had admitted that at least some of this money had come from Watson's pockets.

Mrs Anita Watson, who was now living in St Hilda's Road, Harrogate, told of her meeting with Moore on June 2nd. She had also seen him on June 3rd when she had gone to his house with her uncle, a gentleman named Howe. At one stage, Mr Howe had asked Moore if he had any grievance with the missing man and Moore had said, "Yes I have. Watson sold me a car for £55 and the chassis was broken and he then tried to buy it back for a less (*sic*) figure." Anita also told the court that her husband was carrying about £185 when he left the house on May 31st.

Another of Moore's statements was read out in court. In this he had referred first to the meeting with Watson on May 30th, at the car mart, and had said, "I had full intentions of taking him into the wood and clouting him. He said he had to get back to Leeds, so I arranged to meet him on the Sunday morning. On Sunday we went out around Norwood and Fewston. He was driving, and I was sat in the back.

"I said 'I've seen a pheasant,' and told him to pull up. I got out and shot him. This was at Fewston. I panicked a bit and carried him over the wall into the wood where I dug a trench, put him in and covered him. I shot at him and not at a pheasant. I took £100 odd out of his pocket and hid the gun and spade at my mother's."

It was when Moore stepped into the witness box to tell his own story that a completely new defence was given. To begin with, Moore again referred to the deal with Watson in which he had lost £9. He admitted that this was annoying but it had not affected his friendship with Watson and he had no reason to want him dead. Turning to the day of the shooting, Moore now claimed that it had all been a tragic accident.

On the Saturday, May 30th, he and Watson had driven out to Beckwithshaw and shot at some rabbits with an air rifle which Moore had in his car. Watson had suggested they go out the next day, shooting pheasants, and it had been Watson who told him about Metcalfe having a gun. Watson suggested that Moore should ask to borrow it but if Metcalfe refused, offer to buy it instead and he, Watson, would go 50-50 with him.

On May 31st, the two men met up and drove out towards Fewston. They stopped a few times and took it in turns to take pot shots at pheasants, aiming from the car windows. Watson bagged one and this was placed into the car. Eventually they pulled up in Smithson Lane at Fewston and here it was Moore's turn to take the next shot. Watson moved over to the passenger seat while Moore took aim at a bird through the driver's window. He fired but missed and the bird flew across the front of the car. Without thinking, Moore moved the gun across to take aim again, this time out of the passenger window. However, as he fired, Watson shouted, "What the hell are you doing? You've caught me." He turned and grabbed the gun barrel. Moore still had his finger on the trigger and as Watson pulled, the weapon went off another three or four times.

Seeing what he had done, Moore panicked and decided to bury Watson close by. As he pulled the body over the wall, he felt a wad of notes and took them before placing Watson into his grave. As for his subsequent statements to the police, all of which gave clear indications of his guilt, he had made these believing that he was guilty. After all, he had been responsible for Watson's death, even though it was an accident. This was also why he had tried to gas himself.

Dr Frederick G. Tryhorn, a director of forensic science, said that the gun had been fired from a distance of 2-3ft. This was consistent with both stories Moore had told, the accidental shooting when Watson grabbed the gun, and his original statement that he had fired at him from outside the car.

In his summing up, Mr Justice Stable said that this was not a question of murder or manslaughter, nor was there any claim that Moore was insane at the time he shot Watson. It was for the jury to decide between deliberate murder and an accidental killing. However, the judge also pointed out that no mention had been made of this accidental scenario until the trial itself. Why had Moore not brought forward this defence earlier so that the police could have checked to see if there were any people in the area who had seen Moore and Watson shooting at pheasants?

The jury were out for one hour and 40 minutes before deciding that Moore was guilty as charged. As the sentence of death was passed, one of the female jurors wept. Moore decided to appeal against his conviction and this was heard in December. The main grounds were that the judge, in his summing up, had failed to present fairly and adequately the case for the defence and that he had also failed to put before the jury certain evidence of expert witnesses who, although called by the prosecution, had made statements which were favourable to the defence. Finally, the judge may also have been wrong in not permitting the jury to consider the possibility of a verdict of manslaughter.

Giving his judgement, the Lord Chief Justice, Lord Goddard, said that the defence put forward at the trial was a fantastic story: "This man was guilty of a cruel and deliberate murder. That was the case for the Crown and the jury accepted it." Further, Lord Goddard found no fault with the summing up and therefore the appeal was dismissed.

There was no reprieve and on Tuesday, January 5th, 1954, Robert William Moore, who had by now turned 26, was hanged at Leeds by Stephen Wade who was assisted by Harry Smith.

CHAPTER TWENTY-THREE

UNLUCKY SEVEN

CZELSLAW Kowalewski had not had the happiest of lives. Born in March, 1921, at Skorzewu in Poland, Kowalewski had seen his country overrun by the Germans in 1939 when he was 18 years old. For a few years the young man was allowed to pursue his trade as a joiner before coming to the attention of the occupation forces as someone suitable for slave labour. Kowalewski was sent to France where he was forced to work repairing railways after Allied bombing raids.

For more than two years Kowalewski survived this brutal treatment until he was released by advancing American troops in 1944. Once his background had been checked, Kowalewski was sent to England where he served in the Polish Army. Moving to Scotland after the war ended, the young Pole entered the mining industry, moving back to England and the Leeds area in 1949.

By the year 1953, Kowalewski was living in a room in Grange Avenue, Chapeltown, an address he shared with 29-year-old Doris Douglas, who was also known as Doris Allen. Doris herself had not had things all her own way. The eldest of a family of six, she had left her home at Raynville Crescent, Bramley, when she was only 15. A few years after this, she had taken to using the name Allen and it was as Doris Allen that most people now knew her. Unfortunately, what should have been a simple domestic arrangement was complicated by the fact that Doris did not spend all her time living with Kowalewski but shared her time between two addresses.

Each weekend, Doris Allen would leave the house at Grange Avenue and Kowalewski assumed that she was returning to her family home at Raynville Crescent. It was late September when Kowalewski discovered that every weekend Doris was staying at a third-floor flat, 77 Moynihan House, Quarry Hill Flats, Leeds. The flat was occupied by Mr James Henry McGough and his 16-year-old son, Anthony. When Kowalewski discovered that Doris was sharing a home with another man, his volatile temper got the better of him and a number of violent rows broke out between them, even though she insisted that she was only acting as McGough's house-keeper and there was nothing improper going on. For a couple of weeks the situation simmered until finally, on the night of Monday, October 5th, 1953, it finally boiled over into violence.

That evening, at around 7.00pm, James McGough and Doris Allen went out together to the Marquis of Granby public house. McGough did not stay long as he had promised to join one of the teams in a darts match at another pub. It was around 7.20pm when he left the Marquis and at that time Doris was alone. At the same time, Kowalewski was also drinking alone but he was in another pub, the General Elliott Hotel. At around 8.00pm, Doris walked into that pub and she and Kowalewski began drinking together. They left, still together, shortly afterwards.

Some time around 9.00pm, Kowalewski and Doris were again seen together, this time in the Nag's Head. A Ukrainian named Jan Szyptko was also drinking in that establishment. Although they were not together that evening, Szyptko knew Kowalewski and thought that he was in a fairly aggressive mood. There were certainly harsh words spoken between Kowalewski and Doris, right up to the moment they left the Nag's Head at closing time. Shortly afteward, Kowalewski was in the Rainbow café on Vicar Lane. Szyptko was also there and foolishly made some derogatory remark about Doris.

215

Kowalewski invited him to step outside. A fight ensued and when Kowalewski walked away, Szyptko was left semi-conscious on the pavement. When he was found later he was rushed to hospital and remained there, under treatment, for a number of days. Doris had apparently walked off home alone, but Kowalewski had caught up with her in Briggate and the argument had started all over again.

By 10.00pm, James McGough had arrived home at Moynihan House. The only other person in the house at the time was his son, Anthony, and he was asleep in bed. After half an hour or so, James also went to bed and was soon asleep. It was not long, though, before his slumbers were disturbed by a loud knocking on his front door. By now it was almost midnight and upon opening the door, James McGough saw that it was Doris Allen with a police officer. The skin around her eyes showed signs of bruising and she was distressed and frightened. Doris explained that she had been attacked by Kowalewski and had telephoned the police from a public call box in Vicar Lane. McGough saw that Doris was all right and returned to his bed, as the policeman who had brought her to Moynihan House noted down a statement.

The police officer left the flat just after midnight and Doris, too, retired for the night. Minutes later, though, there was another loud knocking at the door. James McGough answered it to find an irate Czelslaw Kowalewski demanding to see Doris. McGough saw that the Pole was in no mood to be reasoned with and told him to come back in the morning before closing the door in his face. Once more, James McGough went back to bed, but he was to get no rest that night.

No more than two minutes had passed before McGough heard the sound of breaking glass and splintering wood. Even as he was getting out of bed, Doris ran into his bedroom, screaming at the top of her voice, to be followed immediately by Kowalewski who struck out at her and knocked her to the floor. McGough saw Kowalewski kick Doris and then, while she lay on the ground, aim further blows at her head. Only then did James McGough realise that the Pole held a knife in his hand and was stabbing Doris.

Leaping forward, McGough grappled with Kowalewski, suffering a cut finger in the process. Somehow he managed to push him out of the room and down a short flight of stairs. As Kowalewski fled the house, McGough rushed back to Doris and tried to render first aid as he called for his son to run for the police. By the time help arrived it was too late. Doris Allen was already dead.

Detective Chief Inspector Eric Abbott, the officer in charge of the investigation, soon turned up a number of witnesses to the events of the night of October 5th, including Jan Szyptko who was interviewed in hospital. Of Kowalewski, however, there was no sign and on October 7th, his description was published in the newspapers: 'About 5ft 8ins, tall, balding, with a high forehead. Wearing an old pair of trousers and a dirty grey mackintosh.' The same day it was announced that Kowalewski might have left the area because a dagger had been found on the Edinburgh-London express, but in due course this was examined by Professor Cyril John Polson who confirmed that it could not be the murder weapon.

It was not until October 9th that the police received the breakthrough they so badly needed. Samuel Ludbrook ran a shop in Oakwood Lane, Leeds, and on October 7th a man fitting Kowalewski's description had come into his shop to buy some cigarettes and a bottle of wine. Mr Ludbrook's daughter, Pat Howieson, had dialled 999 to report the matter but by the time a radio car had arrived, there was no sign of the suspect. Now, two days later, the same man was back again but this time Mr Ludbrook kept him talking while his son-in-law, Stuart Howieson, called the police. Once more, by the time a police car arrived, the man had left the premises, but driving around the area, Inspector Gordon Marshall soon spotted him in Lawrence Avenue. Kowalewski readily admitted his identity, was cautioned and taken into custody.

At the police station, Kowalewski was interviewed by Detective Superintendent Thomas Bowman and Chief Inspector Abbott, to whom he handed over the knife he still carried. When he was searched, Kowalewski was found to be carrying a number of scraps

of paper on which he had written a sort of diary outlining his movements, actions and thoughts during the period he had remained free.
The first entry, dated Tuesday, October 6th started, 'I am round
where I do not know but I can see the flats where I stab my woman
Doris.' That evening Czelslaw Kowalewski was charged with
murder.

Kowalewski first appeared at the Leeds magistrates' court on
October 10th before the stipendiary magistrate, Mr R. Cleworth,
who shared the bench with the Lord Mayor, Alderman D.G.
Cowling. The prisoner was represented by Mr Ernest Wurzel who
made no objection to a remand until October 16th. Later that day,
Doris Allen was laid to rest at Armley Hill Top cemetery, the service
being conducted by the Reverend Idwal Jenkins, the vicar of the
Church of the Venerable Bede.

Further appearances followed on October 16th, October 23rd
and October 29th, when the evidence was heard and Kowalewski
was sent for trial. That trial opened at Leeds on December 13th
before Mr Justice Stable. The prosecution case was put by Mr Rudolph Lyons and Mr J. McLusky and Kowalewski was defended by
Mr H.R.B. Shepherd and Mr E.J. Parris. The jury consisted of ten
men and two women and the hearing lasted until December 17th.

In addition to his eye-witness account of the stabbing itself, James
McGough said that he had first met Kowalewski three months
before the attack upon Doris Allen. At the time he had been walking
down Vicar Lane when he saw Doris who was with Kowalewski and
introduced them to each other. McGough said that he had not
known, right up until her death, that Doris had earned her living as
a prostitute.

Although James McGough was the only person who saw the fatal
attack, there were other witnesses to earlier events that night. Mrs
Lettie Goodacre also lived in Moynihan House and knew Doris
Allen quite well. At around 11.50pm on October 5th, Lettie heard
a woman's scream. A few seconds later, she heard a second scream
and going to her window to investigate, she saw a woman lying on

the ground outside and a man standing over her, hitting her. After a minute or so, the man walked away, only to return and try to help the woman up. Lettie could see that the woman was Doris Allen and she now screamed at her assailant to leave her alone. The man walked off again and subsequently Lettie had identified that man as Czelslaw Kowalewski.

This argument was also witnessed by Ernest Wakefield, another resident of the flats, who had seen a man and a woman rowing in the street outside. At one stage, the woman shouted, "Send for the police. This man has hit me. I am frightened to death." Wakefield also identified the man involved as Kowalewski.

Constable John Shaw told the court that he had answered a 999 call made from a box in Vicar Lane. He had gone to that box and later escorted Doris to McGough's flat where she made an official complaint about Kowalewski. At this point, Mr Shepherd for the defence objected to Constable Shaw giving details of the complaint as he held that it was hearsay evidence and therefore inadmissible. The jury were told to leave the court while the point was debated, Mr Justice Stable finally deciding that the details could be revealed to them. Constable Shaw went on to say how Doris Allen had told him that Kowalewski had asked her to go home with him that night. When she had refused, he had attacked her. Shaw saw that Doris was calmer and since there were two men in the flat with her, he believed she was safe enough and left her there. Shortly afterwards, though, he was approached by Anthony McGough who told him that there had been a stabbing at Moynihan House and he returned to find that Doris Allen was already dead.

Evidence was called which seemed to indicate that the act of stabbing Doris had been planned and premeditated. Olive Firth worked as a shop assistant for Peter Maturi of Ludgate Hill, off Vicar Lane, Leeds. She testified that on the morning of October 5th she had sold a knife identical to the one produced in court. The knife cost 5s and the customer who purchased it was Kowalewski.

Jan Szyptko told of the altercation he had had with Kowalewski at the rear of the Rainbow café. At one stage, Kowalewski had produced a knife and advanced upon him saying, "I am going to kill you. I am going to catch (*sic*) you up." That knife had also been seen by Mrs Frances Andrews Whitehead who saw it in Kowalewski's trouser pocket while he was in the General Elliott Hotel.

Inspector Marshall said that when he had first stopped Kowalewski he had said, "I am the man you are looking for. This woman, she is dead is she?" Later at the police station, Kowalewski had added, "I know what you want to ask about. Doris stabbed with the knife. She is luckier than me. She is dead. I have hid myself in a bush for four days. I struck her round here [at which point Kowalewski indicated the right side of his head] I was drunk. I do not remember how it was."

The post-mortem on Doris Allen had been carried out by Professor C.J. Polson who described the fatal wound as a deep, penetrating one behind the left ear. The blade had passed through the skull and into the brain and even if medical attention had been immediately available, Doris would not have survived.

Kowalewski gave evidence on his own behalf. He said he had been living with Doris for six months or so and had not known where she went at weekends. Once he discovered the truth, he was angry and jealous and felt that there must be something going on between Doris and Mr McGough. He had not purchased the knife to use on Doris but to defend himself from some Ukrainians who had previously threatened him. Indeed, Doris had been a witness at the August quarter sessions when two of these Ukrainians had been charged with wounding him, but they had been found not guilty.

On the day in question, he had visited several public houses and was already drunk by mid-afternoon. That night he went to the cinema before going to more pubs, in one of which he met Doris. There had been an argument with a foreigner at 10.00pm and that had ended in a fight.

All he could recall of later events was some sort of row with Doris and he seemed to remember running up some steps, but his next memory was of waking up in a field somewhere. He had no memory whatsoever of the attack itself.

Kowalewski's defence team asked the jury to return a verdict of manslaughter. In his summing up, however, the judge pointed out that such a verdict was only possible if they were convinced that Kowalewski was so drunk that he could not have formed the intention to kill and the only evidence of this was his own statement that he had no recollection of what had taken place. The jury took only 15 minutes to decide that this was a case of murder and Kowalewski was guilty as charged.

This was the seventh death sentence passed at this particular assizes, a record number. The other six had been Charles Hall, Robert William Moore, Stanislaw Juras, William Lubina and Patrick and Beatrice Conroy. Of those six, three — Moore, Juras and Lubina — would eventually pay the ultimate penalty.

On December 23rd, Kowalewski's solicitor, Mr Wurzal, announced that after several interviews with his client at Manchester prison it had been decided that he would not enter an appeal, but would petition the Home Secretary for a reprieve. In due course it was announced that no such reprieve would be given and the last hope of the condemned man had passed.

On Friday, January 8th, 1954, Czelslaw Kowalewski, by then 32 years old, was hanged at Strangeways. The only people waiting outside the prison at the time were a small clutch of reporters and the driver of an official car.

CHAPTER TWENTY-FOUR

THE LODGING HOUSE

LOUISE Fairweather ran a large lodging house at 17 Claremont, which was situated in Great Horton Road, Bradford. She shared the house with her daughter and son-in-law, the Mantons, and their nephew. One of her lodgers, 40-year-old Arthur White, had first moved into the house at the beginning of 1949. Another man, 24-year-old Edward Lindsay Reid, became a resident in March 1953 and the two ended up sharing an attic room together at the back of the house. For a time, everyone seemed to live peaceably enough.

On Saturday, April 3rd, 1954, Reid and White were heard arguing while they ate their dinner. The row seemed to be over fairly quickly and that night both men went out drinking in different public houses. White went first to the Little Alec Hotel, at 6.30pm, and later moved on to the Pack Horse in Westgate. It was not until 10.20pm that he left that establishment and made his way back to 17 Claremont. Reid had spent his evening at the Granby Hotel where he had consumed nine pints of beer.

Albert Clough was another of the lodgers at the boarding house and he, too, had been out that Saturday night. It was 10.45pm when Clough returned home and entering the yard at the back, in order to use the outside lavatory, he stumbled over what at first he thought was a bundle of rags. But when he touched the bundle with his foot, Clough realised that it was the body of a man. Looking more closely, he saw that the body was that of his fellow lodger, Arthur White, who was lying in a pool of blood.

Detective Constable Priestley was soon on the scene. He noted that the body lay beneath the attic room window some 35ft above and made the natural assumption that White had been under the influence of drink and had fallen from his bedroom window. When Priestley went upstairs to White's room, however, he found Edward Reid, half undressed and the worse for drink.

Looking around the room and checking the window, Priestley noticed that there was blood on the bottom of the window frame and also on the lead flashing outside. While this might have been explained by a fall, the presence of blood inside the room and upon Reid's face could not. Asked to explain this, Reid said that he had cut himself shaving before he had gone out for the night. His story did not ring true and when Detective Chief Inspector Cheshire arrived, he took Reid to the police station so that he could be questioned more closely.

Cheshire noticed that Reid's right hand was badly swollen, just as might be expected from a man who had been in a fight. Reid, though, continued to insist that he knew nothing about the death of Arthur White. He explained the swelling by saying he had hurt his hand at work and claimed not to have noticed any blood upon his clothing. He said that the last time he had seen his room-mate was at dinner time, although he quickly amended this to tea time. Reid told the chief inspector that after spending the night in the pub, he had returned to his room at 10.40pm, gone straight to bed and been unaware of anything else until the police appeared in his bedroom.

Referring to the argument with White at dinner time on Saturday, Reid told Cheshire that this had been caused by White claiming he had been sick on the dressing table in their room on the Friday evening. Reid denied he was responsible and told White to 'shut his gob'. Despite his protestations of innocence, Reid was told that he was going to be charged with murder, to which he replied, "Nowt to do with that."

On April 5th, Reid made his first appearance at the Bradford City Court. The case for the prosecution was put by Mr P.K. Watkins, who gave only brief details of arrest. Reid was given legal aid and remanded until April 13th. The next day, the inquest on Arthur White opened before Mr A.R.B. Priddin, but only evidence of identification and cause of death was given. By his second court appearance on April 13th, Reid had obtained legal representation in the form of Mr J.H. Cole and further remands followed until April 21st, and then again until April 29th. Only then was the evidence finally heard.

Mr M.D. Hutchinson, who had taken over the case for the Director of Public Prosecutions, explained that the house at Great Horton Road accommodated up to 21 lodgers at any one time and the kitchen was used as a communal dining room. It was for this reason that there were many witnesses to the argument which had taken place between Reid and the dead man at dinner time on April 3rd. Mr Hutchinson went on to explain how Albert Clough had found the body and made a 999 emergency call to the police.

Circumstances at the scene showed that Arthur White had indeed fallen from his bedroom window, for there were bloodstains on the kitchen window sill and medical evidence showed that White had probably banged his head on the sill when he fell. When the police officer entered the attic room which White shared with Reid, the light was on and there were obvious signs of a violent struggle having taken place. The floor of the room was wet and there were marks consistent with blood having recently been wiped up. A damp, bloodstained cloth was lying on the floor.

The window through which White had apparently fallen had two hinges at the top and opened upward and outward. When Constable Priestley first examined the window it was latched and secure, which showed that it must have been closed after White had gone through it. Further, it was of such a small size that a man could not possibly fall through it accidentally. However, if White had been unconscious after a fight or an attack upon him, then his still form could have been manoeuvred through the window without too much difficulty, in order to make his injuries appear accidental.

The hearing of the evidence continued into April 30th when it was decided to send Reid for trial at the next assizes. He was granted legal aid for his defence and when asked if he had anything to say, merely replied, "No sir." The trial opened at Leeds on July 5th before Mr Justice Donovan and lasted for two days. Reid was defended by Mr H.R.B. Shepherd and Mr T.R. Nevin while the case for the prosecution was led by Mr T. Basil Herbert who was assisted by Mr Felix Denny.

Louise Fairweather, the lodging house landlady, stated that over the weekend most of her lodgers went out drinking and she was often left alone in the house. She was there when Reid came in that night and confirmed that it was around 10.40pm. There was nothing unusual about his appearance or behaviour and he went straight up to his room. Mrs Manton had also seen Reid at that time and said he had no obvious bloodstains on him, nor did he have an injured hand.

John Brown and Thomas Garget were two more of the lodgers at 17 Claremont and they had both heard White and Reid arguing earlier in the day, although neither could say exactly what the row was about. Garget had often gone out drinking with White and described him as 'a quiet fellow'.

Detective Constable Priestley said that when he checked the attic window he saw that although it was slightly ajar, it was secured in place by means of a bar held on to a peg. Although there was evidence of bloodstaining in parts of the room, the floor directly underneath the window had recently been wiped over and was still damp. There was also blood in the gutter outside the window. Priestley also noticed a spot of blood on Reid's forehead and on the neck line of his vest. There were signs that Reid had been drinking but when asked how much he had consumed, Reid replied, "I'm not drunk and I don't know what you're talking about. I cut myself when shaving about 6.00pm, before I went out."

Dr Kenneth Sheldon was the police surgeon who had examined Reid at the police station, at 1.05am on April 4th. He testified that Reid smelled of alcohol, although he could not be described as drunk. There was a swelling on the back of Reid's right hand and a scratch over that swelling. In addition, Reid had a graze on his left elbow and blood on his right wrist. There was also dust and dirt rubbed into the skin of both his elbows and upper arms, as might be expected from someone who had been involved in a scuffle.

Reid's clothing had been examined by Dr Frederick G. Tryhorn, the Director of the North Eastern Forensic Science Laboratory and he had found human blood on Reid's trousers, jacket, overcoat and shirt.

The body of Arthur White had been examined by Dr David E. Price at the scene of the crime and he had also performed the post-mortem. He described a large wound across White's forehead and underneath this wound, the skull had been fractured. Part of the bone from that fracture had penetrated the brain and other injuries included a black eye, a fractured cheekbone, a fractured jaw, two broken legs and a broken neck. The cause of death was given as shock and haemorrhage following multiple injuries. More important, Dr Price was able to say that while the wound in the forehead was probably caused by the fall from the window, the other injuries were inflicted several minutes before White's death.

No witnesses were called for the defence and Reid did not go into the witness box to give evidence on his own behalf. The only defence was a speech by Mr Shepherd, his barrister, saying that he did not accept that the prosecution case was strong enough. No motive for murder had been shown and their fellow lodgers had agreed that there was no bad atmosphere between the two men. If a fight had taken place, why had no one else in the house at the time heard it? In Mr Shepherd's opinion it was more likely that White had fallen from the window even before Reid came into the house.

The jury were out for 75 minutes considering their verdict and when they came, it was one of guilty. An appeal was heard on August 17th when the defence claimed that the jury had been misdirected and the charge in the first place should have been one of manslaughter. Referring to that point, one of the appeal court judges, Mr Justice Hallett, said that the only grounds for a reduction of the charge of murder to one of manslaughter was that of provocation and there was no evidence of any provocation in this case. The appeal was dismissed.

On Wednesday September 1st, 1954, Edward Lindsay Reid was hanged at Leeds by Stephen Wade and Harry Smith. There were only two men and a group of reporters outside the prison gates at the time.

CHAPTER TWENTY-FIVE

THE OLDEST MOTIVE

IN 1937, Winston Shaw, who was then 21 years old, married a
girl called Florence. The relationship could hardly have been
described as a great success, however, for the couple lived
together for only two or three months before Shaw moved to Tenter
Street, Windhill, Shipley.

It was 1951 before Shaw met a new love in the shape of Jean Cave
Tate, a woman 15 years his junior. Jean soon moved in with Shaw
and by 1953 she had borne him two children, Barry and Jennifer.
This relationship, too, had its problems which were perhaps not
aided by the fact that eventually Florence Shaw, Winston's legal wife,
moved in with them.

This arrangement lasted for some months but by the beginning
of 1954, Jean Tate was expressing her reservations about the situation
and also about the fact that Shaw was a jealous man who often
treated her cruelly. For his part, Shaw believed that all the problems
stemmed from the home situation and it might be better if he and
Jean lived alone. So it was that on October 25th 1954, the couple
took fresh lodgings at Cunliffe Terrace, Manningham, Bradford. Surprisingly perhaps, the two children remained with Florence Shaw at
Tenter Street.

If Shaw felt that these new living arrangements would bring him and Jean closer together, he was very much mistaken for one month later, on November 25th, Jean Tate was visited, at her own instigation, by Inspector Kelly, an officer of the NSPCC, and two police officers. To these three gentlemen Jean explained that she was, in effect, being kept prisoner by Shaw. He locked her in the house whenever he went out and refused to let her see her children. As a result, she lived in fear of him and desperately wanted to leave. Acting on this information, Inspector Kelly arranged for Jean and the children to be moved to a safe address. That address was, of course, not revealed to Winston Shaw, but Jean and her young family were moved to Flat 1 at Knaresborough Hospital. Shaw, an unemployed radio engineer, spent much of his time trying to trace his estranged lover.

It was on Friday, December 3rd, 1954 that two police officers, Detective Constable Rose and Policewoman Briggs, visited Jean Tate at the hospital flat, about a matter not connected with the treatment she had received at the hands of Winston Shaw. However, while the two officers were talking to Jean, Shaw walked in, carrying a blue teddy bear which he said was for the oldest child, Barry, who was now almost two. Jean was shocked to see Shaw and made it plain that she wanted nothing from him, that their relationship was over and she wanted him out of the flat. Eventually, the police escorted Shaw out and stayed with Jean for an hour or so to make sure that he did not return and cause trouble.

By 4.30pm, the police officers had left Jean's flat and for some hours there was no further incident at the hospital. It was not until 9.15pm, that a woman in a neighbouring flat heard a piercing scream and a loud thud which were followed by the sound of running footsteps. The neighbour went to investigate and upon pushing open the door to Flat 1, discovered Jean Tate lying on the floor, her arms outstretched and covered in blood. Sister Barker from the hospital staff was summoned to give medical assistance but it was too late. Jean Cave Tate was dead.

By the time Constable Hardy called at Winston Shaw's lodgings, it was 11.24pm. Hardy explained that he was investigating the death of Jean Tate. Shaw made no reply but sat down on his bed and began to cry. The constable had already seen an axe head and a broken axe shaft on the dressing table, along with a empty knife sheath, and cautioned Shaw before taking him into custody.

At the police station Shaw was interviewed by Detective Inspector Wilburn and made various statements, all of which incriminated him. At one stage he said, "I remember seeing her face, then everything went black. If you had arrested me this morning, it would never have happened." When told he would be charged, Shaw commented, "It couldn't be any worse than that. I never intended to kill her." Later still he said, "I don't know why I killed her, that's gospel. All I wanted was to make up. I didn't think she was hurt so badly." Finally, as if all this was not enough, Shaw turned to Inspector Wilburn and asked him if he wanted to know where the knife was. He went on to explain that he had hidden it behind some boards in the bathroom at his lodgings.

Shaw made a number of appearances before the magistrates, one of the last taking place on January 17th, 1955, when the case for the prosecution was put by Mr R. Thomas. He explained the details of the case and showed that Shaw had been seen around the hospital long after the police had escorted him from Jean's flat. He was also identified as the man who had purchased an axe and a knife at two local shops on the afternoon of Jean's death. In addition, Shaw had taken lodgings in Jockey Lane, which was just 500 yards from the hospital, at 7.30pm on December 3rd. It all seemed to be a deliberate plan to kill the woman who had left him.

Sent for trial, Winston Shaw appeared before Mr Justice Pearce at Leeds on March 15th, 1955. The trial lasted for three days, the prosecution being led by Sir Godfrey Russell Vick, assisted by Mr Henry C. Scott. Shaw was defended by Mr G.S. Waller and Mr Vivian Hurwitz. Despite his statements and the evidence found linking him to the crime, Shaw pleaded not guilty to murder.

Inspector Kelly of the NSPCC, told of his visit to Shaw's lodgings in Bradford on November 25th. Jean had complained about being beaten by Shaw and of one wound which had required 17 stitches. As he and the two police officers escorted Jean from the premises, Shaw had burst into tears and shouted, "You're not going to leave me Jean, are you?"

One of the policemen who was present during Inspector Kelly's visit was Constable Bairstow. He stated that at one stage Jean Tate had cried, "I have been locked up here for a month by him, and when he goes out he locks me in and takes the key. He has kicked me on the leg and I had to have 17 stitches in it."

The two officers who had visited Jean's flat at the hospital on December 3rd reported that they had arrived at 2.30pm and not long afterwards, Shaw had come in and handed over the blue teddy bear. Jean Tate had shouted, "I want nothing from you for myself or the children. I have finished with you." To this Shaw had said, "You will forgive me won't you?" Far from being mollified, Jean had replied, "I'm all right on my own. I don't want anything to do with you."

The officers reported that Shaw stayed a total of 15 minutes but they remained on the premises until 4.30pm, thinking that it was then safe to leave since Shaw had made no attempt to return

Shaw, though, had not left the area. Mr Smith was the Methodist minister at the hospital and as he arrived on the premises at around 3.15pm Shaw approached him, explained who he was and asked him to intercede on his behalf. Mr Smith went to see Jean but she was adamant that the relationship between her and Shaw was over. The minister returned to where Shaw was waiting and told him that he had been unable to help.

Continuing to trace Shaw's movements, the prosecution now showed that he had visited two shops. In the first he bought an axe and in the second he purchased a sheath knife. Soon after this, at around 7.30pm, he went to the house of Mr Letts in Jockey Lane and rented a room from him. Mr Letts gave evidence that Shaw stayed in his room until around 8.30pm when he went out. He did not return until 9.45pm. Those times, of course, fitted with the time that Jean Tate's neighbour had heard a scream coming from her flat.

Jean's father, Eric Tate, told the court that after Jean had been given the flat at the hospital, Shaw had visited him in order to discover her new address. Eric Tate, of course, refused to help Shaw, whereupon he had said, "Jean has done it to all of us, me and your sons, but she won't do it to anyone else." Shaw told Eric that when he did find her, he would kick her and moved his leg to demonstrate the action.

Inspector Wilburn gave details of the various statements Shaw had made, before and after he had been charged. At one stage, Shaw had said, "You want that knife, don't you? I am beginning to think clearer now. I will tell you where it is." Shaw said that he had hidden the weapon behind some boards in his bathroom at Jockey Lane. The knife was found there, heavily bloodstained.

Evidence was also given that when Shaw was first interviewed by Constable Hardy, he was holding the blue teddy bear, yet earlier, when he had been escorted from Jean's flat, he had left the toy behind. When first spoken to, Shaw had cried and then muttered, "Is she dead then? You don't understand. She has ruined me and now she has brought me to this."

Medical evidence was given by Dr David E. Price, the Home Office pathologist who had examined the scene of the crime and performed a post-mortem on the dead woman. He described at least 20 stab wounds and a further five blows about the head with a different, not so sharp instrument, such as an axe. Death was due to shock and haemorrhage following those multiple wounds.

Winston Shaw entered the witness box on the second day of his trial and the story he told was little short of fantastic. He began by detailing some of the history of his relationship with Jean, during the course of which he denied ever kicking her on the leg, mistreating her, or keeping her prisoner in the flat at Bradford. After Jean had left him, he spent a great deal of time trying to trace her, even going so far as to employ a solicitor. Eventually he was successful and on December 3rd, visited her with the intention of getting her back. He took with him the teddy bear for the eldest child and a powder compact for Jean.

Escorted from the premises, Shaw went for a walk, returning to the hospital just after 3.00pm when he saw the minister, Mr Smith. Aware now that there could be no reconciliation, he walked around the town and did indeed purchase a knife and an axe. The knife was a present for a Boy Scout he knew and the axe was for chopping sticks at home in Shipley.

Thinking it was pointless to return home, Shaw took lodgings with Mr Letts and left those premises at 8.30pm when he went for a couple of drinks. Finding himself back near the hospital, he decided to have one more try to see Jean and walked up to her flat. To his surprise he could hear two voices coming from inside the room, Jean's and a man's. Shaw listened for a few moments, his intention being to hear something that might show Jean was seeing someone else, a fact he would report to the welfare authorities.

Eventually Shaw turned the knob and entered the room to find Jean with a middle-aged man. Seeing Shaw in her room, Jean had said, "What do you want again?" Shaw replied that he would give her more money if she would leave this other man and come back with him. To this, Jean said that she didn't want his money, after which the stranger had asked, "Who is this guy?"

Becoming angry now, Shaw shouted, "Oh I'm nobody. I'm only the father of these children and have kept this woman for the past three years." The stranger threatened to throw Shaw out, to which Shaw said that he would like to see him try. At this, the man picked up a chair and struck Shaw across the head. Shaw happened to have the axe in his hand and lashed out with it to protect himself. At one stage, he heard Jean scream and saw her walk past him towards the doorway where she collapsed. Meanwhile, the man was still hitting him with the chair so Shaw drew out the knife but it was knocked from his hand. Shaw was eventually knocked to the floor and by the time he picked himself up, the man had run out of the room.

Although he was dizzy, Shaw managed to determine that the children were still asleep in bed and Jean was lying on the floor in the doorway. He continued, "After I rested, I pulled Mrs Tate into the room. I tried to lift her but she was too heavy. I kissed her on the forehead and started crying. I was very upset. I saw the axehead and picked it up. I went to the door and slipped because of the blood. I got blood on my hand. I picked up the knife in the passage and also the handle of the axe. I was in a terrible state. I went back into the room and then realised what a position I was in."

Shaw explained how he had wrapped the axe in paper and although he took it and the knife back to his flat, he knew he would have to face the police with what had happened. As Shaw said, "You can never run away from the law. I realised I would have to face them."

Shaw was claiming that he might have been responsible for inflicting the axe wounds on Jean, but if he had done so, it had been accidental. At no stage had he used the knife on Jean. It must have been the other man who stabbed her. In his summing up, Shaw's barrister, Mr Waller, stated that Jean's death was accidental and the jury should return a verdict of manslaughter. Sir Godfrey Russell Vick, for the prosecution, pointed out that at no stage had Shaw gone for help for a woman to whom he claimed he was devoted. Surely if his story were true, that would have been his first action.

In his summing up, Mr Justice Pearce asked why Shaw had carried the knife and the axe with him all evening instead of leaving them in his lodgings if, as he stated, he had bought them for innocent purposes. The judge also asked how Jean had apparently received five blows from an axe and still managed to walk to the doorway. Finally, could the jury accept that while Shaw was lying dazed on the floor, the other man had picked up the knife, stabbed Jean 20 times, then thrown down the weapon and made good his escape.

Not surprisingly, the jury could accept none of Shaw's story and he was found guilty of murder. Asked if he had anything to say, Shaw replied, "My Lord, I would just like to say that I am sorry there has been all this trouble caused to everyone concerned. If that is the verdict, I accept it."

An appeal was entered and this was heard on April 19th, the day that newspapers announced the death, the previous day, of Albert Einstein. Shaw's defence was again that the killing had been accidental, or alternatively, that he had acted in self defence after the other man had attacked him. To this, one of the judges, Mr Justice Hilbery, stated that there could be no possible provocation that would excuse 20 or more stab wounds. Dismissing the appeal, the Lord Chief Justice, Lord Goddard, said, "This was a most terrible murder inspired by the oldest and commonest motive — jealousy."

On Wednesday, May 4th, 1955, 39-year-old Winston Shaw was hanged at Leeds prison by Stephen Wade who was assisted by Harry Smith. It was only the second execution of the year, one in which 11 men and one woman, Ruth Ellis, would die on an English gallows.

CHAPTER TWENTY-SIX

KILLING A DEAD MAN

ELI Myers appeared to be a prosperous man. A successful market trader who dealt in clothes, he traded under the name of Jack Marsh, ran a mobile shop that travelled from market to market, and also owned a shop which was managed by his brother, Louis. All these enterprises were profitable but Eli was also lucky when it came to gambling and, in December 1960, the football syndicate to which he belonged won a substantial amount of money, of which his share was £1,275. He never tired of boasting about his good fortune and it was that which probably led to his violent death.

At 6.15pm on Friday, February 24th, 1961, Eli Myers counted the day's takings, which came to around £40, in his brother's presence. He went back to Louis' house where he had a meal, at one stage counting the money again and handing Louis £5 which he wanted him to use as the cash float in the shop the next day. Eli left his brother's house some time after 9.30pm and travelled to a shop in Harehills Avenue where he had arranged to meet a business contact. The meeting did not take long and it was around 10.00pm when Eli Myers reached his semi-detached home in Chelwood Avenue which was off Street Lane, Leeds.

Hilda Harris lived next door to Eli Myers and it was 10.00pm when she heard what sounded like an argument coming from her neighbour's house. She heard shouting and what appeared to be the sounds of items being thrown about. Although she knew that Eli lived alone, and the noises continued for more than 20 minutes, Hilda Harris did not interfere or telephone the police.

Each working day before he went on his rounds of the markets, Eli Myers would call at the shop run by Louis. When Eli did not put in an appearance on the Saturday morning, Louis became concerned and at 1.15pm went to his brother's house and knocked on the front door. Receiving no reply, he walked around to the back of the house and saw that a pane of glass in the french windows had been broken. Gingerly entering through the open window, he saw that the house was in disarray with drawers thrown open and their contents scattered about. There was worse to come. When he walked into the living room Louis Myers found the battered and bloody body of his brother. The police were called and a murder investigation was under way.

The officer in charge of the case was Detective Chief Superintendent Thomas Bowman and it soon came to his attention that someone had been trying to sell a large quantity of clothing on the night of February 25th, the day after the murder of Eli Myers. A Mr Ballatoni had contacts in the clothing trade and he had been approached in the Nag's Head Hotel in Chapeltown by a man who asked him if he knew of someone who might want to buy 200 to 300 pairs of trousers. Mr Ballatoni did know of someone and in fact had Eli Myers in mind, but once he heard of the murder he contacted the police and passed on the name of the man who had approached him. So it was that in the early hours of February 26th, officers detained Zsiga Pankotia, a 31-year-old Hungarian, who had been living in England for some 12 years.

One of the first things the police did was to examine Pankotia's clothing for blood. There was evidence that there had been a terrific struggle at Chelwood Avenue and the man who had been involved in that fracas with Myers would probably have been bloodstained.

In fact, the only bloodstains were on Pankotia's wristwatch, but these were of the same type as the dead man. More damaging, though, was the fact that the pullover Pankotia was wearing when he was picked up was identified as one that had belonged to Eli Myers. And when Pankotia's home at Woodland Lane, Chapeltown, was searched, officers found a new jacket of the type sold by the dead man from his mobile shop. Finally, a large quantity of new clothing had been found dumped in a derelict garage on the outskirts of town. Worn, bloodstained clothing had also been dumped here and this was shown to have belonged to Pankotia.

Faced with such damning evidence, Pankotia made a statement admitting that he had been the man who broke into Eli's house, grappled with him and killed him. Zsiga Pankotia was charged with murder and since the crime had been committed in the furtherance of theft, this was a capital charge and if found guilty he would face the death penalty.

Pankotia made his first appearance before the magistrate on February 27th. Here brief details of the circumstances of the case were given and at the magistrate's request, Mr Lyth was appointed to handle the defence. Pankotia was remanded to March 6th and then again until March 13th, when he was sent for trial. That trial opened at Leeds on April 24th before Mr Justice Ashworth. The case for the Crown was led by Mr Alastair Sharp, assisted by Mr Gilbert Hartley, while Pankotia's defence lay in the hands of Mr Henry C. Scott and Mr Charles Raymond Dean. The proceedings lasted for three days.

In addition to the evidence of Louis Myers, outlining his brother's movements, and that of the neighbour, Hilda Harris, who gave details of the argument she had heard, further information was given by Mr J. Spence, a young man who was driving up Chelwood Avenue, with his fiancée, at around 10.30pm on February 24th. They had noticed a van backing out of Eli Myers' driveway and the inference was that this was Pankotia, leaving the scene of the crime.

Medical and forensic evidence was given by Dr Alastair Stuart

Ritchie Sinton and Professor Cyril J. Polson. They reported that the dining-room carpet at Chelwood Avenue, was heavily bloodstained and a bread-knife, also covered in blood, was lying on the table in the kitchen. A wallet lay on the floor, close by Eli's body, and although this was identified by Louis as the one Eli had owned, it was now empty of cash.

Details of the injuries inflicted on Eli Myers was given. There were multiple injuries on the scalp and face caused by some kind of blunt instrument, possibly a chair and other injuries which had been inflicted by means of the bread knife. Eli's nasal bones had been fractured and the upper teeth had been displaced. The direct cause of death had been haemorrhage and a blockage of the nasal air passage.

Pankotia stepped into the witness box to give evidence on his own behalf. He explained that he had lived in Leeds since September, 1952 and while living there had got to know some fellow Hungarians including one named Pepo who worked for Eli Myers. In early February, Pepo had met Zsiga in a public house and suggested that he knew of a job he might be interested in. According to Pepo, Eli Myers had a habit of carrying perhaps £200 or even £300 on him, especially on Fridays and Saturdays, and it should be relatively easy to take this cash from him. Pepo went on to explain that he could not carry out the robbery himself in case he was recognised, and Pankotia agreed to do the job for him.

On the morning of February 24th, Pepo again spoke to Pankotia and told him that he had seen his employer carrying two bundles of cash, so this might be a perfect time to commit the robbery. That evening Pankotia, who was wearing overalls, a leather jacket, a black cap and gloves, broke into Eli Myers' house through the french windows. There was no one in the house when he arrived so, using the torch which he had brought with him, he began to search the rooms, beginning upstairs. At one stage, Pankotia even tore out the light fittings from the kitchen and put the bulbs into the sink so that if Myers should come home suddenly, he would be unable to switch on the lights and Pankotia would be able to escape without being seen. In the event, Myers did come home and finding someone moving about his house, confronted him and a struggle began which lasted for a full half hour. At the end of this time, Pankotia picked up a bread knife from a table and plunged it into Myers before finally making good his escape.

Having heard all the evidence, the jury had little trouble in returning a guilty verdict and since Pankotia's prime reason for being at the scene was to commit a robbery, he was sentenced to death. An appeal was entered and this was heard on June 5th before Justices Slade, Glyn-Jones and Megaw. Here Pankotia's defence team said that they were not disputing that he had broken into the house and had a fight with Myers in which the latter suffered injuries. There was, however, some dispute as to whether those injuries were the cause of death.

The evidence of Professor Polson was read out in court. He had stated that death was due to shock caused by the multiple injuries in association with a disease of the arteries. Professor Polson had stated at the trial that the injuries precipitated death which might have occurred at any time from arterial disease. Mr Justice Slade, hearing this, remarked that the professor appeared to agree that there was a chance, albeit remote, that the injuries inflicted by Pankotia had nothing to do with Eli Myers' death. However, the appeal was dismissed. The judges ruled that Pankotia had engaged in a fight which lasted almost half and hour and Mr Myers had died from shock only after some considerable time. It was therefore much more likely that it had been the injuries inflicted which led to his death and Pankotia admitted he was responsible for those injuries.

Less than 24 hours before he was due to die, Pankotia was received into the Church of England by the Bishop of Ripon, the Right Reverend John Moorman. The next morning, Thursday, June 29th, 1961, Zsiga Pankotia was hanged at Leeds by Harry Allen and Harry Robinson. There was no crowd outside the prison.

LIST OF EXECUTIONS AT LEEDS

Although this book covers all the Leeds and Bradford crimes for which the ultimate penalty of death by hanging was administered, there were other executions at Armley jail since the turn of the century. Here is a list of all those hanged at that establishment since 1900:

Charles Benjamin Backhouse, 16th August, 1900

Thomas Mellor, 16th August, 1900

Charles Oliver Blewitt, 28th August, 1900

John Gallagher and Emily Swann, 29th December, 1903

James Henry Clarkson, 29th March, 1904

John Thomas Kay, 16th August, 1904

Edmund Hall, 20th December, 1904

Arthur Jeffries, 29th December, 1904

Thomas George Tattersall, 15th August, 1905

George Smith, 28th December, 1905

John Ellwood, 3rd December, 1908

Thomas Mead, 12th March, 1909

John Raper Coulson, 9th August, 1910

Henry Ison, 29th December, 1910

John William Thompson, 27th March, 1917

Robert Gadsby, 18th April, 1917

John William Walsh, 17th December, 1918

Benjamin Hindle Benson, 7th January, 1919

George Walter Cardwell and

Percy George Barnett, 8th January, 1919

Lewis Massey, 6th January, 1920

Miles McHugh, 16th April, 1920

Thomas Hargreaves Wilson, 6th May, 1920

Edwin Sowerby, 30th December, 1920

Lee Doon, 5th January, 1923

John William Eastwood, 28th December, 1923

William Horsely Wardell, 18th June, 1924

Alfred Bostock, 3rd September, 1925

William Fowler, 3rd September, 1925

Lawrence Fowler, 4th September, 1925

Lorraine Lax, 7th January, 1926

William Cornelius Jones, 5th January, 1927

Arthur Harnett, 2nd September, 1927

Samuel Case, 7th January, 1928

Arthur Leslie Raveny, 14th August, 1929

Frederick Gill, 4th February, 1931

John Henry Roberts, 28th April, 1932

Thomas Riley, 28th April, 1932

Ernest Brown, 6th February, 1934

Louis Hamilton, 6th April, 1934

Frederick Rushworth, 1st January, 1935

David Maskill Blake, 7th February, 1935

Andrew Bagley, 10th February, 1937

Trevor Elvin, 10th September, 1943

Mervin Clare McEwen, 3rd February, 1944

Arthur Thompson, 31st January, 1945

Thomas Eric Richardson, 7th September, 1945

William Batty, 8th January, 1946

Albert Sabin, 30th January, 1947

Eric Charles Briggs, 20th June, 1947

William Smedley, 14th August, 1947

John Edward Gartside, 21st August, 1947

George Henry Whelpton, 7th January, 1948

Arthur George Osborne, 30th December, 1948

Dennis Neville, 2nd June, 1949

Walter Sharpe, 30th March, 1950

Alfred Moore, 6th February, 1952

Philip Henry, 30th July, 1953

Robert Moore, 5th January, 1954

Wilhelm Lubina, 27th January, 1954

Albert George Hall, 22nd April, 1954

Edward Reid, 1st September, 1954

Winston Shaw, 4th May, 1955

Alec Wilkinson, 12th August, 1955

Ernest Jones, 10th February, 1959

Bernard Hugh Walden, 14th August, 1959

Zsiga Pankotia, 29th June, 1961

The execution of Gallagher and Swann, on December 29th, 1903, was the only occasion this century when a man and a woman were hanged at the same prison at the same time for the same crime. It may also interest the true crime aficionado to know that despite the fact that Albert Pierrepoint is arguably the best known executioner in England, he only officiated at one execution at Leeds prison, that of Phillip Henry, in 1953, when he was assisted by Royston Rickard.

BIBLIOGRAPHY

NEWSPAPERS

Bradford Daily Telegraph

Bradford Telegraph and Argus

Telegraph and Argus

The Times

Yorkshire Post

Yorkshire Evening Post

ASSIZES DOCUMENTS

ASSI 45 84/4 Wardell

ASSI 45 92/5 Roberts

ASSI 45 94/2 Hamilton

ASSI 45 94/14 Blake

ASSI 45 105/17 Richardson

ASSI 45 104/13 Thompson

ASSI 45 105/4 Batty

ASSI 45 106/7 Sabin

ASSI 45 107/3 Briggs

ASSI 45 110/9 Sharpe

INDEX